RELEASE 2.25

GAMS

A USER'S GUIDE

RELEASE 2.25
GAMS
A USER'S GUIDE

by

Anthony Brooke
GAMS Development Corp.

David Kendrick
The University of Texas
Austin

Alexander Meeraus
GAMS Development Corp

Tutorial by
Richard E. Rosenthal
Naval Postgraduate School, Monterey

boyd & fraser publishing company

 The Scientific Press Series

Production Editor: Gene Smith
Text Design: Gene Smith
Cover Design: Rogondino & Associates

Gams: A User's Guide, Release 2.25
by Anthony Brooke, David Kendrick, and Alexander Meeraus

Originally published by the Scientific Press © 1988, 1992

boyd & fraser publishing company
One Corporate Place • Ferncroft Village
Danvers, Massachusetts 01923

 The Scientific Press Series

I(T)P
International Thomson Publishing
boyd & fraser publishing company is an ITP company.
The ITP trademark is used under license.

Manufactured in the United States of America

ISBN 0-89426-215-7

6 7 8 9 10 M 8 7 6 5 4

CONTENTS

PART 2 THE GAMS LANGUAGE 33

3 GAMS Programs 35

4 Set Definitions 43

5 Data Entry: Parameters, Scalars & Tables 51

PREFACE

Release 2.25 (Summer 1992)

GAMS 2.25 incorporates improvements and new capabilities which have been developed and rigorously tested over the past four years. What follows is a brief description of each of the major new features.

Speed. Internal modifications allow GAMS 2.25 to run up to 10 times faster than earlier versions, and the optimization of file structures has improved reading and writing by a factor of 10 over character files (MPS).

Input. An include facility ($INCLUDE) has been added to allow parts of a model to be placed in different files. Data tables can be separated this way from the model formulation itself. At the point where an include statement is found, the compiler reads that file and then switches back to the original file continuing where it left off. Include files can be nested up to 10 levels deep. Also, MS/DOS batch file-like features add limited macro capabilities, and input line length has been extended to 255 characters.

Output. When using GAMS with other systems, there is often the need for a more flexible and powerful way of outputting values so that they can directly read what GAMS is producing. The new PUT statement in GAMS 2.25 now allows the user to create complex management style reports and to write machine readable files.

With the new $INCLUDE and PUT facilities, moving data from and to spreadsheets such as Lotus 1-2-3® and Quattro® has been vastly simplified.

Solves Within a Loop. The LOOP statement is a very powerful device, and it is described extensively in this manual. With GAMS 2.25, it is now possible to do SOLVES within a loop giving the user the capability of doing a solve, changing some parameters or levels, and then repeating the process.

Flow Control. A new IF–ELSE statement has been added to the GAMS language to provide additional control structures. The syntax closely follows that of the LOOP statement and is particularly useful in branching conditionally around a group of statements.

Solvers & Computing Platforms. Links to, and GAMS specific versions of many of the major solvers such as CPlex,® OSL,® and MINOS® either exist now or are in development. The same is true for the constantly changing world of computing platforms and operating systems. So, for the latest information contact your distributor.

Finally, except in rare instances, GAMS 2.25 is backwards compatible with all previous versions of GAMS. All of the new features are detailed in the Addendum for Release 2.25 on page 273.

Alexander Meeraus
GAMS Development Corp.

PREFACE

Release 2.05 (Summer 1988)

This study guide describes the main features of GAMS (the acronym stands for General Algebraic Modeling System) and explains how to use it. GAMS is designed to make the construction and solution of large and complex mathematical programming models more straightforward for programmers and more comprehensible to users of models from other disciplines, e.g., economists. Because it can make concise algebraic statements of models in a language that is easily read by both modelers and computers, GAMS can substantially improve the productivity of modelers and greatly expand the extent and usefulness of mathematical programming applications in policy analysis and decision making.

The impetus for the development of GAMS arose out of the frustrating experiences of an economic modeling group at the World Bank. Even the then best available techniques for developing and solving, e.g., multisectoral economywide models or large simulation and optimization models in sectors such as agriculture, steel, and fertilizer had serious flaws. The programmers in the group wrote FORTRAN programs to prepare each model for solution; the work was dull but demanding, and errors were easy to make and hard to find. Meanwhile, the economists involved frequently found the computer representations of their models complicated and time-consuming to understand and work with; the model's programmer was often the only person who knew exactly how it functioned. Thus, if a programmer quit, it took months for a successor to master the model. Models were also difficult and expensive to change, especially if the contemplated change had not been foreseen and planned for. In seminar presentations modelers had to defend existing versions of their models, sometimes quite irrationally, because the time and money needed to make proposed modifications were prohibitive. These models could not be moved to other environments, not only because of the specialized programming knowledge needed, but also because data formats and solution methods were not portable. GAMS is designed to change this situation by providing a system structure and programming language in which conciseness of expression, generality, and portability are easily maintained and by using the computer to keep track of as many of the programming details as possible.

In view of the system's origins, it is hardly surprising that the developers of GAMS owe a considerable debt of gratitude to the World Bank. Research and development work on GAMS was funded by the Bank's Research Committee (RPO 671-58 and 673-06) and carried out under the direction of Alexander Meeraus in the Development Research Center (later Department) in Washington, D.C. Many people have participated in the design and implementation of the system at different times; since exact attribution to each of them is impossible, we here simply list their names in alphabetical order: Masood Ahmad, John Ayler, Jan Bisschop, Piet Bleyendaal, Tony Brooke, Henrik Dahl, Arne Drud, Paul van der Eijk, Richard Inman, David Kendrick, Mohammed Ketabchi, Yonatan Levi, Alex Meeraus, Soren Nielsen, Sethu Palaniappan, Helen Patton, Skip Paules, Peter Pellemans, Mohammed Pourghadiri, and Ardy Stoutjesdijk. The main authors of the software are Tony Brooke, Paul van der Eijk, and Alexander Meeraus.

Without the support, understanding, and commitment of senior management, the project would have been impossible. In chronological order, J. Duloy, A. Stoutjesdijk, and G. Ingram were the responsible department directors, and Hollis B. Chenery and Anne O. Kreuger were the Vice Presidents. B. Balassa, B. King and D. Lal were Research Administrators. We all owe them a great deal.

We also owe a great deal to Alan Manne and to Michael Saunders. They have tirelessly reviewed successive versions of this book and have helped to make it clearer, less verbose, and a more effective teaching tool. Peter Bocock has done a splendid professional editing job on the final draft, and we have also received helpful comments and suggestions from J. Colias, P. Manouchehri-Adib, B. McCullough, B. Paulin, S. Rogers, and R. Rosenthal.

We are also grateful to Roy Marsten and Michael Saunders for giving freely of their time while ZOOM and MINOS were being modified to run with GAMS. We also thank those who have written parts of this book: Rick Rosenthal for Chapter 2, the tutorial; Philip Gill, Walter Murray, Bruce Murtagh, Michael Saunders, and Margaret Wright for Appendix D on GAMS/MINOS; and Roy Marsten and Jaya Singhal for Appendix E on GAMS/ZOOM. Thanks also to all the GAMS users, too many to mention individually, who have commented on the software, showed us their models, or reported errors.

Anthony Brooke
The World Bank

David Kendrick
The University of Texas

Alexander Meeraus
The World Bank

PART 1

Introduction

1 Introduction

2 A GAMS Tutorial

INTRODUCTION 1

1.1 MOTIVATION ■

Substantial progress was made in the 1950s and 1960s with the development of algorithms and computer codes to solve large mathematical programming problems. The number of applications of these tools in the 1970s was less than expected, however, because the solution procedures formed only a small part of the overall modeling effort. A large part of the time required to develop a model involved data preparation and transformation and report preparation. Each model required many hours of analyst and programming time to organize the data and write the programs that would transform the data into the form required by the mathematical programming optimizers. Furthermore, it was difficult to detect and eliminate errors because the programs that performed the data operations were only accessible to the specialist who wrote them and not to the analysts in charge of the project.

GAMS was developed to improve on this situation by

- Providing a high-level language for the compact representation of large and complex models
- Allowing changes to be made in model specifications simply and safely
- Allowing unambiguous statements of algebraic relationships
- Permitting model descriptions that are independent of solution algorithms

1.2 BASIC FEATURES OF GAMS ■

1.2 (a) General Principles ■

The design of GAMS has incorporated ideas drawn from relational database theory and mathematical programming and has attempted to merge these ideas to suit the needs of strategic modelers. Relational databases provide a structured framework for developing general data organization and transformation capabilities. Mathematical programming

3

provides a way of describing a problem and a variety of methods for solving it. The following principles were used in designing the system:

- All existing algorithmic methods should be available without changing the user's model representation. Introduction of new methods, or of new implementations of existing methods, should be possible without requiring changes in existing models. Linear, nonlinear, and mixed integer optimizations can currently be accommodated, as well as the special cases of simultaneous linear or nonlinear systems; extensions are planned to linear (and later to nonlinear) complementarity problems.

- The optimization problem should be expressible independently of the data it uses. This separation of logic and data allows problems to be increased in size without causing an increase in the complexity of the representation.

- The use of the relational data model requires that the allocation of computer resources be automated. This means that large and complex models can be constructed without the user having to worry about details such as array sizes and scratch storage.

1.2 (b)   Documentation   ∎

The GAMS model representation is in a form that can be easily read by people and by computers. This means that the GAMS program itself is the documentation of the model, and that the separate description required in the past (which was a burden to maintain, and which was seldom up-to-date) is no longer needed. Moreover, the design of GAMS incorporates the following features that specifically address the user's documentation needs:

- A GAMS model representation is concise, and makes full use of the elegance of the mathematical representation.

- All data transformations are specified concisely and algebraically. This means that all data can be entered in their most elemental form and that all transformations made in constructing the model and in reporting are available for inspection.

- Explanatory text can be made part of the definition of all symbols and is reproduced whenever associated values are displayed.

- All information needed to understand the model is in one document.

Of course some discipline is needed to take full advantage of these design features, but the aim is to make models more accessible, more understandable, more verifiable, and hence more credible.

1.2 (c)   Portability   ∎

The GAMS system is designed so that models can be solved on different types of computers with no change. A model developed on a small personal computer can later be solved on a large mainframe. One person can develop a model that is later used by others, who may be physically distant from the original developer. In contrast to previous approaches, only one document need be moved—the GAMS statement of the model, which rarely exceeds a few hundred lines of information and always fits on a diskette. It contains all the data and logical specifications needed to solve the model.

1.2 (d)   User Interface   ■

Portability concerns also have implications for the user interface. The basic GAMS system is file-oriented, and no special editor or graphical input and output routines exist. Rather than burden the user with having to learn yet another set of editing commands, GAMS offers an open architecture in which each user can use his word processor or editor of choice. This basic user interface facilitates the integration of GAMS with a variety of existing and future user environments.

1.2 (e)   Model Library   ■

When architects begin to design a new building, they develop the new structure by using ideas and techniques that have been tested in previous structures. The same is true in other fields: design elements from previous projects serve as sources of ideas for new developments.

From the early stages of the development of GAMS we have collected models to be used in a library of examples. Many of these are standard textbook examples and can be used in classes on problem formulation or to illustrate points about GAMS. Others are models that have been used in policy or sector analysis and are interesting for both the methods and the data they use. All the substantive models in the library are described in the open literature. The entire collection of models is now included with all mainframe GAMS systems, along with a database to help users locate examples that cover countries, sectors, or topics of interest to them. The model library is also available separately (on diskettes) to users of DOS-based personal computers, although some of the models are too large to be solved on DOS machines.

1.3   ORGANIZATION OF THE BOOK   ■

Some introductions to software systems are like reference manuals: they describe each command in detail. Others take you step by step through a small number of examples. This book uses elements of both approaches. The text is divided into three parts. The first part (Chapters 1 and 2) is introductory. Chapter 2 is a self-contained tutorial that guides you through a single example, a small transportation model, in some detail: you can quickly investigate the flavor of GAMS by reading it.

The second part (Chapters 3 to 12) comprises the meat of the book. The components of the GAMS language are introduced in an informal but ordered way, interspersed with detailed examples that are often drawn from the model library. Some specialized material has deliberately been omitted in this process because our primary aim is to make GAMS accessible to the widest possible audience, especially those without extensive experience with computers or mathematical programming systems. (We do, however, assume familiarity with quantitative methods and mathematical representations.)

The third part (Chapters 13 to 19) consists of specialized discussions of advanced topics and can be studied as needed. Users with large, complex, or expensive models will find much useful material in this part. The topics include the DISPLAY statement, the work file, nonlinear models, mixed integer models, large models, and the model library. Finally, the Appendices contain additional material for the advanced or curious user.

1.4 GETTING STARTED ■

Before you can use GAMS on a personal computer, the system must be installed from the distribution diskettes to your hard disk. If this has not been done, you should carefully follow the installation instructions that come with the diskettes: these are reproduced in the last section of this book, Installation Guide. If you have the restricted "student" version of GAMS, details of the restrictions can be found on page 274 in the Installation Guide.

GAMS systems on mainframe computers are normally installed and administered by the group that has arranged for the license. Once GAMS has been installed, individual users typically need to incorporate access information into their local environment. This causes an automatic "link" to be made to GAMS whenever the computer is used. Check with the computer center or whoever is handling the administration of GAMS for details.

A GAMS TUTORIAL 2

by Richard E. Rosenthal

2.1 INTRODUCTION ■

The introductory part of this book ends with a detailed example of the use of GAMS for formulating, solving, and analyzing a small and simple optimization problem. It was written by Richard E. Rosenthal of the Naval Postgraduate School in Monterey, California. The example is a quick but complete overview of GAMS and its features. Many references are made to other parts of the book, but they are only to tell you where to look for more details; the material here can be read profitably without reference to the rest of the book.

The example is an instance of the transportation problem of linear programming, which has historically served as a "laboratory animal" in the development of optimization technology. [See, for example, Dantzig (1963).] It is a good choice for illustrating the power of algebraic modeling languages like GAMS because the transportation problem, no matter how large the instance at hand, possesses a simple, exploitable algebraic structure. You will see that almost all of the statements in the GAMS input file we are about to present would remain unchanged if a much larger transportation problem were considered.

In the familiar transportation problem, we are given the supplies at several plants and the demands at several markets for a single commodity, and we are given the unit costs of shipping the commodity from plants to markets. The economic question is: how much shipment should there be between each plant and each market so as to minimize total transport cost?

The algebraic representation of this problem is usually presented in a format similar to the following.

Indices:

i = plants
j = markets

Given Data:

a_i = supply of commodity at plant i (in cases)
b_j = demand for commodity at market j (cases)
c_{ij} = cost per unit shipment between plant i and market j ($/case)

Decision Variables:

x_{ij} = amount of commodity to ship from plant i to market j (cases),
where $x_{ij} \geq 0$, for all i, j

Constraints:

Observe supply limit at plant i:	$\sum_j x_{ij} \leq a_i$, *for all i*	(cases)
Satisfy demand at market j:	$\sum_i x_{ij} \geq b_j$, *for all j*	(cases)

Objective Function:

Minimize $\sum_i \sum_j c_{ij} x_{ij}$ ($K)

Note that this simple example reveals some modeling practices that we regard as good habits in general and that are consistent with GAMS's design. First, all the entities of the model are identified (and grouped) by type. Second, the ordering of entities is chosen so that no symbol is referred to before it is defined. Third, the units of all entities are specified, and, fourth, the units are chosen to a scale such that the numerical values to be encountered by the optimizer have relatively small absolute orders of magnitude. (The symbol $K here means thousands of dollars.)

The names of the types of entities may differ among modelers. For example, economists use the terms "exogenous variable" and "endogenous variable" for "given data" and "decision variable," respectively. In GAMS, the terminology adopted is as follows: indices are called SETS, given data are called PARAMETERS, decision variables are called VARIABLES, and constraints and the objective function are called EQUATIONS.

The GAMS representation of the transportation problem closely resembles the algebraic representation above. The most important difference, however, is that the GAMS version can be read and processed by a computer.

As an instance of the transportation problem, suppose there are two canning plants and three markets, with the given data as follows. (This example is adapted from Dantzig, 1963, Chapter 3.)

		Markets		
	New York	*Chicago*	*Topeka*	
Plants		*Shipping Distances*		*Supplies*
Seattle	2.5	1.7	1.8	350
San Diego	2.5	1.8	1.4	600
Demands	325	300	275	

Shipping distances are in thousands of miles, and shipping costs are assumed to be $90.00 per case per thousand miles.

The GAMS representation of this problem is as follows:

```
SETS
     I    canning plants    / SEATTLE, SAN-DIEGO /
     J    markets           / NEW-YORK, CHICAGO, TOPEKA / ;
```

```
PARAMETERS

    A(I)  capacity of plant i in cases
      /  SEATTLE     350
         SAN-DIEGO   600  /

    B(J)  demand at market j in cases
      /  NEW-YORK    325
         CHICAGO     300
         TOPEKA      275  / ;

TABLE D(I,J)  distance in thousands of miles
                  NEW-YORK      CHICAGO      TOPEKA
    SEATTLE         2.5           1.7          1.8
    SAN-DIEGO       2.5           1.8          1.4  ;

SCALAR F  freight in dollars per case per thousand miles  /90/ ;

PARAMETER C(I,J)  transport cost in thousands of dollars per case ;

       C(I,J) = F * D(I,J) / 1000 ;

VARIABLES
    X(I,J)  shipment quantities in cases
    Z       total transportation costs in thousands of dollars ;

POSITIVE VARIABLE X ;

EQUATIONS
    COST        define objective function
    SUPPLY(I)   observe supply limit at plant i
    DEMAND(J)   satisfy demand at market j ;

COST ..        Z  =E=  SUM((I,J), C(I,J)*X(I,J)) ;

SUPPLY(I) ..  SUM(J, X(I,J))  =L=  A(I) ;

DEMAND(J) ..  SUM(I, X(I,J))  =G=  B(J) ;

MODEL TRANSPORT /ALL/ ;

SOLVE TRANSPORT USING LP MINIMIZING Z ;

DISPLAY X.L, X.M ;
```

If you submit a file containing the statements above as input to the GAMS program, the transportation model will be formulated and solved. Appendix A gives detailed instructions on how to invoke GAMS on several kinds of computers, but the simplest ("no frills") way to call GAMS is to enter the word GAMS followed by the input file's name.* You will see a number of terse lines describing the progress GAMS is making, including the name of the file onto which the output is being written. When GAMS has finished,

---

*When using the "no frills" call, you may omit the file's type or extension, but you are obligated to make certain choices. For example, on DOS-based personal computers, the input file's extension (if omitted) must be ".GMS," and on mainframes with the CMS operating system, the input file's type must be "GAMS."

examine this file, and if all has gone well the optimal shipments will be displayed at the bottom as follows.

	NEW-YORK	CHICAGO	TOPEKA
SEATTLE	50.000	300.000	
SAN-DIEGO	275.000		275.000

You will also receive the marginal costs (simplex multipliers) below.

	CHICAGO	TOPEKA
SEATTLE		0.036
SAN-DIEGO	0.009	

These results indicate, for example, that it is optimal to send nothing from Seattle to Topeka, but if you insist on sending one case it will add .036 $K (or $36.00) to the optimal cost. (Can you prove that this figure is correct from the optimal shipments and the given data?*)

2.2 Structure of a GAMS Model ■

For the remainder of the tutorial, we will discuss the basic components of a GAMS model, with reference to the example above. The basic components are

Inputs

SETS

Declaration
Assignment of members

Data (PARAMETERS, TABLES, SCALARS)

Declaration
Assignment of values

VARIABLES

Declaration
Assignment of type
(Optional) Assignment of bounds and/or initial values

EQUATIONS

Declaration
Definition

MODEL and SOLVE statements

(Optional) DISPLAY statements

---

*If you send one case from Seattle to Topeka, then, to maintain the supply/demand balance, you must send one less case from San Diego to Topeka, one more case from San Diego to New York, and one less case from Seattle to New York. The net increase in shipping distance is $+1800 - 1400 + 2500 - 2500 = 400$ miles, which costs $36 at the given shipping rate.

Outputs

Echo Print

Reference Maps

Equation Listings

Status Reports

Results

There are optional input components, such as edit checks for bad data and requests for customized reports of results. Other optional advanced features include saving and restoring old models, and creating multiple models in a single run, but this tutorial will discuss only the basic components.

Before treating the individual components, we give a few general remarks.

1. A GAMS model is a collection of statements in the GAMS language. The only rule governing the ordering of statements is that an entity of the model cannot be referenced before it is declared to exist.

2. GAMS statements may be laid out typographically in almost any style that is appealing to the user. Multiple lines per statement, embedded blank lines, and multiple statements per line are allowed. You will get a good idea of what is allowed from the examples in this tutorial, but precise rules of the road are given in Chapter 3.

3. When you are a beginning GAMS user, you should terminate every statement with a semicolon, as in our examples. The rules for relaxed punctuation are given in Chapter 18.

4. The GAMS compiler does not distinguish between upper- and lowercase letters, so you are free to use either. The style adopted and recommended here is to always use uppercase for any word or symbol that is part of the GAMS language or that is an entity declared to exist in a particular GAMS model. We recommend reserving lowercase only for words that appear in the GAMS input for documentation.

5. Documentation is crucial to the usefulness of mathematical models. It is all the more useful (and most likely to be accurate) if it is embedded within the model itself rather than written up separately. There are at least two ways to insert documentation within a GAMS model. First, any line that starts with an asterisk in column 1 is disregarded as a comment line by the GAMS compiler. Second, perhaps more important, documentary text can be inserted within specific GAMS statements. All the lowercase words in the transportation model are examples of the second form of documentation.

6. As you can see from the list of input components above, the creation of GAMS entities involves two steps: a declaration and an assignment or definition. "Declaration" means declaring the existence of something and giving it a name. "Assignment" or "definition" means giving something a specific value or form. In the case of equations, you must make the declaration and definition in separate GAMS statements. For all other GAMS entities, however, you have the option of making declarations and assignments in the same statement or separately.

7. The names given to the entities of the model must start with a letter and can be followed by up to nine more letters or digits.

2.3   SETS ■

Sets are the basic building blocks of a GAMS model, corresponding exactly to the indices in the algebraic representations of models. The transportation example above contains just one SET statement:

```
SETS
      I   canning plants   / SEATTLE, SAN-DIEGO /
      J   markets          / NEW-YORK, CHICAGO, TOPEKA / ;
```

The effects of this statement are probably self-evident. We declared two sets and gave them the names I and J. We also assigned members to the sets as follows:

$I = \{\text{Seattle, San Diego}\}$

$J = \{\text{New York, Chicago, Topeka}\}.$

You should note the typographical differences between the GAMS format and the usual mathematical format for listing the elements of a set. GAMS uses slashes "/" rather than curly braces "{ }" to delineate the set simply because not all computer keyboards have keys for curly braces. Note also that multiword names like "New York" are not allowed, so hyphens are inserted.

The lowercase words in the SETS statement above are called "text." Text is optional. It is there only for internal documentation, serving no formal purpose in the model. The GAMS compiler makes no attempt to interpret the text, but it saves the text and "parrots" it back to you at various times for your convenience.*

It was not necessary to combine the creation of sets I and J in one statement. We could have put them into separate statements as follows:

```
SET   I   canning plants   / SEATTLE, SAN-DIEGO / ;
SET   J   markets          / NEW-YORK, CHICAGO, TOPEKA / ;
```

The placement of blank spaces and lines (as well as the choice of upper- or lowercase) is up to you. Each GAMS user tends to develop individual stylistic conventions. (The use of the singular SET or the plural SETS is also up to you. Using SET in a statement that makes a single declaration and SETS in one that makes several is good English, but GAMS treats the singular and plural synonymously.)

A convenient feature to use when you are assigning members to a set is the asterisk. It applies to cases when the elements follow a sequence. For example, the following are valid SET statements in GAMS.

```
SET   T   time periods   / 1991 * 2000 / ;
SET   M   machines       / MACH1 * MACH24 / ;
```

---

*The text must fit on one line and cannot exceed 80 characters in length. It should not start with one of GAM's reserved words or contain any of the following special characters: equal sign (=), comma (,), semicolon (;), or slash (/).

Here the effect is to assign

$$T = \{1991, 1992, 1993, \ldots, 2000\}$$
$$M = \{\text{MACH}_1, \text{MACH}_2, \ldots, \text{MACH}_{24}\}.$$

Note that set elements are stored as character strings, so the elements of T are not numbers.

Another convenient feature is the ALIAS statement, which is used to give another name to a previously declared set. In the following example,

```
ALIAS (T,TP) ;
```

the name TP is like a T' in mathematical notation. It is useful in models that are concerned with the interactions of elements within the same set.

The sets I, J, T, and M in the statements above are examples of static sets, i.e., they are assigned their members directly by the user and do not change. GAMS has several capabilities for creating dynamic sets, which acquire their members through the execution of set-theoretic and logical operations. Dynamic sets are discussed in Chapter 11. Another valuable advanced feature is multidimensional sets which, are discussed in Chapter 4.

2.4 DATA ∎

The GAMS model of the transportation problem demonstrates all of the three fundamentally different formats that are allowable for entering data. The three formats are

1. Lists
2. Tables
3. Direct assignments

2.4 (a) Data Entry by Lists ∎

The first format is illustrated by the first PARAMETERS statement of the example, which is repeated below.

```
PARAMETERS

    A(I)   capacity of plant i in cases
        /  SEATTLE     350
           SAN-DIEGO   600  /

    B(J)   demand at market j in cases
        /  NEW-YORK    325
           CHICAGO     300
           TOPEKA      275  / ;
```

This statement has several effects. Again, they may be self-evident, but it is worthwhile to analyze them in detail. The statement declares the existence of two parameters, gives them the names A and B, and declares their "domains" to be I and J, respectively. (A domain is the set, or tuple of sets, over which a parameter, variable, or equation is defined.) The statement also gives documentary text for each parameter and assigns values of A(I) and B(J) for each element of I and J. It is perfectly acceptable to break this one statement into two, if you prefer, as follows.

```
PARAMETER  A(I)   capacity of plant i in cases
     /  SEATTLE    350
        SAN-DIEGO  600  / ;

PARAMETER  B(J)   demand at market j in cases
     /  NEW-YORK   325
        CHICAGO    300
        TOPEKA     275  / ;
```

Here are some points to remember when using the list format.

1. The list of domain elements and their respective parameter values can be laid out in almost any way you like. The only rules are that the entire list must be enclosed in slashes and that the element-value pairs must be separated by commas or entered on separate lines.

2. There is no semicolon separating the element-value list from the name, domain, and text that precede it. This is because the same statement is being used for declaration and assignment when you use the list format. (An element-value list by itself is not interpretable by GAMS and will result in an error message.)

3. The GAMS compiler has an unusual feature called "domain checking," which verifies that each domain element in the list is in fact a member of the appropriate set. For example, if you were to spell "Seattle" correctly in the statement declaring SET I but misspell it as "Seatle" in a subsequent element-value list, the GAMS compiler would give you an error message that the element Seatle does not belong to the set I.

4. Zero is the default value for all parameters. Therefore, you only need to include the nonzero entries in the element-value list, and these can be entered in any order.

5. A scalar is regarded as a parameter that has no domain. It can be declared and assigned with a SCALAR statement containing a "degenerate" list of only one value, as in the following statement from the transportation model.

```
SCALAR F freight in dollars per case per thousand miles /90/ ;
```

If a parameter's domain has two or more dimensions, it can still have its values entered by the list format. This is very useful for entering arrays that are sparse (having few nonzeros) and supersparse (having few distinct nonzeros). This is discussed in Chapter 5.

2.4 (b)   Data Entry by Tables   ■

Optimization practitioners have noticed for some time that many of the input data for a large model are derived from relatively small tables of numbers. Thus, it is very useful to have the table format for data entry. An example of a two-dimensional table (or matrix) is provided in the transportation model:

```
TABLE D(I,J)  distance in thousands of miles
                NEW-YORK      CHICAGO      TOPEKA
    SEATTLE        2.5          1.7         1.8
    SAN-DIEGO      2.5          1.8         1.4  ;
```

The effect of this statement is to declare the parameter D and to specify its domain as the set of ordered pairs in the Cartesian product of I and J. The values of D are also given in this statement under the appropriate heading. If there are blank entries in a table, they are interpreted as zeroes.

As in the list format, GAMS will perform domain checking to make sure that the row and column names of the table are members of the appropriate sets. Formats for entering tables with more columns than you can fit on one line and for entering tables with more than two dimensions are given in Chapter 5.

2.4 (c) Data Entry by Direct Assignment ■

The direct assignment method of data entry differs from the list and table methods in that it divides the tasks of parameter declaration and parameter assignment between separate statements. The transportation model contains the following example of this method.

```
PARAMETER C(I,J)  transportation cost in dollars per case ;
          C(I,J) = F * D(I,J) / 1000 ;
```

It is important to emphasize the presence of the semicolon at the end of the first line. Without it, the GAMS compiler would attempt to interpret both lines as parts of the same statement. (GAMS would fail to discern a valid interpretation, so it would send you a terse but helpful error message.)

The effects of the first statement above are to declare the parameter C, to specify the domain (I,J), and to provide some documentary text. The second statement assigns to C(I,J) the product of the values of the parameters F and D(I,J). Naturally, this is legal in GAMS only if you have already assigned values to F and D(I,J) in previous statements.

The direct assignment above applies to all (I,J) pairs in the domain of C. If you wish to make assignments for specific elements in the domain, you enclose the element names in quotes. For example,

```
C("SEATTLE","NEW-YORK") = 0.40 ;
```

is a valid GAMS assignment statement.

The same parameter can be assigned value more than once. Each assignment statement takes effect immediately and overrides any previous values. (In contrast, the same parameter *may not be declared more than once*. This is a GAMS error check to keep you from accidentally using the same name for two different things.)

The right-hand side of an assignment statement can contain a great variety of mathematical expressions and built-in functions. If you are familiar with a scientific programming language such as FORTRAN, you will have no trouble in becoming comfortable writing assignment statements in GAMS. (Notice, however, that GAMS has some efficiencies not shared by FORTRAN. For example, we were able to assign C(I,J) values for all (I,J) pairs without constructing "do loops.")

The GAMS standard operations and supplied functions are given in Table 6.1. Here are some examples of valid assignments. In all cases, assume the left-hand-side parameter has already been declared and the right-hand-side parameters have already been assigned values in previous statements.

```
CSQUARED = SQR(C) ;
E = M * CSQUARED ;
W = L / LAMDA ;
```

```
EOQ(I)  =  SQRT( 2 * DEMAND(I) * ORDCOST(I) / HOLDCOST(I) ) ;
T(I) = MIN( P(I), Q(I)/R(I), LOG(S(I)) ) ;
EUCLIDEAN(I,J) = SQRT( SQR(X1(I) - X1(J)) + SQR(X2(I) - X2(J))) ;
PRESENT(J) = FUTURE(J) * EXP( - INTEREST * TIME(J) ) ;
```

The summation and product operators to be introduced later can also be used in direct assignments.

2.5 VARIABLES ∎

The decision variables (or endogenous variables) of a GAMS-expressed model must be declared with a VARIABLES statement. Each variable is given a name, a domain if appropriate, and (optionally) text. The transportation model contains the following example of a VARIABLES statement.

```
VARIABLES
    X(I,J )   shipment quantities in cases
    Z         total transportation costs in thousands of dollars ;
```

This statement results in the declaration of a shipment variable for each i,j pair. (You will see in Chapter 8 how GAMS can handle the typical real-world situation in which only a subset of the i,j pairs is allowable for shipment.)

The Z variable is declared without a domain because it is a scalar quantity. Every GAMS optimization model must contain one such variable to serve as the quantity to be minimized or maximized.

Once declared, every variable must be assigned a type. The permissible types are give below.

Name of Variable Type	Allowed Range of Variable
FREE (default type)	$-\infty$ to $+\infty$
POSITIVE	0 to $+\infty$
NEGATIVE	$-\infty$ to 0
BINARY	0 or 1
INTEGER	$0, 1, \ldots, 100$

The variable that serves as the quantity to be optimized *must be* a scalar and *must be* of the FREE type. In our transportation example, Z is kept free by default, but X(I,J) is constrained to nonnegativity by the following statement.

```
POSITIVE VARIABLE X;
```

Note that the domain of X should not be repeated in the type assignment. All entries in the domain automatically have the same variable type.

Section 2.10 describes how to assign lower bounds, upper bounds, and initial values to variables.

2.6   EQUATIONS   ■

The power of algebraic modeling languages like GAMS is most apparent in the creation of the equations and inequalities that comprise the model under construction. This is because whenever a group of equations or inequalities has the same algebraic structure, all the members of the group are created simultaneously, not individually.

2.6 (a)   Equation Declaration   ■

Equations must be declared and defined in separate statements. The format of the declaration is the same as for other GAMS entities. First comes the keyword, EQUATIONS in this case, followed by the name, domain and text of one or more groups of equations or inequalities being declared. Our transportation model contains the following equation declaration:

```
EQUATIONS
        COST            define objective function
        SUPPLY(I)       observe supply limit at plant i
        DEMAND(J)       satisfy demand at market j;
```

Keep in mind that the word "EQUATION" has a broad meaning in GAMS. It encompasses both equality and inequality relationships, and a GAMS equation with a single name can refer to one or several of these relationships. For example, COST has no domain so it is a single equation, but SUPPLY refers to a set of inequalities defined over the domain I.

2.6 (b) GAMS Summation (and Product) Notation   ■

Before going into equation definition we describe GAMS's notation for summations. Remember that GAMS is designed for standard keyboards and line-by-line input readers, so it is not possible (nor would it be convenient for the user) to employ the standard mathematical notation for summations.

GAMS's summation notation can be used for simple and complex expressions. Its format is based on the idea of always thinking of a summation as an operator with two arguments:

```
SUM( index of summation, summand )
```

The two arguments are separated by a comma, and if the first argument requires a comma then it should be in parentheses. The second argument can be any mathematical expression including another summation.

As a simple example, the transportation problem contains the expression

```
SUM( J, X(I,J) )
```

that is equivalent to $\sum_j x_{ij}$.

A slightly more complex summation is used in the following example:

```
SUM( (I,J), C(I,J)*X(I,J) )
```

that is equivalent to $\sum_i \sum_j c_{ij} x_{ij}$.

The last expression could also have been written as a nested summation as follows:

```
SUM( I, SUM( J, C(I,J)*X(I,J) ) )
```

In Chapters 6 and 8 we describe how to use the "dollar" operator to impose restrictions on the summation operator so that only the elements of I and J that satisfy specified conditions are included in the summation.

Products are defined in GAMS using exactly the same format as summations, replacing "SUM" by "PROD." For example,

```
PROD( J, X(I,J) )
```

is equivalent to $\prod_j x_{ij}$.

Summation and product operators may be used in direct assignment statements for parameters. For example,

```
SCALAR TOTSUPPLY  total supply over all plants ;
TOTSUPPLY = SUM( I, B(I) ) ;
```

2.6 (c) Equation Definition ∎

Equation definitions are the most complex statements in GAMS in terms of their variety. The components of an equation definition are, in order:

1. The name of the equation being defined
2. The domain
3. (Optional) domain restriction condition
4. The symbol "`..`"
5. Left-hand-side expression
6. Relational operator: `=L=`, `=E=`, or `=G=`
7. Right-hand-side expression

The transportation example contains three of these statements.

```
COST ..        Z =E= SUM((I,J), C(I,J)*X(I,J)) ;
SUPPLY(I) ..   SUM(J, X(I,J))  =L=  A(I) ;
DEMAND(J) ..   SUM(I, X(I,J))  =G=  B(J) ;
```

Here are some points to remember.

1. The power to create multiple equations with a single GAMS statement is controlled by the domain. For example, the DEMAND definition will result in the creation of one constraint for each element of the domain J, as shown in the following excerpt from the GAMS output.

```
DEMAND(NEW-YORK).. X(SEATTLE,NEW-YORK) + X(SAN-DIEGO,NEW-YORK) =G= 325 ;
DEMAND(CHICAGO).. X(SEATTLE,CHICAGO) + X(SAN-DIEGO,CHICAGO) =G= 300 ;
DEMAND(TOPEKA).. X(SEATTLE,TOPEKA) + X(SAN-DIEGO,TOPEKA) =G= 275 ;
```

The key idea here is that the definition of the demand constraints is exactly the same whether we are solving the toy-sized example above or a 20,000-node real-world problem. In either case, the user enters just one generic equation algebraically, and GAMS creates the specific equations that are appropriate for the model instance at hand. (Using some other optimization packages, something like the extract above would be part of the input, not the output.)

2. In many real-world problems, some of the members of an equation's domain need to be omitted or differentiated from the pattern of the others because of an exception of some kind. GAMS can readily accommodate this loss of structure using a powerful feature known as the "dollar" or "such-that" operator, which is not illustrated here but is discussed in Chapter 8. The domain restriction feature can be absolutely essential for keeping the size of a real-world model within the range of solvability.

3. The relational operators have the following meanings:

=L=   less than or equal to

=G=   greater than or equal to

=E=   equal to

   It is important to understand the difference between the symbols "=" and "=E=." The "=" symbol is used only in direct assignments, and the "=E=" symbol is used only in equation definitions. These two contexts are very different. A direct assignment gives a desired value to a parameter before the solver is called. An equation definition also describes a desired relationship, but it cannot be satisfied until after the solver is called. It follows that equation definitions must contain variables and direct assignments must not.

4. Variables can appear on the left- or right-hand side of an equation or both. The same variable can appear in an equation more than once. The GAMS processor will automatically convert the equation to its equivalent standard form (variables on the left, no duplicate appearances) before calling the solver.

5. An equation definition can appear anywhere in the GAMS input, provided the equation and all variables and parameters to which it refers are previously declared. (Note that it is permissible for a parameter appearing in the equation to be assigned or reassigned a value after the definition. This is useful when doing multiple model runs with one GAMS input.) The equations need not be defined in the same order in which they are declared.

2.7   OBJECTIVE FUNCTION   ■

This is just a reminder that GAMS has no explicit entity called the "objective function." To specify the function to be optimized, you must create a variable, which is free (unconstrained in sign) and scalar-valued (has no domain) and which appears in an equation definition that equates it to your objective function.

2.8   MODEL AND SOLVE STATEMENTS   ■

The word "MODEL" has a very precise meaning in GAMS. It is simply a collection of EQUATIONS. Like other GAMS entities, it must be given a name in a declaration. The format of the declaration is the keyword MODEL followed by the model's name, followed by a list of equation names enclosed in slashes. If all previously defined equations are to be included, you can enter /ALL/ in place of the explicit list. In our example, there is one MODEL statement:

    MODEL TRANSPORT /ALL/ ;

This statement may seem superfluous, but it is useful to advanced users who may create several models in one GAMS run. If we were to use the explicit list rather than the shortcut /ALL/, the statement would be written as

    MODEL TRANSPORT / COST, SUPPLY, DEMAND / ;

The domains are omitted from the list since they are not part of the equation name. The list option is used when only a subset of the existing equations comprise a specific model (or submodel) being generated.

Once a model has been declared and assigned equations, we are ready to call the solver. This is done with a SOLVE statement, which in our example is written as

    SOLVE TRANSPORT USING LP MINIMIZING Z ;

The format of the SOLVE statement is as follows:

1. The keyword "SOLVE"
2. The name of the model to be solved
3. The keyword "USING"
4. An available solution procedure, such as

    "LP" for linear programming
    "NLP" for nonlinear programming
    "MIP" for mixed integer programming
    "RMIP" for relaxed mixed integer programming

5. The keyword "MINIMIZING" or "MAXIMIZING"
6. The name of the variable to be optimized

2.9 DISPLAY STATEMENTS ■

The SOLVE statement will cause several things to happen when it is executed. The specific instance of interest of the model will be generated, the appropriate data structures for inputting this problem to the solver will be created, the solver will be invoked, and the solver's output will be printed to a file. To get the optimal values of the primal and/or dual variables, we can look at the solver's output, or, if we wish, we can request a display of these results from GAMS. Our example contains the following statement:

    DISPLAY X.L, X.M ;

that calls for a printout of the final levels, X.L, and marginals (or reduced costs), X.M, of the shipment variables, X(I,J). GAMS will automatically format this printout in two-dimensional tables with appropriate headings.

2.10   THE ".LO, .L, .UP, .M" DATABASE   ∎

GAMS was designed with a small database system in which records are maintained for the variables and equations. There are four fields in each record:

.LO = lower bound

.L = level or primal value

.UP = upper bound

.M = marginal or dual value

The format for referencing these quantities is the variable or equation's name followed by the field's name, followed (if necessary) by the domain (or an element of the domain).

GAMS allows the user complete read- and write-access to the database. This may not seem remarkable to you now, but it can become a greatly appreciated feature in advanced use. Some examples of use of the database follow.

2.10 (a)   Assignment of Variable Bounds and/or Initial Values   ∎

The lower and upper bounds of a variable are set automatically according to the variable's type (FREE, POSITIVE, NEGATIVE, BINARY, or INTEGER), but these bounds can be overwritten by the GAMS user. Some examples follow.

```
X.UP(I,J) = CAPACITY(I,J) ;
X.LO(I,J) = 10.0 ;
X.UP("SEATTLE","NEW-YORK") = 1.2 * CAPACITY("SEATTLE","NEW-YORK") ;
```

It is assumed in the first and third examples that CAPACITY(I,J) is a parameter that was previously declared and assigned values. These statements must appear after the variable declaration and before the SOLVE statement. All the mathematical expressions available for direct assignments are usable on the right-hand side.

In nonlinear programming, it is very important for the modeler to help the solver by specifying as narrow a range as possible between lower and upper bounds. It is also very helpful to specify an initial solution from which the solver can start searching for the optimum. For example, in a constrained inventory model, the variables are QUANTITY(I), and it is known that the optimal solution to the unconstrained version of the problem is a parameter called EOQ(I). As a guess for the optimum of the constrained problem we enter

```
QUANTITY.L(I) = 0.5 * EOQ(I) ;
```

(The default initial level is zero unless zero is not within the bounded range, in which case it is the bound closest to zero.)

It is important to understand that the .LO and .UP fields are entirely under the control of the GAMS user. The .L and .M fields, in contrast, can be initialized by the user but are then controlled by the solver.

2.10 (b)   Transformation and Display of Optimal Values   ∎

(This section can be skipped on first reading if desired.)

After the optimizer is called via the SOLVE statement, the values it computes for the primal and dual variables are placed in the database in the .L and .M fields. We can then read these results and transform and display them with GAMS statements.

For example, in the transportation problem, suppose we wish to know the percentage of each market's demand that is filled by each plant. After the SOLVE statement, we would enter

```
PARAMETER  PCTX(I,J)  percent of market j's demand filled by plant i ;

PCTX(I,J)  =  100.0 * X.L(I,J) / B(J) ;

DISPLAY PCTX ;
```

Appending these commands to the original transportation problem input results in the following output:

```
PCTX        PERCENT OF MARKET J'S DEMAND FILLED BY PLANT I

            NEW-YORK     CHICAGO      TOPEKA

SEATTLE       15.385     100.000
SAN-DIEGO     84.615                  100.000
```

For an example involving marginals, we briefly consider the "ratio constraints" that commonly appear in blending and refining problems. These linear programming models are concerned with determining the optimal amount of each of several available raw materials to put into each of several desired finished products. Let $Y(I,J)$ be the variable for the number of tons of raw material i put into finished product j. Let $Q(J)$ be the variable for the number of tons of product j produced. Suppose the "ratio constraint" is that no product can consist of more than 25 percent of one ingredient, that is,

```
Y(I,J) / Q(J)  =L=  .25
```

for all i, j. To keep the model linear, the constraint is written as

```
RATIO(I,J)..  Y(I,J) - .25 * Q(J)  =L=  0.0 ;
```

rather than explicitly as a ratio.

The problem here is that RATIO.M(I,J), the marginal value associated with the linear form of the constraint, has no intrinsic meaning. At optimality, it tells us by at most how much we can benefit from relaxing the linear constraint to

```
Y(I,J) - .25 * Q(J)  =L= 1.0 ;
```

Unfortunately, this relaxed constraint has no realistic significance. The constraint we are interested in relaxing (or tightening) is the nonlinear form of the ratio constraint. For example, we would like to know the marginal benefit arising from changing the ratio constraint to

```
Y(I,J) / Q(J)  =L=  .26 ;
```

We can in fact obtain the desired marginals by entering the following transformation on the undesired marginals:

```
PARAMETER  AMR(I,J)  appropriate marginal for ratio constraint ;

AMR(I,J)  =  RATIO.M(I,J) * 0.01 * Q.L(J) ;

DISPLAY AMR ;
```

Notice that the assignment statement for AMR accesses both .M and .L records from the database. The idea behind the transformation is to notice that

```
Y(I,J) / Q(J) =L= .26 ;
```

is equivalent to

```
Y(I,J) - .25 * Q(J) =L= 0.01 * Q(J) ;
```

2.11   GAMS OUTPUT   ■

The default output of a GAMS run is extensive and informative. For a complete discussion, see Chapter 10. This tutorial discusses output partially as follows:

Outputs

Echo Print	*or*	Echo Print
Error Messages		Reference Maps
Reference Maps		Equation Listings
		Model Statistics
		Status Reports
		Solution Reports

A great deal of unnecessary anxiety has been caused by textbooks and users' manuals that give the reader the false impression that flawless use of advanced software should be easy for anyone with a positive pulse rate. GAMS is designed with the understanding that even the most experienced users will make errors. GAMS attempts to catch the errors as soon as possible and to minimize their consequences.

2.11 (a)   Echo Print   ■

Whether or not errors prevent your optimization problem from being solved, the first section of output from a GAMS run is an echo, or copy, of your input file. For the sake of future reference, GAMS puts line numbers on the left-hand side of the echo. For our transportation example, which luckily contained no errors, the echo print is as follows:

```
 3
 4    SETS
 5         I   canning plants   / SEATTLE, SAN-DIEGO /
 6         J   markets          / NEW-YORK, CHICAGO, TOPEKA / ;
 7
 8    PARAMETERS
 9
10         A(I)  capacity of plant i in cases
11             / SEATTLE      350
12               SAN-DIEGO    600  /
13
```

```
14         B(J)  demand at market j in cases
15            /  NEW-YORK    325
16               CHICAGO     300
17               TOPEKA      275  / ;
18
19   TABLE D(I,J)  distance in thousands of miles
20                     NEW-YORK      CHICAGO       TOPEKA
21      SEATTLE          2.5           1.7          1.8
22      SAN-DIEGO        2.5           1.8          1.4  ;
23
24   SCALAR F  freight in dollars per case per thousand miles  /90/ ;
25
26   PARAMETER C(I,J)  transport cost in thousands of dollars per case ;
27
28            C(I,J) = F * D(I,J) / 1000 ;
29
30   VARIABLES
31       X(I,J)   shipment quantities in cases
32       Z        total transportation costs in thousands of dollars ;
33
34   POSITIVE VARIABLE X ;
35
36   EQUATIONS
37       COST         define objective function
38       SUPPLY(I)    observe supply limit at plant i
39       DEMAND(J)    satisfy demand at market j ;
40
41   COST ..        Z  =E=  SUM((I,J), C(I,J)*X(I,J)) ;
42
43   SUPPLY(I) ..   SUM(J, X(I,J))  =L=  A(I) ;
44
45   DEMAND(J) ..   SUM(I, X(I,J))  =G=  B(J) ;
46
47   MODEL TRANSPORT /ALL/ ;
48
49   SOLVE TRANSPORT USING LP MINIMIZING Z ;
50
51   DISPLAY X.L, X.M ;
```

The reason this echo print starts with line number 3 rather than line number 1 is because the input file contains two "dollar-print-control" statements. This type of instruction controls the output printing, but since it has nothing to do with defining the optimization model, it is omitted from the echo. The dollar print controls must start in column 1. The two used in our example are as follows.

```
$TITLE  A TRANSPORTATION MODEL
$OFFUPPER
```

The $TITLE statement causes the subsequent text to be printed at the top of each page of output. The $OFFUPPER statement is needed for the echo to contain mixed upper- and lowercase. Other available instructions are given in Chapter 10 and Appendix B.

2.11 (b)   Error Messages   ■

When the GAMS compiler encounters an error in the input file, it inserts a coded error message inside the echo print on the line immediately following the scene of the offense. These messages always start with "****" and contain a "$" directly below the point at which the compiler thinks the error occured. The $ is followed by a numerical error code, which is explained after the echo print. Several examples follow.

Example 1: Entering the statement

```
        SET  Q  quarterly time periods  / SPRING, SUM, FALL, WTR / ;
```

results in the echo

```
    1    SET  Q  QUARTERLY TIME PERIODS  / SPRING, SUM, FALL, WTR / ;
****                                                    $160
```

In this case, the GAMS compiler indicates that something is wrong with the set element "SUM." At the bottom of the echo print, we see the interpretation of error code 160:

```
ERROR MESSAGES
 160    UNIQUE ELEMENT EXPECTED
```

The problem is that "SUM" is a reserved word meaning "summation," so our set element must have a unique name like "SUMMER." This is a common beginner's error. The complete list of reserved words is shown in Table 3.2.

Example 2: Another common error is the omission of a semicolon preceding a direct assignment or equation definition. In our transportation example, suppose we omit the semicolon prior to the assignment of $C(I,J)$, as follows.

```
        PARAMETER C(I,J)  transport cost in thousands of dollars per case
                  C(I,J) = F * D(I,J) / 1000 ;
```

Here is the resulting output.

```
   16    PARAMETER C(I,J)  transport cost in thousands of dollars per case
   17             C(I,J) = F * D(I,J) / 1000 ;
****               $97        $195$96$194$1
ERROR MESSAGES
    1    REAL NUMBER EXPECTED
   96    BLANK NEEDED BETWEEN IDENTIFIER AND TEXT
           (-OR-ILLEGAL CHARACTER IN IDENTIFIER)
           (-OR-CHECK FOR MISSING ';' ON PREVIOUS LINE)
   97    EXPLANATORY TEXT CAN NOT START WITH '$', '=', or '..'
           (-OR-CHECK FOR MISSING ';' ON PREVIOUS LINE)
  194    SYMBOL REDEFINED
  195    SYMBOL REDEFINED WITH A DIFFERENT TYPE
```

It is not uncommon for one little offense like our missing semicolon to generate five intimidating error messages. The lesson here is: concentrate on fixing the first error and ignore the others! The first error detected (in line 17), code 97, indicates that GAMS thinks the symbols in line 17 are a continuation of the documentary text at the end of line 16 rather than a direct assignment as we intended. The error message also appropriately advises us to check the preceding line for a missing semicolon.

Unfortunately, you cannot always expect error messages to be so accurate in their advice. The compiler cannot read your mind. It will at times fail to comprehend your intentions, so learn to detect the causes of errors by picking up the clues that abound in the GAMS output. For example, the missing semicolon could have been detected by looking up the C entry in the cross-reference list (to be explained in the next section) and noticing that it was never assigned.

```
SYMBOL     TYPE   REFERENCES
C          PARAM  DECLARED      15     REF      17
```

Example 3: Many errors are caused merely by spelling mistakes and are caught before they can be damaging. For example, with "Seattle" spelled in the table differently from the way it was introduced in the set declaration, we get the following error message.

```
    4   SETS
    5       I    canning plants   / SEATTLE, SAN-DIEGO /
    6       J    markets          / NEW-YORK, CHICAGO, TOPEKA / ;
    7
    8   TABLE D(I,J)  distance in thousands of miles
    9                    NEW-YORK        CHICAGO        TOPEKA
   10       SEATLE          2.5            1.7           1.8
****             $170
   11       SAN-DIEGO       2.5            1.8           1.4  ;

    ERROR MESSAGES
    170  DOMAIN VIOLATION FOR ELEMENT
```

Example 4: Similarly, if we mistakenly enter DEM(J) instead of B(J) as the right-hand side of the demand constraint, the result is

```
   45   DEMAND(J) ..   SUM(I, X(I,J))   =G=  DEM(J) ;
****                                          $140

    ERROR MESSAGES
    140  UNKNOWN SYMBOL, ENTERED AS PARAMETER
```

Example 5: The next example is a mathematical error, which is sometimes committed by novice modelers and which GAMS is adept at catching. The following is mathematically inconsistent and, hence, is not an interpretable statement.

For all i, $\sum_i x_{ij} = 100$.

There are two errors in this equation, both having to do with the control of indices. Index i is overcontrolled and index j is undercontrolled.

You should see that index i is getting conflicting orders. By appearing in the quantifier "for all i," it is supposed to remain fixed for each instance of the equation. Yet, by appearing as an index of summation, it is supposed to vary. It can't do both. On the other hand, index j is not controlled in any way, so we have no way of knowing which of its possible values to use.

If we enter this meaningless equation into GAMS, both errors are correctly diagnosed.

```
        MEANINGLSS(I) ..   SUM(I, X(I,J))  =E=  100 ;
****                       $125   $149
```

ERROR MESSAGES

125 SET IS UNDER CONTROL ALREADY   [This refers to set I.]
149 UNCONTROLLED SET ENTERED AS CONSTANT   [This refers to set J.]

A great deal more information about error reporting is given in Chapter 10. Comprehensive error detection and well-designed error messages are a big help in getting models implemented quickly and correctly.

2.11 (c)   Reference Maps ∎

The next section of output, which is the last if errors have been detected, is a pair of "reference maps" that contain summaries and analyses of the input file for the purposes of debugging and documentation.

The first reference map is a "cross-reference map" such as one finds in most modern compilers. It is an alphabetical, cross-referenced list of all the entities (sets, parameters, variables, and equations) of the model. The list shows the type of each entity and a coded reference for each appearance of the entity in the input. The cross-reference map for our transportation example is as follows.

SYMBOL	TYPE	REFERENCES					
A	PARAM	DECLARED	10	DEFINED	11	REF	43
B	PARAM	DECLARED	14	DEFINED	15	REF	45
C	PARAM	DECLARED	26	ASSIGNED	28	REF	41
COST	EQU	DECLARED	37	DEFINED	41	IMPL-ASN	49
		REF	47				
D	PARAM	DECLARED	19	DEFINED	19	REF	28
DEMAND	EQU	DECLARED	39	DEFINED	45	IMPL-ASN	49
		REF	47				
F	PARAM	DECLARED	24	DEFINED	24	REF•	28
I	SET	DECLARED	5	DEFINED	5	REF	10
		19	26	28	31	38	2*41
		2*43	45	CONTROL	28	41	43
		45					
J	SET	DECLARED	6	DEFINED	6	REF	14
		19	26	28	31	39	2*41
		43	2*45	CONTROL	28	41	43
		45					
SUPPLY	EQU	DECLARED	38	DEFINED	43	IMPL-ASN	49
		REF	47				

TRANSPORT	MODEL	DECLARED	47	DEFINED	47	REF	49
X	VAR	DECLARED	31	IMPL-ASN	49	REF	34
		41	43	45	2*51		
Z	VAR	DECLARED	32	IMPL-ASN	49	REF	41
		49					

For example, the cross-reference list tells us that the symbol A is a parameter that was declared in line 10, defined (assigned value) in line 11, and referenced in line 43. The symbol I has a more complicated entry in the cross-reference list. It is shown to be a set that was declared and defined in line 5. It is referenced once in lines 10, 19, 26, 28, 31, 38, and 45 and referenced twice in lines 41 and 43. Set I is also used as a controlling index in a summation, equation definition or direct parameter assignment in lines 28, 41, 43, and 45.

For the GAMS novice, the detailed analysis of the cross-reference list may not be important. Perhaps the most likely benefit he or she will get from the reference maps will be the discovery of an unwanted entity that mistakenly entered the model owing to a punctuation or syntax error.

The second part of the reference map is a list of model entities grouped by type and listed with their associated documentary text. For our example, this list is as follows.

```
SETS
I              CANNING PLANTS
J              MARKETS

PARAMETERS
A              CAPACITY OF PLANT I IN CASES
B              DEMAND AT MARKET J IN CASES
C              TRANSPORT COST IN THOUSANDS OF DOLLARS PER CASE
D              DISTANCE IN THOUSANDS OF MILES
F              FREIGHT IN DOLLARS PER CASE PER THOUSAND MILES

VARIABLES
X              SHIPMENT QUANTITIES IN CASES
Z              TOTAL TRANSPORTATION COSTS IN THOUSANDS OF DOLLARS

EQUATIONS
COST           DEFINE OBJECTIVE FUNCTION
DEMAND         SATISFY DEMAND AT MARKET J
SUPPLY         OBSERVE SUPPLY LIMIT AT PLANT I

MODELS
TRANSPORT
```

2.11 (d) Equation Listings ■

Once you succeed in building an input file devoid of compilation errors, GAMS is able to generate a model. The question remains, and only you can answer it, does GAMS generate the model you intended?

The equation listing is probably the best device for studying this extremely important question. A product of the SOLVE command, the equation listing shows the specific instance of the model that is created when the current values of the sets and parameters are plugged into the general algebraic form of the model. For example, the generic demand constraint given in the input file for the transportation model is

```
DEMAND(J) ..    SUM(I, X(I,J))  =G=  B(J) ;
```

while the equation listing of specific constraints is

```
-------- DEMAND      =G=  SATISFY DEMAND AT MARKET J

DEMAND(NEW-YORK).. X(SEATTLE,NEW-YORK) + X(SAN-DIEGO,NEW-YORK) =G= 325 ;

DEMAND(CHICAGO).. X(SEATTLE,CHICAGO) + X(SAN-DIEGO,CHICAGO) =G= 300 ;

DEMAND(TOPEKA).. X(SEATTLE,TOPEKA) + X(SAN-DIEGO,TOPEKA) =G= 275 ;
```

The default output is a maximum of three specific equations for each generic equation. To change the default, insert an input statement prior to the SOLVE statement:

```
OPTION LIMROW = r ;
```

where r is the desired number.

The default output also contains a section called the column listing, analogous to the equation listing, which shows the coefficients of three specific variables for each generic variable. This listing would be particularly useful for verifying a GAMS model that was previously implemented in MPS format. To change the default number of specific column printouts per generic variable, the above command can be extended:

```
OPTION LIMROW = r, LIMCOL = c ;
```

where c is the desired number of columns. (Setting LIMROW = 0 and LIMCOL = 0 is a good way to save paper after your model has been debugged.)

In nonlinear models, the GAMS equation listing shows first-order Taylor approximations of the nonlinear equations. The approximations are taken at the starting values of the variables.

2.11 (e)   Model Statistics   ∎

The last section of output that GAMS produces before invoking the solver is a group of statistics about the model's size, as shown below for the transportation example.

```
MODEL STATISTICS

BLOCKS OF EQUATIONS    3      SINGLE EQUATIONS    6
BLOCKS OF VARIABLES    2      SINGLE VARIABLES    7
NON ZERO ELEMENTS      19
```

The "BLOCK" counts refer to the number of generic equations and variables. The "SINGLE" counts refer to individual rows and columns in the specific model instance being generated. For nonlinear models, some other statistics are given to describe the degree of nonlinearity in the problem.

2.11 (f)   Status Reports   ∎

After the solver executes, GAMS prints out a brief "SOLVE SUMMARY," whose two most important entries are "SOLVER STATUS" and the "MODEL STATUS." For our transportation problem the solve summary is as follows:

```
                    S O L V E      S U M M A R Y
        MODEL   TRANSPORT          OBJECTIVE   Z
        TYPE    LP                 DIRECTION   MINIMIZE
        SOLVER  BDMLP              FROM LINE   49

    **** SOLVER STATUS     1. NORMAL COMPLETION
    **** MODEL STATUS      1 OPTIMAL
    **** OBJECTIVE VALUE              153.6750

        RESOURCE USAGE, LIMIT        0.050      1000.000
        ITERATION COUNT, LIMIT       4          1000
```

The status reports are preceded by the same "****" string as an error message, so you should probably develop the habit of searching for all occurrences of this string whenever you look at an output file for the first time. The desired solver status is "1 NORMAL COMPLETION," but there are five other possibilities, documented in Chapter 10, which relate to various types of errors and mishaps.

There are eleven possible model statuses, including the usual linear programming termination states ("1 OPTIMAL," "3 UNBOUNDED," "4 INFEASIBLE"), and others relating to nonlinear and integer programming. In nonlinear programming, the status to look for is "2 LOCALLY OPTIMAL." The most the software can guarantee for nonlinear programming is a local optimum. The user is responsible for analyzing the convexity of the problem to determine whether local optimality is sufficient for global optimality.

In integer programming, the status to look for is "8 INTEGER SOLUTION." This means that a feasible integer solution has been found. More detail follows as to whether the solution meets the relative and absolute optimality tolerances that the user specifies.

2.11 (g) Solution Reports

If the solver status and model status are acceptable, then you will be interested in examining the results of the optimization. The results are first presented in a standard mathematical programming output format, with the added feature that rows and columns are grouped and labeled according to names that are appropriate for the specific model just solved. In this format, there is a line of printout for each row and column giving the lower limit, level, upper limit, and marginal. The row output is grouped by generic equation block and the column output by generic variable block. Set element names are embedded in the output for easy reading. In the transportation example, the solver outputs for SUPPLY(I), DEMAND(J), and X(I,J) are as follows:

```
    ---- EQU SUPPLY      OBSERVE SUPPLY LIMIT AT PLANT I

                  LOWER     LEVEL     UPPER    MARGINAL
    SEATTLE       -INF     350.000   350.000    EPS
    SAN-DIEGO     -INF     550.000   600.000     .

    ---- EQU DEMAND      SATISFY DEMAND AT MARKET J

                  LOWER     LEVEL     UPPER    MARGINAL
    NEW-YORK     325.000   325.000   +INF      0.225
    CHICAGO      300.000   300.000   +INF      0.153
    TOPEKA       275.000   275.000   +INF      0.126
```

```
---- VAR X              SHIPMENT QUANTITIES IN CASES

                    LOWER      LEVEL      UPPER     MARGINAL
SEATTLE   .NEW-YORK     .       50.000    +INF        .
SEATTLE   .CHICAGO      .      300.000    +INF        .
SEATTLE   .TOPEKA       .          .      +INF      0.036
SAN-DIEGO.NEW-YORK      .      275.000    +INF        .
SAN-DIEGO.CHICAGO       .          .      +INF      0.009
SAN-DIEGO.TOPEKA        .      275.000    +INF        .
```

The single dots "." in the output represent zeroes. The entry "EPS," which stands for "epsilon," means very small but nonzero. In this case, EPS indicates degeneracy. (The slack variable for the Seattle supply constraint is in the basis at zero level. The marginal is marked with EPS rather than zero to facilitate restarting the optimizer from the old basis.)

If the solver's results contain either infeasibilities or marginal costs of the wrong sign, then the offending entries are marked with "INFES" or "NOPT," respectively. If the problem terminates unbounded, then the rows and columns corresponding to extreme rays are marked "UNBND."

At the end of the solver's solution report is a very important "report summary," which gives a tally of the total number of nonoptimal, infeasible, and unbounded rows and columns. For our example, the report summary shows all zero tallies as desired.

```
**** REPORT SUMMARY :      0     NONOPT
                           0    INFEASIBLE
                           0    UNBOUNDED
```

After the solver's report is written, control is returned from the solver back to GAMS. All the levels and marginals obtained by the solver are entered into the GAMS database in the .L and .M fields. These values can then be transformed and displayed in any desired report. As noted earlier, the user merely lists the quantities to be displayed, and GAMS automatically formats and labels an appropriate array. For example, the input statement

```
DISPLAY X.L, X.M ;
```

results in the following output.

```
----      51 VARIABLE  X.L          SHIPMENT QUANTITIES IN CASES

               NEW-YORK     CHICAGO      TOPEKA
SEATTLE         50.000     300.000
SAN-DIEGO      275.000                  275.000


----      51 VARIABLE  X.M          SHIPMENT QUANTITIES IN CASES

               CHICAGO      TOPEKA
SEATTLE                      0.036
SAN-DIEGO       0.009
```

As seen in reference maps, equation listings, solution reports, and optional displays, GAMS saves the documentary text and "parrots" it back throughout the output to help keep the model well documented.

2.12 CONCLUSIONS ■

This tutorial has demonstrated several of the features of GAMS's design that enable you to build practical optimization models quickly and effectively. The following discussion summarizes the advantages of using an algebraic modeling language such as GAMS versus a matrix generator or conversational solver.*

1. By using an algebra-based notation, you can describe an optimization model to a computer nearly as easily as you can describe it to another mathematically trained person.

2. Because an algebraic description of a problem has generality, most of the statements in a GAMS model are reusable when new instances of the same or related problems arise. This is especially important in environments where models are constantly changing.

3. You save time and reduce generation errors by creating whole sets of closely related constraints in one statement.

4. You can save time and reduce input errors by providing formulae for calculating the data rather than entering them explicitly.

5. The model is self-documenting. Since the tasks of model development and model documentation can be done simultaneously, the modeler is much more likely to be conscientious about keeping the documentation accurate and up to date.

6. The output of GAMS is easy to read and use. The solver's solution report is automatically reformatted so that related equations and variables are grouped together and appropriately labeled. Also, the DISPLAY command allows you to modify and tabulate results very easily.

7. If you are teaching or learning modeling, you can benefit from the GAMS compiler's insistence that every equation be mathematically consistent. Even if you are an experienced modeler, the hundreds of ways in which errors are deleted should greatly reduce development time.

8. By using the "dollar" operator and other advanced features not covered in this tutorial, you could efficiently implement large-scale models. Specific applications of the dollar operator include the following:

    (a) It can enforce logical restrictions on the allowable combinations of indices for the variables and equations to be included in the model. You can thereby screen out unnecessary rows and columns and keep the size of the problem within the range of solvability.

    (b) It can be used to build complex summations and products, which can then be used in equations or customized reports.

    (c) It can be used for issuing warning messages or for terminating prematurely conditioned upon context-specific data edits.

---

*For information concerning other algebraic modeling languages that are available or in development, see Fourer (1983); Fourer, Gay, and Kernighan (1987); Geoffrion (1987); Schrage (1987); and Welch (1987).

PART 2

The GAMS Language

GAMS PROGRAMS 3

In Part II of this book (Chapters 3 to 12) we will show you how to write models in GAMS. This chapter provides a look at the structure of the GAMS language and its components. We emphasize again that GAMS is a programming language, and that you must write programs in the language to use it. A GAMS program is contained in a disk file which is normally constructed with the text editor of your choice. When you "run" GAMS you submit the file containing your program (the input file) to be processed (as we show later in Appendix A). After this processing has finished you inspect the results, which are on the output file, with a text editor or file lister. On many machines a few terse lines appear on your screen while GAMS runs, telling you something about progress and error detection. But it is your responsibility to inspect the output file carefully to see the results and to diagnose any errors.

This chapter can be skipped by the first time or casual reader: the discussion of specific parts of the language in Chapters 4 to 12 does not assume an understanding of this chapter.

3.1 THE STRUCTURE OF GAMS PROGRAMS ■

GAMS programs consist of one or more statements (sentences) that define data structures, initial values, data modifications, and symbolic relationships (equations). While there is no fixed order in which statements have to be arranged, the order in which data modifications are carried out is important. Symbols must be declared as to type before they are used, and must have values assigned before they can be referenced in assignment statements. The structure of a GAMS program is illustrated below.

```
                         statement;
                         statement;
GAMS Program              . . . ;
                          . . . ;
                          . . . ;
                         statement
```

Each statement is followed by a semicolon except the last statement, where a semicolon is optional.

GAMS input is free format. A statement can be placed anywhere on a line, multiple statements can appear on a line, or a statement can be continued over any number of lines as follows:

```
statement;

statement;

statement; statement; statement;
              the words that you are now reading exemplify a very long
statement which is stretched over two lines;
```

Blanks and end-of-lines can generally be used freely between individual symbols or words. GAMS is not case sensitive, meaning that lower and upper case letters can be mixed freely but are treated identically. Up to 120 characters can be placed on one line and completely blank lines can be inserted for easier reading.

Not all lines are a part of the GAMS language. Two special symbols, the asterisk "*" and the dollar symbol "$" can be used in the first position on a line to indicate a non-language input line. An asterisk in column one means that the line will not be processed, but treated as a comment. A dollar symbol in the same position indicates that compiler options are contained in the rest of the line.

Each statement in GAMS is classified into one of two groups:

1. declaration and definition statements; or

2. execution statements

Declaration statements describe the class of symbols. Often initial values are provided in a declaration, and then it may be called a definition. The specification of symbolic relationships for an equation is a definition. The declaration and definition statements are:

acronym	parameter	equation declaration
set	scalar	equation definition
alias	table	model
	variable	

Execution statements are instructions to carry out actions such as data transformation, model solution, and report generation. The execution statements are:

option	display	abort
assignment	loop	solve

Although there is great freedom about the order in which statements can be placed in a GAMS program, certain orders are commonly used. The two most common arrangements are discussed next.

3.2   ORGANIZATION OF GAMS PROGRAMS ■

One common style of organizing GAMS statements places the data first, followed by the model and then the solution statements:

set declarations and definitions
parameter declarations and definitions
assignments
displays
} data

variable declarations
equation declarations
equation definitions
model definition
} model

solve
displays
} solution

In this style of organization, the sets are placed first. Then the data are specified with parameter, scalar, and table statements. Next the model is defined with the variable, equation declaration, equation definition, and model statements. Finally the model is solved and the results are displayed.

A second style emphasizes the model by placing it before the data. This is a particularly useful order when the model may be solved repeatedly with different data sets. This order is:

set declarations
parameter declarations
variable definitions
equation declarations
equation definitions
model definition
} model

set definitions
parameter definitions
assignments
displays
} data

solve
displays
} solution

In this order there is a separation between declaration and definition. For example a set may be declared with the statement

        SET   C   CROPS;

and then defined later with a statement

        SET   C   /WHEAT,CLOVER,BEANS/;

The first statement declares that the identifier C is a set and the second defines the elements in the set. Also a parameter may first be declared as

        PARAMETER YIELD   Crop yield;

and then defined later in the program with

```
PARAMETER YIELD /  WHEAT    1.5
                   CLOVER   6.5
                   BEANS    1.0  /;
```

Sets and parameters used in the equations must be *declared* before the equations are specified; they can be *defined*, however, after the equation specifications but before a specific equation is used in a solve statement. This gives GAMS programs substantial organizational flexibility.

3.3 DATA TYPES AND DEFINITIONS ■

There are six basic GAMS data types and each symbol or identifier must be declared to belong to one of the following groups:

SETS	VARIABLES
PARAMETERS (SCALAR, TABLE)	EQUATIONS
ACRONYMS	MODELS

SCALARs and TABLEs are not separate data types but are a shorthand way to declare a symbol to be a PARAMETER, and to use a particular format for initializing the numeric data. ACRONYMs are used mainly in connection with HERCULES (see Drud and Kendrick, 1986) and we will not refer to them further.

Definitions have common characteristics, for example:

PARAMETER	A	(I,J)	INPUT–OUTPUT MATRIX
data-type-keyword	identifier	domain list	text

The domain list and the text are always optional characteristics. Other examples are:

```
SET      TIME     Time periods;
MODEL    TURKEY   Turkish fertilizer model;
VARIABLES X, Y, Z;
```

In the last example a number of identifiers (separated by commas) are declared in one statement.

3.4 LANGUAGE ITEMS ■

Before proceeding with more language details, we need to define a few basic symbols and the rules for recognizing and writing them in GAMS. These basic symbols are often called lexical items and form the building blocks of the language. The items are:

- characters
- reserved words and tokens
- identifiers (idents)
- labels

- text
- numbers
- delimiters
- comments

As noted previously, we can use any mix of lower and upper case. GAMS makes no distinction between upper and lower case.

3.4 (a)   Characters   ■

A few characters are not allowed in a GAMS program because they are illegal or ambiguous on some machines. Generally all unprintable or control characters are illegal. Of the ones you might use deliberately, the most likely to cause trouble are the tab (control-I on personal computers), square brackets "[]", braces "{ }", exclamation mark "!", and hat "^". The only place where any character is legal is in an 'ontext-offtext' block as illustrated in the section on comments below. For completeness we list the full set of legal characters in Table 3.1. Most of the uncommon punctuation characters are not part of the language, but can be used freely in text or comments.

Table 3.1:   Legal Characters

A to Z	(alphabet)	a to z	(alphabet)	0 to 9	(numerals)
&	(ampersand)	"	(double quote)	#	(pound sign)
*	(asterisk)	=	(equals)	?	(question mark)
@	(at sign)	>	(greater than)	;	(semicolon)
\	(back slash)	<	(less than)	'	(single quote)
:	(colon)	–	(minus)	/	(slash)
,	(comma)	( )	(parentheses)		(space)
$	(dollar)	%	(percent)	_	(underscore)
.	(dot)	+	(plus)		

3.4 (b)   Reserved Words and Tokens.   ■

GAMS, like computer languages such as C and Pascal, uses reserved words (often also called keywords) that have predefined meanings. You may not use any of these for your own definitions, either as identifiers or labels. These words are listed in Table 3.2. In addition, a small number of symbols constructed from non-alphanumeric characters have a meaning in GAMS.*

3.4 (c)   Identifiers   ■

Identifiers are the names given to SETS, PARAMETERS, VARIABLES, MODELS, etc. A name used for one data type can not be reused for another. GAMS follows rules similar to those for other programming languages and requires an identifier to start with a letter followed by more letters or digits. The length of an identifier is limited to 10 characters. Identifiers can only contain alphanumeric characters (letters or numbers). Examples of legal identifiers are:

        A   A15   REVENUE   X0051

whereas the following identifiers are incorrect:

        15    $CASH   MUCHTOOLONG   MILK&MEAT

3.4 (d)   Labels   ■

Labels are set elements. They may be up to 10 characters long and can be used in quoted or unquoted form. The unquoted form is simpler to use but places restrictions on characters

---

*The meaning and uses of the alphanumeric and non-alphanumeric symbols will be introduced in later chapters.

Table 3.2: Reserved Words and Symbols

ABORT	CARD	GT	MODEL	OPTIONS	SCALARS	SUM
ACRONYM	DISPLAY	INF	MODELS	OR	SET	SYSTEM
ACRONYMS	EPS	INTEGER	NA	ORD	SETS	TABLE
ALIAS	EQ	LE	NE	PARAMETER	SMAX	USING
ALL	EQUATION	LOOP	NEGATIVE	PARAMETERS	SMIN	VARIABLE
AND	EQUATIONS	LT	NO	POSITIVE	SOLVE	VARIABLES
ASSIGN	FREE	MAXIMIZING	NOT	PROD	SOS1	XOR
BINARY	GE	MINIMIZING	OPTION	SCALAR	SOS2	YES

The reserved non-alphanumeric symbols are

..	=L=	=G=	=E=	=N=	--	++	**

used, in that any unquoted label must start with a letter or digit and can only be followed by letters, digits, or the sign characters "+" and "-". Examples of unquoted labels are:

PHOS-ACID	1986	1952-53	A
SEPTEMBER	H2S04	LINE-1	

In quoted labels, quotes are used to delimit the label, which may begin with and/or include any legal character. Either single or double quotes can be used but the closing quote has to match the opening one. A label quoted with double quotes can contain a single quote (and vice versa). Most experienced users avoid quoted labels because they can be tedious to enter and confusing to read. There are a couple of special circumstances. If you want to make a label stand out, then to put asterisks in it and indent it, as below, is common. A more subtle example is that you can use GAMS keywords as labels if they are quoted. If you need to use labels like "NO", "NE" or "SUM" then you will have to quote them. Examples of quoted labels are:

```
"   *TOTAL*"    'MATCH'   "10%-INCR"   '12"  /  FOOT'   "LINE 1"
```

Labels do not have a value. The label "1986" does not have the numerical value 1986 and the label "01" is different from the label "1". To summarize, set names are identifiers and set elements are labels. The rules for constructing identifiers and labels are as shown in Table 3.3.

3.4 (e) Text ∎

Identifiers and simple labels can also be associated with a line of descriptive text. This text is more than a comment: it is retained by GAMS and is displayed whenever results are written for the identifier.

Text can be quoted or unquoted. Quoted text can contain any character except the quote character used. Single or double quotes can be used but must match. Text has to fit on one line and cannot exceed 80 characters in length. (Remember that lines can be up to 120 characters long.) Text is normally used in unquoted form, which introduces a number of mild restrictions. Unquoted text cannot start with a reserved word, ".." or "=".

Table 3.3:   Rules for Constructing Identifiers and Labels

	Identifiers	*Unquoted Labels*	*Quoted Labels*
Number of Characters	10	10	10
Must Begin With	A letter	A letter or a number	Any character
Permitted Special Characters	None	+ or – characters	Any but the starting quote

Semicolon ";", commas ",", slashes "/" and end of line terminates a text. These restrictions are a direct consequence of the GAMS syntax and are usually followed naturally by the user. Some examples are:

```
THIS IS TEXT
FINAL PRODUCT SHIPMENT (TPY)
"QUOTED TEXT CONTAINING OTHERWISE ILLEGAL CHARACTERS ;/,"
'USE SINGLE QUOTES TO PUT A "DOUBLE" QUOTE IN TEXT'
```

3.4 (f)   Numbers   ∎

Numeric values are entered in a style similar to that in other computer languages. Blanks can not be used in a number: GAMS treats a blank as a separator. If you use a number without a decimal point it is still stored as a real number, since the common distinction between real and integer data types does not exist in GAMS. In addition, GAMS uses an extended range arithmetic that contains special symbols for infinity (INF), negative infinity (-INF), undefined (UNDF), epsilon (EPS), and not available (NA). You cannot enter UNDF; it is only produced by an operation that does not have a proper result, such as division by zero. The other special symbols can be entered and used as if they were ordinary numbers. The following example shows various legal ways of entering numbers:

```
0        156.70    -135      .095      1.
2E10     2E+10     15.E-2    .314E-5   +17.7
0.0      .0        0.        INF       NA
```

The letter E denotes the well known scientific notation allowing convenient representation of very large or small numbers. For example:

$$1E-5 \ = \ 1 \ \times \ 10^{-5} \ = \ 0.00001$$
$$3.56E6 \ = \ 3.56 \ \times \ 10^{6} \ = \ 3,560,000$$

Two warnings are in order on number entry. First, GAMS uses a smaller range of numbers than many computers are able to handle. This has been done to ensure that GAMS programs will behave in the same way on a wide variety of machines, including personal computers. A good general rule is to avoid using or creating numbers with absolute values greater than 1.0E+20. Second, a number can be entered with up to ten significant digits on all machines, and more on some. There are more details on this in Appendix B.

3.4 (g)   Delimiters   ∎

As we said above, statements are separated by a semicolon ";". However, if the next statement begins with a reserved word (often called keyword in succeeding chapters), then GAMS does not require that the semicolon be used. We will be strict about using semicolons in this book, but be warned that many example models in the GAMS Library use "relaxed" punctuation. A full discussion is given in Chapter 18.

The characters comma "," and slash "/" are used as delimiters in data lists, to be introduced in Chapters 4 and 5. The comma terminates a data element (as does an end-of-line) and the slash terminates a data list.

3.4 (h)   Comments   ∎

A comment is explanatory text not processed or retained by the computer. There are two ways to include comments in a GAMS program. The first, already mentioned above, is to start a line with an asterisk "*" in the first character position. The remaining characters on the line are ignored but printed on the output file. The second is to use special 'block' delimiters that cause GAMS to ignore an entire section of your program. The $ symbol must be in the first character position. Which of these two ways you choose is a matter of individual taste or utility. The block comment is illustrated below.

```
$ONTEXT
    Following an $ONTEXT directive in column 1 all lines are
    ignored by GAMS but printed on the output file until the
    matching $OFFTEXT is encountered, also in column 1.

    This facility is often used to logically remove parts of
    programs that are not used every time, such as statements
    producing voluminous reports.

    Every $ONTEXT must have a matching $OFFTEXT in the same file
$OFFTEXT
```

3.5   SUMMARY   ∎

This completes our discussion of the components of the GAMS language. Interested readers will find a formal language definition in Appendix F, on Language Grammar. Many unfamiliar terms used in this chapter have been further explained in the Glossary. We now move on to our discussion of particular parts of the language, beginning with sets.

SET DEFINITIONS 4

This chapter begins our detailed discussion of the GAMS language. From here until the end of Chapter 12 we will illustrate concepts mostly by example, starting with simple notions and gradually increasing their complexity. In this way we hope to make the book useful to a wide audience. This material is designed to be studied sequentially: we have tried to introduce the concepts in a naturally ordered way. The disadvantage of this incremental approach is that it is not possible to go to one section and find out all there is to know about a particular topic, for example, domain checking. In Chapters 13 and following we will revert to the "random access" approach by providing detailed discussions of special topics.

Sets are fundamental building blocks in any GAMS model. They allow the model to be succinctly stated and easily read. In this chapter we will discuss how sets are declared and initialized. There are some more advanced set concepts, such as assignments to sets as well as lag and lead operations, but these are are not introduced until much later in the book. However the topics covered in this chapter will be enough to provide a good start on most models.

4.1 SIMPLE SETS ■

A set S that contains the elements a, b and c is written, using normal mathematical notation, as

$$S = \{a, b, c\}$$

In GAMS notation, because of character set limitations, the same set must be written as

```
SET    S   /a, b, c/
```

The SET statement begins with the keyword SET (or SETS). S is the name of the set, and its members are a, b, and c. They are labels, but are often referred to as elements or members. The order in which the set members are listed is normally not important. However, if the members represent, for example, time periods, then we may want to be able to refer to the 'next' or 'previous' member. There are special operations to do this, and they will be discussed in Chapter 12. For now it is enough to remember that the order in which set elements are specified is not relevant, unless and until some operation implying order is used. At that time the rules change, and the set becomes what we will later call an ordered set.

The name of the set is an identifier. As we discussed in the previous chapter, identifiers can be up to ten characters long. This is enough to construct meaningful names, and explanatory text can be used to provide more details. It is also possible to associate text with each set member or element. For example, label text for the set of final products in [SHALE]* contained details of the units of measurement. (We will use lower case for text. It doesn't matter to the computer, and it makes life easier for humans.)

```
SET      CF       Final products

         /  SYNCRUDE    Refined crude (million barrels)
            LPG         Liquefied petroleum gas (million barrels)
            AMMONIA     Ammonia (million tons)
            COKE        Coke (million tons)
            SULFUR      Sulfur (million tons)  /;
```

Notice that text may have embedded blanks, and may include special characters such as parentheses. There are, however, restrictions on special characters in text. Do not include slashes, commas or semicolons because the GAMS compiler will interpret these characters as ending the text. Thus a SET definition like

```
SET      PRICES    Prices of commodities

         /  GOLD-PRICE   Price of gold in dollars/ounce
            SIL-PRICE    Price of silver in dollars/ounce  /;
```

will cause errors since the slash between dollars and ounce will signal the end of the set definition, and the GAMS compiler will treat ounce as the name of a second set. If it is necessary to use special characters in the text, then enclose the text in quotes:

```
'Price of gold in dollars/ounce'
```

Remember that explanatory text must not exceed 80 characters and must all be contained on the same line as the identifier or label it describes.

Each element in a set must be separated from other elements by a comma or by an end-of-line. In contrast, each element is separated from any associated text by a blank. Thus the set of fertilizer nutrients in the Egyptian fertilizer model in [FERTS] could be written as

```
SET      CQ      NUTRIENTS    / N, P205 /;
```

or as

```
SET      CQ      NUTRIENTS    / N
                                P205   /;
```

If text were associated with each element, the set could be written as

```
SET      CQ      NUTRIENTS    / N        Nitrogen, P205 Phosphorus /;
```

---

*Throughout this book, references to models from the GAMS Library are cited by the model name enclosed by brackets. A listing of the models in the library is contained in Chapter 19.

or as

```
SET     CQ     NUTRIENTS   / N       Nitrogen
                             P205    Phosphorus  /;
```

The keyword SET (if you prefer, say SETS instead: the two are entirely equivalent) does not need to be used for each set, rather only at the beginning of a group of sets. It is often convenient to put a group of set declarations together at the beginning of the program. When this is done the SET keyword need only be used once. If you prefer to intermingle set declarations with other statements, you will have to use a new SET statement for each additional group of sets. The example below shows how two sets can be declared together. The semicolon is used only after the last one.

```
SETS

      S   Sector   /   MANUF
                       AGRI
                       SERVICES
                       GOVERNMENT   /

      R   Regions  /   NORTH
                       EASTCOAST
                       MIDWEST
                       SUNBELT  /;
```

When you first use GAMS you may find it tempting to use short names for set elements. Experience has shown that it is well worthwhile to embed as much meaning as possible into the names of set elements, since it makes your model easier for others to understand. Look at the definitions below and compare them with the ones above.

```
SETS
      S   Sector   / 1, 2, 3, 4 /
      R   Regions  / R1, R2, R3, R4 /;
```

In contrast to meaningful element labels, it is usually desirable to have relatively short set names. Set names are used in the specification of equations in the way that indices are used in mathematics, and complicated equations are easier to read if the set names are relatively short.

The asterisk "*" plays a special role in set definitions. It is used to relieve the tedium of typing a sequence of elements for a set, and to make intent clearer. For example in a simulation model there might be ten annual time periods from 1991 to 2000. Instead of typing all ten years, the elements of this set can be written as

```
SET     T    Time    / 1991 * 2000 /;
```

which means that the set includes the ten elements 1991, 1992, . . . , 2000. GAMS builds up these label lists by looking at the differences between the two labels. If the only characters that differ are digits, and if the number (say L) formed by these digits in the left one is less than that from the right one (R), then a label is constructed for every integer in the sequence L to R. Any non-numeric differences or other inconsistencies cause errors.

For example, the following is the most general form of the "asterisked" definition:

```
SET   G   General definition   / A1BC * A20BC /;
```

Note that this is *not* the same as

```
SET   D   A different definition   / A01BC * A20BC /;
```

although the sets, which have 20 members each, have 11 members in common. As a last example, the following are all illegal because they are not consistent with the rule given above for making lists:

```
SET   ILLEGAL1   / A20BC * A10BC /
      ILLEGAL2   / A1X1 * A9X9 /
      ILLEGAL3   / A1 * B9 /;
```

Note one last time that set elements (often referred to as labels) can contain the sign characters "-" and "+" as well as letters and numbers.

4.2   THE ALIAS STATEMENT: MULTIPLE NAMES FOR A SET   ■

It is sometimes necessary to have more than one name for the same set. In input-output models, for example, each commodity may be used in the production of all other commodities and it is necessary to have two names for the set of commodities to specify the problem without ambiguity. In the general equilibrium model [ORANI], the set of commodities is written

```
SET   C   Commodities / FOOD, CLOTHING /;
```

and a second name for the set C is established with the statement

```
ALIAS(C,CP);
```

where CP stands for *C* prime. ALIAS is a keyword, and the ALIAS statement terminates the declaration of a group of sets. If more sets are to be declared, the SET keyword must be used in a new SET statement:

```
SET   C   Commodities / FOOD, CLOTHING /;

ALIAS (C,CP);

SET   F   Factors / LABOR, CAPITAL /;
```

We will not demonstrate the use of set aliases until later, in Chapter 6. Just remember they are used for cases when a set has to be referred to by more than one name.

4.3   SUBSETS AND DOMAIN CHECKING   ■

It is often necessary to define sets whose members must all be members of some larger set. For instance, we may wish to define the sectors in an economic model following the style in [CHENERY] as below:

```
SET
  I     All sectors
                / LIGHT-IND, FOOD+AGR, HEAVY-IND, SERVICES /
  T(I)  Traded sectors
                / LIGHT-IND, FOOD+AGR, HEAVY-IND /
* NOTE: The definition following has no domain checking
* It is for illustration, not for copying
  NT    Non-traded sectors
                / SERVICES /;
```

Some types of economic activity, for example exporting and importing, may be logically restricted to a subset of all sectors. In order to model the trade balance, for example, we need to know which sectors are traded, and one obvious way is to list them explicitly, as in the definition of the set T above. The specification T(I) means that each member of the set T must also be a member of the set I. GAMS will enforce this relationship, which is called domain checking. Obviously the order of declaration is important: the membership of I must be known before T is declared for checking to be done. There will be much more on this topic in succeeding chapters. For now it is important to note that domain checking will find any spelling errors that might be made in establishing the members of the set T. These would cause errors in the model if they went undetected.

It is legal but unwise to define a subset without reference to the larger set, as is done above for the set NT. If SERVICES were misspelled no error would be marked, but the model would give incorrect results. So we urge you to use domain checking whenever possible. It catches errors and allows you to write models that are conceptually cleaner because logical relationships are made explicit.

This completes the discussion of sets in which the elements are simple. This is sufficient for most GAMS applications; however, there are a variety of problems for which it is useful to have sets whose elements contain two or more labels.

4.4 MULTI-DIMENSIONAL SETS AND MAPPINGS   ■

Consider a set whose elements are pairs:

```
A = { (b,d), (a,c), (c,e) }
```

In this set there are three elements and each element consists of a pair of letters. This kind of set is useful in many types of modeling. In the world aluminum model [ALUM], for example, it is necessary to associate with each bauxite-supplying country a port that is near to the bauxite mines. The set of countries is

```
SET   C   Countries

          / JAMAICA
            HAITI
            GUYANA
            BRAZIL /;
```

and the set of ports is

```
SET    P    Ports

       / KINGSTON
         S-DOMINGO
         GEORGETOWN
         BELEM /;
```

Then a set can be created to associate each port with its country, viz.,

```
SET    PTOC(P,C)   Port to country relationship

       /  KINGSTON   .JAMAICA
          S-DOMINGO  .HAITI
          GEORGETOWN .GUYANA
          BELEM      .BRAZIL /;
```

The dot between KINGSTON and JAMAICA is used to create one such pair. Blanks may be used freely around the dot for readability. The set PTOC has four elements, and each element consists of a port-country pair. The notation (P,C) after the set name PTOC indicates that the first member of each pair must be a member of the set P of ports, and that the second must be in the set C of countries. This is a second example of domain checking. GAMS will check the set elements to ensure that all members belong to the appropriate sets.

Another example of the use of pairs is a crude oil tag in a refinery model. These tags are used to label each intermediate product with the crude oil from which it is produced, since there are subtle but important differences in intermediate products depending on their origin. For example, in the small refinery model [MARCO] the crude oils are

```
SET    CR    Crude oils
             / WESTEX     West Texas
               MIDCON     Mid continent /;
```

and some of the intermediate products are

```
SET

       CI    Intermediate products
             / NAPHTHA
               GASOIL
               DISTILLATE /;
```

and the set of all tagged intermediate products is therefore

```
SET    CICR(CI,CR)    Tagged Intermediate products /

                      NAPHTHA.    WESTEX
                      NAPHTHA.    MIDCON
                      GASOIL.     WESTEX
                      GASOIL.     MIDCON
                      DISTILLATE.WESTEX
                      DISTILLATE.MIDCON  /;
```

There are six tagged intermediate products in the set. This set can be written more compactly as:

```
SET     CICR(CI,CR)   Tagged Intermediate products /

              NAPHTHA.    (WESTEX, MIDCON)
              GASOIL.     (WESTEX, MIDCON)
              DISTILLATE.(WESTEX, MIDCON)   /;
```

The dot produces a one-to-one mapping and the dot combined with the list in parentheses provides a one-to-many mapping, i.e., NAPHTHA.WESTEX is a one-to-one mapping and NAPHTHA.(WESTEX, MIDCON) is a one-to-many mapping. An even more succinct representation is therefore:

```
SET     CICR(CI,CR)   Tagged Intermediate products

        / (NAPHTHA, GASOIL, DISTILLATE).(WESTEX, MIDCON) /;

  DISPLAY CICR;
```

A many-to-many mapping is used in this case. When complex sets like this are created, it is important to check that the desired set has been obtained. The checking can be done by using a DISPLAY statement as shown above. It will cause GAMS to print the elements of the set CICR during the execution phase of the GAMS system.

These concepts may be generalized to sets with more than two labels per set element. Mathematically these are called 3-tuples, 4-tuples, or more generally, n-tuples. This section ends with some examples to illustrate definitions of multi-label set elements.

In the relational database example from a department store [ZLOOF], there are items of different colors and sizes. The basic sets in this example are

```
SETS
    ITEM    / DISK, INK, LIPSTICK, PEN, PENCIL, PERFUME /
    COLOR   / WHITE, RED, GREEN, BLUE /
    SIZE    / SMALL, MEDIUM, LARGE /;
```

Then the available types of pencils can be specified as follows:

```
SET   TYPE (ITEM, COLOR, SIZE)
          / PENCIL.RED.LARGE
            PENCIL.BLUE.LARGE
            PENCIL.GREEN.SMALL /;
```

There are three elements in this set and each element is a three-tuple. The set could be entered in a more compact form as

```
/ PENCIL.(RED.LARGE, BLUE.LARGE, GREEN.SMALL) /
```

or in a still more compact form as

```
/ PENCIL.((RED,BLUE).LARGE, GREEN.SMALL) /
```

Other examples of the compact representation of sets of n-tuples using combinations of dots, parentheses and commas are:

Construct .	*Result*
(A,B).C.D	A.C.D., B.C.D
(A,B).(C,D).E	A.C.E., B.C.E, A.D.E, B.D.E

The asterisk can also be used in conjunction with the dot. Recall that the elements of the list 1*4 are {1,2,3,4} when examining the following examples:

Construct	*Result*
(A.1*3, B.(4,7)).C	(A.1, A.2, A.3, B.(4,7).C
or	(A.1, A.2, A.3, B.4, B.7).C
or	A.1.C, A.2.C, A.3.C, B.4.C, B.7.C
1*3.1*3.1*3	1.1.1, 1.1.2, 1.1.3, . . . , 3.3.3

4.5 SUMMARY   ■

In GAMS, a simple SET consists of a set name and the elements of the set. Both the name and the elements may have associated text that explains the name or the elements in more detail. More complex sets have elements that are pairs or even *n*-tuples. These sets with pairs and *n*-tuples are ideal for establishing relationships between the elements in different sets, such as ports and countries. GAMS also uses a domain checking capability to help catch labeling inconsistencies and typographical errors made during the definition of related sets.

The discussion here has been limited to sets whose members are all specified as the set is being declared. For many models this is all you need to know about sets. Later we will discuss more complicated concepts, such as sets whose membership changes in different parts of the model (assignment to sets) and other set operations such as unions, complements and intersections.

DATA ENTRY: PARAMETERS, SCALARS & TABLES 5

Data handling is of crucial importance in all modeling applications. The quality of the numbers and the intelligence with which they are used is likely to be at least as important as the logic of the model in determining if an application is successful or not. GAMS has been designed to have a complete set of facilities for entering information, manipulating it and reporting on the results. In this chapter we will concentrate on data entry while alluding to some of the reporting features. Chapter 6 will deal with data manipulations.

One very important principle will motivate all of our discussions about data.

- *Data should be entered in its most basic form, and each data item should be entered only once.*

There are two reasons for adopting this principle. Numbers are almost certain to change, and when they do we want to be able to make the process of changing them as easy and safe as possible. We also want to make our model easy for others to read and understand. Keeping the amount of data as small as possible certainly helps. All the data transformations are shown explicitly in the GAMS representation, which makes it possible to reproduce the results of the study and shows the reader all the assumptions made during data manipulation. Another advantage is that everything needed to run or change the model is included in one program that can easily be moved from place to place or from one machine to another.

In this chapter we will discuss data entry. This is normally done by specifying numbers as part of parameter definitions using PARAMETER, SCALAR or TABLE statements. Initialization of data can only be done once for parameters; thereafter data must be modified with assignment statements, the subject of the next chapter.

5.1 PARAMETERS ∎

Data, by which we mean numbers that will be used in a model to produce (for example) matrix coefficients or right-hand side values, are normally associated with the GAMS data type called PARAMETER. Again we will use examples to introduce the concepts. A parameter can be defined in a similar way to that used with a set. The fragment below is adapted from [MEXSS]. We also show the set definitions because they make the example clearer.

```
SET I     Steel plants  / AHMSA     Altos Hornos - Monclova
                          FUNDIDORA  Monterrey
                          SICARTSA   Lazaro Cardenas
                          HYLSA      Monterrey
                          HYLSAP     Puebla
                                                          /

    J    Markets        / MEXICO-DF, MONTERREY, GUADALAJA /;

PARAMETERS  MUF(I,J) Transport rate for final products ($US per ton)
            DD(J)    Distribution of demand
                     / MEXICO-DF   55,
                       MONTERREY   30,
                       GUADALAJA   15 /;
```

The parameters declared here are MUF and DD. Both have domain lists and explanatory text. Let us first look at DD. The domain checking specification means that there will be a vector of data associated with it, one number corresponding to every member of the set J. Evidently these numbers are attributes of the markets in the model. The numbers are specified along with the declaration in a format very reminiscent of the way we specified sets: in this simple case a label followed by a blank separator and then a value. Any of the legal number entry formats are allowable for the value. The default data value is zero. If we had, for example, left MONTERREY out of the data list, then the value associated with DD("MONTERREY"), the market share in MONTERREY, would be zero. A careful modeler would include a check somewhere that the market shares add up to 100, since GAMS cannot check all of a user's intentions. We will go into how to do this later, when we discuss the ABORT statement.

Look now at the declaration of MUF. This is two dimensional, and the domain checking implies that there can be one value associated with every combination of plant (I) and market (J). Given five plants and three markets, this data structure may contain up to 15 numbers. Notice that no data are listed. They will presumably be specified later, perhaps in another PARAMETER statement, but more likely in a TABLE or with an assignment statement. Any attempt to use data associated with MUF will cause an error condition until these numbers have been specified.

An immediate extension of data initialization in parameter statements is to higher dimensionality:

```
PARAMETER  SALARIES(EMPLOYEE,MANAGER,DEPARTMENT)
           / ANDERSON.MURPHY.TOY       = 6000
             HENRY   .SMITH .TOY       = 9000
             HOFFMAN .MORGAN.COSMETICS = 8000 /;
```

Notice that an equals sign can be used to separate the label combination from the value. We can also put several data elements on a line, separated by commas:

```
PARAMETER  A(I)  Available supplies (cases daily)

  /SEATTLE  =  350, SAN-DIEGO = 600/;
```

As with sets, commas are optional at end-of-line. All the mechanisms using asterisks and parenthesized lists that we introduced in our discussion of sets are available here as well. Below is an artificial example, in which a very small fraction of the total data points are initialized. GAMS will mark an error if the same label combination (or label-tuple) appears more than once in a data list.

```
SET   ROW    / ROW1 * ROW10 /,
      COL    / COL1 * COL10 /;

PARAMETER A(ROW,COL)
                /(ROW1, ROW4) . COL2 * COL7   12
                     ROW10 . COL10            17
              ROW1 * ROW7 . COL10             33 /;
```

In this example, the twelve elements ROW1.COL2 to ROW1.COL7 and ROW4.COL2 to ROW4.COL7 are all initialized at 12, the single element ROW10.COL10 at 17, and the seven elements ROW1.COL10 to ROW7.COL10 at 33. The other 80 elements (out of a total of 100) remain at their default value, which is 0. This example shows GAMS' ability to provide a concise initialization, or definition, for a sparse data structure.

In summary, parameters initialization requires a list of data elements, each consisting of a label-tuple and a value. Slashes must be used at the beginning and end of the list, and commas must separate data elements entered more than one to a line. An equals sign or a blank may be used to separate the label-tuple from its associated value. However in practice, except for one dimensional lists where the PARAMETER statement is required, most data are entered in GAMS using the TABLE statement, discussed in Section 5.3 below. Meanwhile, let us briefly define the SCALAR statement.

5.2 SCALARS

The SCALAR statement is used to declare and (optionally) initialize a GAMS parameter of dimensionality zero. That means there are no associated sets, and that there is therefore exactly one number associated with the parameter. Note that the use of domain checking implies set association, and is therefore illegal in the SCALAR statement. An example:

```
SCALARS  RHO     Discount rate  /.15/
         IRR     Internal rate of return
         LIFE    Financial lifetime of productive units  /20/;
```

The statement above initializes RHO and LIFE, but not IRR. Later on we will have to either use another SCALAR statement to initialize IRR, or, (looking ahead to a notion we will develop in the next chapter), we could use an assignment statement to provide the value:

```
IRR = 0.07;
```

5.3 SIMPLE TABLES

A parameter may also be declared and given initial values in a TABLE statement. For 2- and higher-dimensional parameters this provides a more concise and easier method of data entry than the PARAMETER statement, since each label appears only once (at least in small tables). The example below is from [KORPET] and is preceded by the appropriate set definitions.

```
SETS   I     Plants
       / INCHON, ULSAN, YOSU /

       M     Productive units

       / ATMOS-DIST  Atmospheric distillation unit
         STEAM-CR    Steam cracker
         CAT-REFORM  Catalytic reformer
         BUTAD-EXT   Butadiene extracter
         PLATFINER   Platfiner
         AROMATICS   Aromatics unit
         HYDRODEAL   Hydrodealkylator / ;

TABLE  KA(M,I)   Initial capacity of productive units (1000 tons per year)

              INCHON     ULSAN      YOSU

ATMOS-DIST    3702       12910      9875
STEAM-CR                 517        1207
CAT-REFORM    369        1200       790
BUTAD-EXT                45         94
PLATFINER                201
AROMATICS                181        148
HYDRODEAL                180                      ;
```

The rules for forming simple tables are straightforward. The components of the header line are the by now familiar keyword-identifier-domain-list-text sequence, the domain-list and text being optional. The body of the table is in free format. Labels are used on the top and the left to map out a rectangular grid that contains the data values. The order of labels is unimportant, but if domain checking has been specified each label must match one in the associated set. In the example above, the row labels are drawn from the set M, and those on the column from the set I. Labels must not be repeated, but can be left out if the corresponding numbers are all zero or logically not needed. Blank entries imply that the default value (zero) will be associated with that label combination. If there is any uncertainty about which data column a number goes with, GAMS will protest with an error message and mark the ambiguous entry. At least one blank must separate all labels and data entries. Notice also that, in contrast to the SET, PARAMETER, and SCALAR statements, only one identifier (which must be a parameter) can be declared and initialized in a TABLE statement.

5.4   CONTINUED TABLES   ■

If a table has too many columns to fit nicely on a single line, then the columns that don't fit can be entered below. We use the same example to illustrate:

```
TABLE  KA(M,I)  Initial capacity of productive units (1000 tons per year)

                    INCHON     ULSAN

ATMOS-DIST          3702       12910
STEAM-CR                         517
CAT-REFORM           369        1200
BUTAD-EXT                         45
PLATFINER                        201
AROMATICS                        181
HYDRODEAL                        180


    +               YOSU
ATMOS-DIST          9875
STEAM-CR            1207
CAT-REFORM           790
BUTAD-EXT             94
AROMATICS           148    ;
```

The crucial item is the plus "+" sign above the row labels and to the left of the column labels in the continued part of the TABLE. The row labels have been duplicated, except that those for PLATFINER and HYDRODEAL have been left out, not having associated data. Tables can be continued as many times as necessary.

5.5   TABLES WITH MORE THAN TWO DIMENSIONS ■

A table, like a set, can have up 10 dimensions. Dots are again used to separate adjacent labels, and can be used in the row or column position. The label on the left of the row corresponds to the first set in the domain list, and that on the right of each column header to the last. Obviously there must be the same number of labels associated with each number in the table as there are sets in the domain list.

The actual layout chosen will depend on the size of the controlling sets and the amount of data, and the ideal choice should be the one that provides the most intuitively satisfactory way of organizing and inspecting the data. Most people can more easily look down a column of numbers than across a row, but to put extra labels on the row leads to a greater density of information. The example is from [MARCO]. The first layout shown is probably the best. The spaces around the dots are optional.

```
SETS  CI  Commodities : intermediate
      /  NAPHTHA    Naphtha
         DIST          Distillate
         GAS-OIL       Gas oil /

      CR  Commodities : crude oils
      /  MID-C       Mid-continent
         W-TEX       West Texas /

      Q Attributes of intermediate products
      /  DENSITY, SULFUR  /  ;
```

```
TABLE  ATTRIB(CI,CR,Q)  Blending attributes

                         DENSITY SULFUR

NAPHTHA.MID-C              272    .283
NAPHTHA.W-TEX              272   1.48
DIST   .MID-C             292    .526
DIST   .W-TEX             297   2.83
GAS-OIL.MID.C             295    .98
GAS-OIL.W-TEX            303   5.05   ;
```

The same table could be laid out as shown below:

```
         TABLE  ATTRIB(CI,CR,Q)  Blending attributes

         W-TEX.DENSITY  MID-C.DENSITY  W-TEX.SULFUR  MID-C.SULFUR

NAPHTHA       272            272           1.48          .283
DIST          297            297           2.83          .526
GAS-OIL       303            303           5.05           .98      ;
```

Another example showing how repeated columns or rows can be condensed with asterisks and lists in parentheses follows. The set membership is not shown, but can easily be inferred.

```
         TABLE  UPGRADE(STRAT,SIZE,TECH)
    *    Fraction of farm types that move up in each period
    *    under alternative strategies

         TABLE  ATTRIB(CI,CR,Q) Blending attributes
              SMALL.TECH1 SMALL.TECH2 MEDIUM.TECH1 MEDIUM.TECH2
    STRATEGY-1    .05         .05          .05          .05
    STRATEGY-2    .2          .2           .2           .2
    STRATEGY-3    .2          .2           .2           .2
    STRATEGY-4                             .2           .2
```

```
TABLE  UPGRADX(STRAT,SIZE,TECH) Alternative way of writing the same table

                                      TECH1*TECH2

         STRATEGY-1.(SMALL,MEDIUM)         .05

STRATEGY-2*STRATEGY-3.(SMALL,MEDIUM)       .2
         STRATEGY-4.MEDIUM                 .2
```

```
DISPLAY UPGRADE, UPGRADX;
```

Here we encounter the DISPLAY statement again. It causes the data associated with UPGRADE and UPGRADX to be listed on the output file if no compilation errors (discussed in the section following) are detected.

It is wise when considering table layout to imagine how the table will look on the output file. We will give complete details and examples in Chapter 10. Here, however, it is enough to note that long lines in tables will be broken if the print width (PW: see Appendix A) on the output file is not large enough to accommodate them. Many models brought from mainframes to personal computers are affected by this. It is possible to continue the row labels in a table on a second, or even third, line in order to accommodate a reasonable number of columns. An example of part of a big table from [INDUS] is used to illustrate. As written, this table actually has nine columns and a great many rows: we have just reproduced a small part to show continued row label-tuples. The break must come *after* a dot, and the rest of each line containing an incomplete row label-tuple must be blank.

```
TABLE YIELD(C,T,S,W,Z)  CROP YIELD (METRIC TONS PER ACRE)
                                              NWFP      PMW
WHEAT. (BULLOCK,SEMI-MECH). LA-PLANT.
                          (HEAVY,JANUARY)     .385      .338
WHEAT. (BULLOCK,SEMI-MECH). LA-PLANT. LIGHT   .506      .446
WHEAT. (BULLOCK,SEMI-MECH). LA-PLANT. STANDARD .592     .524
WHEAT. (BULLOCK,SEMI-MECH).(QK-HARV,STANDARD).
                          (HEAVY,JANUARY)     .439      .387
WHEAT.(BULLOCK,SEMI-MECH).(QK-HARV,STANDARD).LIGHT .573 .506
WHEAT. (BULLOCK,SEMI-MECH).(QK-HARV,STANDARD).
                                    STANDARD  .675      .595
ORCHARD.(BULLOCK,SEMI-MECH).STANDARD.STANDARD  3.9      3.9
```

5.6   ERROR REPORTING DURING COMPILATION ■

Several times since we began our discussion of sets we have remarked that certain ways of writing things are not allowed. It is time to demonstrate what actually happens if GAMS objects to something.

GAMS has been designed around the assumption that everyone makes errors, but that the computer is better at checking details of spelling and consistency than humans are. All possible checks are made as early in the processing of your GAMS program as possible, and we have tried to ensure that error recovery is graceful and that the error messages are helpful and self-explanatory.

There are two distinct phases during which error conditions may be detected. The first is during what we often call compilation: this is when GAMS is processing your program and checking that what you have entered follows the rules and is intelligible and internally consistent. All of the errors we have mentioned so far are of this type, and we try to make all possible checks at this stage, before too much time (or money) have been used. When GAMS detects a compilation error it marks the position with a dollar "$" sign and a number on a line that starts with 4 asterisks "****". At the end of the listing there is a section labeled ERROR MESSAGES where a brief explanation is given of the probable cause of the error. Some errors may not be detected on the line on which they are made: if a required semicolon is forgotten, for example, the error will not be detected until the next line. Below is a program fragment showing the listing and the messages for tables containing errors. The first is caused because SOUTH is not a member of the set S, the second by the ambiguous position of the number 123.4 in the body of the table.

```
GAMS 2.04 PC AT/XT
G E N E R A L   A L G E B R A I C   M O D E L I N G
C O M P I L A T I O N

    2    SET D     / NORTH, EAST, SOUTH, WEST /
    3        S(D) / NORTH, EAST /;
    4
    5        TABLE LEN(D,S)
    6             NORTH    SOUTH
****                      $170
    7    EAST    22.6    27.2
    8    WEST          123.4       ;
****                      $224


GAMS 2.04 PC AT/XT
G E N E R A L   A L G E B R A I C   M O D E L I N G
ERROR MESSAGES


170   DOMAIN VIOLATION FOR ELEMENT
224   OVERLAPPING ENTRY IGNORED
```

The other type of error occurs while GAMS is doing calculations or generating models. Division by zero is an example. These are called execution or run-time errors, and will be discussed in the next chapter since we have not yet explained how you might produce them.

5.7   TABLE AND PARAMETER STATEMENTS ▪
THAT ARE NOT DOMAIN CHECKED

As we have mentioned before, domain checking is not compulsory. If you enter a statement such as:

```
PARAMETER RHO Discount Rate;
```

then GAMS makes no assumptions about RHO until you provide more information. You can later decide to domain check it by continuing the definition, as in:

```
PARAMETER RHO(T) / 1988 0.07, 1989*1994 0.10, 1995 0.09 /;
```

(which assumes that T has already been declared to contain at least the labels 1988*1995). Or you can choose not to domain check it, as is shown in the deliberately nonsensical (but legal) statement below:

```
PARAMETER RHO / 1988.JANUARY 0.07, STRATEGY-1.COST 4400,
                CAT-CRACKR.CAPACITY 99 /;
```

If a parameter is not domain checked, the only restriction is that the dimensionality must be constant. Once the number of labels per data item has been established it is frozen; to refer to the parameter differently is an error.

It may sometimes be useful to domain check some but not all of the index positions associated with a parameter. In the table below, various costs are established, but because (as it turns out but is not demonstrated here) there is no logical connection in the algebra between the labels heading the columns, an asterisk is put in the second index position in the domain list.

```
TABLE INV(M,*) INVESTMENT COST TABLE

                     H        PHI        BETA

  BLAST-FURN        1.5       250         .6
  BOF               1.5       120         .6
  DIRECT-RED         .8       100         .6
  ELEC-ARC           .5        42         .6
```

The alternative to the formulation above would be to define a set whose only purpose is to check the column headers. Many experienced GAMS users, not all of them paranoid, would do it that way. This "wildcard" domain specifier means that any label can be used in the corresponding index position, the last in this case. This facility is often useful in generating reports, which may involve labels that are entered only once. It is not possible to misspell such labels. An entirely unchecked table may be written with a list of asterisks (which allows GAMS to check the dimensionality, and is therefore encouraged), or without, as shown in the tiny artificial examples below.

```
TABLE  TABLE1 This is an example of a table with no domain list at all
                 DEM-DMSTC      DEM-EXPRT
  AGRIC.1988         233           256
  MANUF.1988*1990    207           219       ;

TABLE  TABLE2(*,*) This is not domain checked but will be 2-dimensional
                 1988      1989
  AGRIC           44        67
  MANUF           47        55
  SERVICES        39        44     ;
```

We have demonstrated the use of unchecked symbols and of unchecked index positions (the asterisk domain specifier) using TABLE statements for examples. However the same mechanisms can be used in any declarations of sets, parameters, variables and equations.

5.8 CONCLUSION ■

Two general points should be made before we finish this discussion of data initialization. All data are stored internally using what computer scientists call real numbers, regardless of how the numbers are written. There is no integer data type or mixed mode arithmetic in GAMS. Secondly, all data known to a GAMS program must be entered or produced using statements in the GAMS language. Currently GAMS cannot extract data from databases or read files of numbers. This is a deliberate design decision, stemming from the notion that all parts of a model should be available in one place in both human and machine readable form. We expect that in the future GAMS will be able to import data, but the problems of how to provide safeguards against errors and how to verify later what has been done are difficult ones.

In this chapter we have discussed the declaration and initialization of parameters with the PARAMETER, SCALAR and TABLE statement. In the next we will discuss how data can be changed with assignment statements.

DATA MANIPULATIONS WITH PARAMETERS 6

In this chapter we will deal explicitly only with parameter manipulation, but we will cover all aspects of data handling except assignments to sets and the LOOP statement. The material in this chapter may be more difficult to follow than what we have covered until now, but if you are seriously interested in learning how to use GAMS, then the effort is required. As with learning other computer languages it is often instructive to construct small examples and have GAMS process them to see if the results are as anticipated. (In Section 6.2 we describe the DISPLAY statement, needed to inspect results of data manipulations.) A thorough grasp of the concepts in this chapter will make your dealings with GAMS much more effective.

6.1 THE ASSIGNMENT STATEMENT ■

The assignment statement is the fundamental data manipulation statement in GAMS. It may be used to define or alter values associated with any sets, parameters, variables or equations. As before, we will illustrate by example.

A simple assignment is written in the style associated with many other computer languages. GAMS uses the traditional symbols for addition, subtraction, multiplication and division (+ - * /). We will use them in the examples that follow, and give more details in Section 6.3. Consider the following artificial sequence:

```
SCALAR X / 1.5 /;
X = 1.2;
X = X + 2;
```

The SCALAR X is initialized to be 1.5. The second statement listed changes the value to 1.2, and the third changes it yet again to 3.2. The second and third statements are assignments, whose the effect is to replace the previous value of X, if any, with a new one. Notice that an assignment is guaranteed *not* to start with a reserved word, and that the semicolon is therefore *required* as a delimiter before all assignments. A formal description of the assignment statement is quite elaborate, and is given in Appendix F on language grammar. The rest of the chapter will be devoted to explaining all the ramifications: indexed assignments, functions, index operations (SUM and so forth) and the dollar control.

Now consider the following fragment:

```
SET D / NORTH, SOUTH /
PARAMETER DA(D) / NORTH 21.7, SOUTH 3.07 /
          DJ(D) ;
DJ(D) = 2.75*DA(D);
```

The assignment statement means that, for every member of the set D, a value is assigned to DJ. The value is 2.75 multiplied by the corresponding value in DA, and so the value 59.675 is assigned to DJ('NORTH'), and 8.4425 to DJ('SOUTH'). This assignment is known technically as an indexed assignment, and we will often refer to the set D as the controlling index or controlling set. Since this operation offers what may be thought of as simultaneous or parallel assignment it provides a concise way of specifying changes in large amounts of data. Mathematically, this assignment would be written:

$$DJ_d = 2.75\,DA_d, \quad \text{for all } d \tag{6.1}$$

More examples follow. We will intersperse them with text to explain the principles involved, which are important. Study these examples carefully. The declarations that follow apply to all examples until the end of this section. In the following section (on displays) there are examples showing the results of assignment statements similar to these.

```
SET ROW      / ROW-1*ROW-10 /
    COL      / COL-1*COL-10 /
    SRO(ROW) / ROW-7*ROW-10 /;
PARAMETER A(ROW,COL),
          B(ROW,ROW),
          R(ROW) / ROW-1 22, ROW-4*ROW-7 4.7 ,(ROW-2, ROW-9) 2.4 /,
          C(COL) / COL-4 17.4, COL-1 8.8, COL-9*COL-10 11.1 /;
```

The next statement assigns a constant value to one element of A. All other elements of A remain unchanged. Either single or double quotes can be used to delimit the labels. Domain checking is enforced here and in all following examples, since all the parameters declared above are domain checked.

```
A('ROW-7','COL-4') = -2.36;
```

Next is an assignment to the 10 values associated with 'COL-3'.

```
A(ROW,'COL-3') = 7.73 + 0.5*R(ROW);
```

We can safely use the same symbol on the left and right of the = sign. The new values are not available until the calculations are complete, and the operation below gives the expected results.

```
R(ROW) = 3 * R(ROW);
```

Next we make an assignment over a subset, which works because the proper relationship has been established between the sets ROW and SRO. In general, wherever a set name can occur in an indexed assignment, a subset (or even a label) can be used instead if you need to make the assignment over a subset instead of the whole domain.

```
A(SRO,'COL-10') = 2.44 - 33*R(SRO);
```

Now come two errors. In the first statement, what is apparently a controlling index on the right of the = sign is not matched on the left. In the second, there is an illegal reference to C(ROW): C has been declared as C(COL).

```
A(ROW,'COL-2') = 22 - C(COL) ;
A(ROW,'COL-3') = 4.3 + C(ROW) ;
```

Next is an assignment to all 100 data elements of A.

```
A(ROW,COL) = 13.2 + R(ROW)*C(COL);
```

For each unique two-label combination that can be formed from the elements of ROW and COL the calculation above is carried out. The first of these is, explicitly, A('ROW-1','COL-1') = 13.2 + R('ROW-1')*C('COL-1'). This assignment has two controlling indices, and the extension to more should be apparent.

The next example is not straightforward.

```
B(ROW,ROW) = 7.7 - R(ROW);
```

This assigns exactly 10 values! The assignment is done successively for each member of the set ROW, resulting in assignments to B('ROW-1','ROW-1') and so forth, but to none of the off-diagonal elements. To understand why, it may be easiest to look at the expression and note that there is only one controlling index (ROW), and that if we step through the elements of ROW one at a time we will make assignments only to the diagonal entries in B. To make an assignment over all the elements of B, we need to recall our discussion of the ALIAS statement from Chapter 4. If we provide an additional name for ROW and use it in the second index position, then there will be two controlling indices and GAMS will make assignments over the full Cartesian product, all 100 values:

```
ALIAS(ROW, ROWP);
B(ROW, ROWP) = 7.7 - R(ROW) + R(ROWP);
```

It is possible to have fewer controlling indices on the right of the = sign than on the left. The first example sets all elements of A to a constant; the second assigns a constant value for each member of the set ROW:

```
A(ROW, COL) = 1 ; A(ROW, COL) = 9 - C(COL) ;
```

The GAMS 'extended range' identifiers can also be used in assignment statements, as in

```
A(ROW, 'COL-10') = INF; A(ROW, 'COL-1') = -INF;
```

We will discuss extended range arithmetic in Section 6.3 (d) below. The values most often used are NA in incomplete tables, and INF for variable bounds.

For parameters that are not domain checked, the only restriction is, as before, that identifiers retain constant dimensionality. It is possible to make assignments to Z(A) and Z(B), for example, where A and B are entirely unrelated sets, if domain checking has been suppressed for Z. But we emphasize again that we regard this as unwise, even in play models, that could be copied by others.

6.2   THE DISPLAY STATEMENT   ■

The DISPLAY statement is used with parameters to write all the values associated with the identifier onto the output file, properly labeled. The general form of the DISPLAY statement (for parameters or sets; a small extension is needed for variables and equations) is

```
DISPLAY identifier,identifier, . . . , "quoted text", . . ;
```

where identifier is the name (*without* parentheses or domain lists) of an initialized or assigned set or parameter, and quoted text is arbitrary text between quote symbols. Text and identifiers can be intermixed in any order, but, as previously, text must be contained on one line and can not exceed 80 characters. Text is used to put explanatory material onto the output file. An example is needed of display output and then a short discussion. This tiny fragment has been designed to show features of index assignments. First the listing of the input as echoed back by the GAMS compiler; this contains line numbers, and so is useful in interpreting the output:

```
GAMS 2.04 PC AT/XT
G E N E R A L   A L G E B R A I C   M O D E L I N G
C O M P I L A T I O N
   1   SET R     LABELS FOR THE ROWS        / R-1 * R-3 /,
   2       C     LABELS FOR THE COLUMNS     / C-1 * C-3 /,
   3   SR(R) A SUBSET OF THE ROW LABELS / R-2, R-3 /;
   4
   5   PARAMETER A(R,C) A SIMPLE 3 BY 3 PARAMETER
   6             B(R) / R-1 1, R-2 2, R-3 3 /;
   7
   8   A(R, C) = -1;
   9
  10   DISPLAY 'A AFTER EXECUTING A(R,C) = -1', A;
  11
  12   A('R-3','C-3') = 2;
  13
  14   DISPLAY "A AFTER EXECUTING A('R-3','C-3') = 2;" , A;
  15
  16   A(R,'C-2') = 1.2 + 3 * B(R);
  17
  18   DISPLAY "A AFTER EXECUTING A(R,'C-2') = 1.2 + 3 * B(R); ",
  19           'ONLY A SINGLE COLUMN HAS CHANGED', A;
  20
  21   A(SR,C) = 3;
  22
  23   DISPLAY 'A AFTER EXECUTING A(SR,C) = 3;',
  24           'ONLY A SUBSET OF THE ROWS HAVE CHANGED', A;
```

Now follows the output produced by the four DISPLAYs above:

```
GAMS 2.04 PC AT/XT
G E N E R A L   A L G E B R A I C   M O D E L I N G
E X E C U T I N G

----      10 A AFTER EXECUTING A(R,C) = -1

----      10 PARAMETER A              A SIMPLE 3 BY 3 PARAMETER

              C-1         C-2         C-3
R-1        -1.000      -1.000      -1.000
R-2        -1.000      -1.000      -1.000
R-3        -1.000      -1.000      -1.000

----      14 A AFTER EXECUTING A('R-3','C-3') = 2;

----      14 PARAMETER A              A SIMPLE 3 BY 3 PARAMETER

              C-1         C-2         C-3
R-1        -1.000      -1.000      -1.000
R-2        -1.000      -1.000      -1.000
R-3        -1.000      -1.000       2.000

----      18 A AFTER EXECUTING A(R,'C-2') = 1.2 + 3 * B(R);
             ONLY A SINGLE COLUMN HAS CHANGED

----      18 PARAMETER A              A SIMPLE 3 BY 3 PARAMETER

              C-1         C-2         C-3
R-1        -1.000       4.200      -1.000
R-2        -1.000       7.200      -1.000
R-3        -1.000      10.200       2.000

----      23 A AFTER EXECUTING A(SR,C) = 3;
             ONLY A SUBSET OF THE ROWS HAVE CHANGED

----      23 PARAMETER A              A SIMPLE 3 BY 3 PARAMETER

              C-1         C-2         C-3
R-1        -1.000       4.200      -1.000
R-2         3.000       3.000       3.000
R-3         3.000       3.000       3.000
```

The four dashes "----" are useful in finding display output with a lister or editor. Then comes the line number of the DISPLAY statement from the compiler listing, useful if the same symbol is displayed several times as values are modified. The symbol type and name and any associated text are written in upper case (as is all output produced after the listing of the input, which can optionally be in the case entered by the user). GAMS has a facility to vary the format of display output which we will discuss in Chapter 13; here we confine the discussion to the default layout. Symbols with one index are listed in parameter initialization style; if there are n indices, where n is two or more, they are listed in table style. If n is more than three, several tables are used, one for each single label combination needed over the domain of the first $(n - 3)$ indices. The order of the label list for a given index is the order in which GAMS first encountered the labels. Three places of decimals are shown for the values, but scientific notation is used if individual values require it. Blanks are used for zeroes and all zero rows or columns are suppressed. An all zero parameter (not uninitialized or unassigned: it is illegal to display these) produces the output (ALL ZERO). Displays of sets look similar to parameters except the word YES appears instead of numbers.

At this stage the DISPLAY statement's most obvious use is to inspect the results of assignment statements to see if they are as expected.

6.3 SIMPLE EXPRESSIONS ■

In this section we will continue our discussion of parameter assignments by showing in more detail what can be used on the right of the = sign. We will cover all numerical facilities available in both standard and 'extended' arithmetic, and also error reporting during data manipulations. In the next section we will cover relational operators and exception handling.

6.3 (a) Standard arithmetic operations ■

The standard arithmetic symbols and operations are:

**		exponentiation
*	/	multiplication and division
+	-	addition and subtraction (including unary operations)

They are listed here in what is known as precedence order, which determines the order of evaluation in an expression without parentheses. Consider, for example:

```
X = 5 + 4 * 3 ** 2;
```

For clarity, this could have been written:

```
X = 5 + (4 * (3 ** 2));
```

In both cases the result is 41. It is better to use parentheses than to rely on the precedence of operators, since it prevents errors and makes your intentions clear. An expression is an arbitrarily complicated specification for a calculation, with parentheses nested as needed for clarity and intent. Expressions may be freely continued over many lines: an end-of-line is permissible at any point where a blank may be used. Blanks may be used for readability around identifiers, parentheses, operator symbols and so forth. Blanks are not allowed within identifiers or numbers, and are significant inside the quote marks used to delimit labels. These rules will seem quite natural if you are familiar with structured programming languages such as C or Pascal. Some quite complex expressions are shown as examples in this chapter, and we have deliberately not been consistent in our use of blanks so that different styles of presentation are shown.

We noted earlier that GAMS uses only real values for arithmetic: there is no need to worry about FORTRAN style division with truncation. But there is a potential difficulty with exponentiation, which will again sound familiar to Pascal users. If you enter, for example, X**N (or even X**3), then GAMS assumes that this is a real number to be raised to a real power. This operation is not defined if X has a negative value, and an error will result. If you know that the exponent is an integer, and if you want to admit the possibility of negative values for X, then a function call, POWER(X,N), is available that checks if the exponent is an integer and produces the desired result if it is (and an error message if it is not).

Three additional capabilities are available to add power and flexibility to expression calculations. They are indexed operations, functions and extended range arithmetic.

6.3 (b)   Indexed Operations   ■

The indexed operations are SUM, PROD, SMIN and SMAX.

The most common of these is SUM, which is used to calculate totals over the domain of a set. We use an example from [ANDEAN].

```
SETS I    Plants
      /   BARANQUILL    Baranquilla in Colombia
          CARTAGENA     Cartagena in Colombia
          CALLAO        Callao in Peru
          CUZCO         Cuzco in Peru
          MORON         Moron in Venezuela /

      M    Productive units
      /   NITR-ACID     Nitric acid
          SULF-ACID     Sulfuric acid
          AMM-NITR      Ammonium nitrate
          AMM-SULF      Ammonium sulfate /;
```

```
TABLE CAPACITY(I,M)  Capacity in tons per day
```

	NITR-ACID	SULF-ACID	AMM-NITR	AMM-SULF
BARANQUILL	230	162		212
CARTAGENA	68			
CALLAO	107		140	50
CUZCO	90		118	
MORON	88	1200		200

These five plants each contain some of the productive units. In order to calculate total capacity for each process we would form totals over the SET of plants as below:

```
PARAMETER TOTCAP(M)    Total capacity by process;
TOTCAP(M) = SUM(I, CAPACITY(I,M));
DISPLAY TOTCAP;
```

This would be written, using normal mathematical representation, as

$$TOTC_m = \sum_i C_{im} \qquad (6.2)$$

In the GAMS representation, the index over which the summation is done, I, is separated from the reserved word SUM by a left parenthesis and from the data term CAPACITY(I,M) by a comma. I is again called the controlling index for this operation. The scope of the control is the pair of parentheses ( ) that starts immediately after the SUM. It is illegal for the controlling index to appear outside this scope. (Actually it is legal but not likely to be useful to have two independent index operations controlled by the same index.) It is also possible to SUM simultaneously over the domain of two or more sets, in which case more parentheses are needed. Also, of course, an arithmetic expression may be used instead of an identifier:

```
COUNT = SUM((I,J), A(I,J)); EMP = SUM(T, L(T)*H(T));
```

Again we show equivalent mathematical forms:

$$COUNT = \sum_i \sum_j A_{ij} \quad \text{and} \quad EMP = \sum_t L_t M_t \tag{6.3}$$

The PROD operator takes the *product* over the domain of the controlling sets in an analogous way. A good example is that of a Cobb-Douglas economic production function, in which the parameter SHARE(I) denotes the exponent associated with INPUT(I).

```
OUTPUT = PROD(I, INPUT(I)**SHARE(I) ) ;
```

The SMIN and SMAX operations are used to find largest and smallest values over the domain of the index set or sets. From the [ANDEAN] example above, for example, we can obtain the minimum and maximum capacities for each type of productive unit by using SMIN and SMAX.

```
PARAMETER
   MINCAP(M)   Minimum capacity across plants for productive units
   MAXCAP(M)   Maximum capacity across plants for productive units;

MINCAP (M) = SMIN(I, CAPACITY(I,M));
MAXCAP (M) = SMAX(I, CAPACITY(I,M));
DISPLAY MINCAP, MAXCAP;
```

The index for the SMIN and SMAX operators is specified in the same manner as is the index for the SUM operator. To find the unit of any type with the largest capacity, we could run the operation over both sets:

```
LRGUNIT = SMAX((I,M), CAPACITY(I,M)); or LRGUNIT = SMAX(M, MAXCAP(M));
```

6.3 (c) Functions   ■

GAMS provides commonly used standard functions such as exponentiation, logarithms, and the trigonometric functions. An example is the assignment statement

```
X(J) = LOG(Y(J)) ;
```

which replaces the current value of X with the natural logarithm of Y over the domain of the index set J. Table 6.1 lists the available functions, along with a description, definition, and the number of arguments expected for each. There are further cautions when functions appear in equations: these are dealt with in Chapter 8.

The following GAMS program shows the results of some less common functions. We have ignored our own advice and left the second index position on TAB unchecked:

Table 6.1: GAMS Standard Functions

Name	Description	Definition	Number of Arguments
ABS	Absolute value	$\lvert \text{arg} \rvert$	1
ARCTAN	Arctangent	arctan(arg); result in radians	1
CEIL	Ceiling	smallest integer $\geq$ arg	1
COS	Cosine	cos(arg); argument in radians	1
ERRORF	Error function	integral of the standard normal distribution from $-\infty$ to arg	1
EXP	Exponential	e^{arg}	1
FLOOR	Floor	largest integer $\leq$ arg	1
LOG	Natural logarithm	log base e of arg	1
LOG10	Common logarithm	log base 10 of arg	1
MAPVAL	Mapping function	Assigns unique numbers to special values	1
MAX	Largest value	max(arg1,arg2,arg3, ...)	>1
MIN	Smallest value	min(arg1,arg2,arg3, ...)	>1
MOD	Remainder	$\text{arg1} - \text{trunc(arg1/arg2)} \times \text{arg2}$	2
NORMAL	Normal random	random number normally distributed with mean arg1 and standard deviation arg2	2*
POWER	Integer power	$\text{arg1}^{\text{arg2}}$, where arg2 must be an integer	2
ROUND	Rounding	round(arg) round to the nearest integer round(arg1,arg2) rounds arg1 to arg2 decimal places right ($+$) or left ($-$) to the decimal point	1 or 2
SIGN	Sign	$\text{sign(arg)} = \begin{cases} +1 \text{ if arg} > 0 \\ -1 \text{ if arg} < 0 \\ 0 \text{ if arg} = 0 \end{cases}$	1
SIN	Sine	sin(arg); arg in radians	1
SQR	Square	$\text{arg} \times \text{arg}$	1
SQRT	Square root	$\sqrt{\text{arg}}$	1
TRUNC	Truncation	sign (arg) times floor (abs(arg))	1
UNIFORM	Uniform random	random number with uniform distribution between arg1 and arg2	2*

*The pseudo random number generators NORMAL and UNIFORM must not appear in equations. The seed can be reset by OPTION SEED = number. The seed is preserved over continued compilations, and the functions generate the same sequence on different machines within the precision of the hardware.

since each label occurs only once, typographical errors made entering them will never be detected. We have also edited the results to show the calculated zeroes explicitly.

```
Set  i  numbers      / n1*n5 /

Parameter x(i)    arguments
                / n1 = -1.5, n2 = -.5, n4 = .5, n5 = 1.5 /
```

```
                    tab(i,*) summary table ;

    tab(i,'argument') =        x(i) ;
    tab(i,'ceil    ') = ceil  (x(i));
    tab(i,'floor   ') = floor (x(i));
    tab(i,'trunc   ') = trunc (x(i));
    tab(i,'sign    ') = sign  (x(i));

    display tab;

    -----    13 PARAMETER TAB        SUMMARY TABLE

                ARGUMENT    CEIL    FLOOR   TRUNC    SIGN
    N1             -1.5    -1.0     -2.0    -1.0    -1.0
    N2              -.5      .0     -1.0      .0    -1.0
    N3               0        0        0       0       0
    N4               .5     1.0       .0      .0     1.0
    N5              1.5     2.0      1.0     1.0     1.0
```

6.3 (d)   Extended Range Arithmetic and Error Handling   ■

GAMS uses an 'extended range' arithmetic to handle missing data, the results of undefined operations, and the representation of bounds that solver systems regard as 'infinite.' The special symbols are listed in Table 6.2, with a brief explanation of the meaning of each.

Table 6.2:   Special Symbols for Extended Arithmetic

INF	Plus infinity. A very large positive number.
-INF	Minus infinity. A very large negative number.
NA	Not available. Used for missing data. Any operation that uses the value NA will produce the result NA.
UNDF	Undefined. The result of an undefined or illegal operation. The user can not directly set a value to UNDF.
EPS	Very close to zero, but different from zero.

GAMS has defined the results of all arithmetic operations and all function values using these special values. The results can be inspected by running the library problem [CRAZY], and a few are illustrated below. They are as expected: 1 + INF evaluates to INF, 1 + EPS to 1, and similarly for others.

The range of values available with ordinary numbers is quite small compared to the range that most computers can handle, because we are concerned that models give the same results on all types of machines. You should avoid creating or using numbers with absolute values larger than 1.0E+20, or smaller than 1.0E-20. If a number is too large, you run the risk that it will be treated by GAMS as undefined (UNDF), and you will not be able to use any values derived from it in a model. Always use INF (or -INF) explicitly for arbitrarily large numbers.

When an attempted arithmetic operation is illegal or has undefined results because of the value of arguments (division by zero is the normal example), an error is reported and the result is set to undefined (UNDF). The error is marked on the output file in a similar way to that used during the syntactic check. The row of four asterisks "****" again appears, making this sequence a good search target in your editor. GAMS will also report the line number in the input file where the statement causing the error was entered, and give as much detail as possible about the cause. From there on, UNDF is treated as a proper data value and does not trigger additional error messages.

The important thing to remember is that GAMS will not solve a model if an error has been detected, but will terminate with an error condition. It is thus always necessary to anticipate conditions that will cause errors, such as divide by zero. This is most easily done with the dollar control, and will be discussed in the next section.

Table 6.3 shows a selection of results for exponentiation and division for a variety of input parameters.

Table 6.3:   Exponentiation and Division

| *Value* | | | *Operation* | |
a	b	a**b	power(a,b)	a/b
2	2	4	4	1
-2	2	UNDF	4	-1
2	2.1	4.287	UNDF	.952
NA	2.5	NA	NA	NA
3	0	1	1	UNDF
INF	2	INF	INF	INF
2	INF	UNDF	UNDF	0

6.4   EXCEPTION HANDLING ■

In this section we deal with the way in which exceptions are handled. The index operations already described are very powerful, but it is necessary to allow for exceptions of one sort or another. For example, heavy trucks may not be able to use a particular route because of a weak bridge, or some sectors in an economy may not produce exportable products. We have already seen that the use of a subset in an indexed expression provides some ability to handle exceptions. Here we will cover other ways.

6.4 (a)   Relational Operators ■

Let us first deal with the relational operators available. For completeness we list all operators, relational and arithmetic, in precedence order:

$	dollar operator
**	exponentiation
* /	multiplication, division
– *	unary and binary
LT LE EQ NE GE GT	less than, less than-or-equal, equal, not equal, etc.
NOT	
AND	
OR XOR	or, either or

GAMS does not have a boolean data type, but follows the convention that the result of a relational operation is zero if the assertion is false, and one if true. For the results of boolean operations, GAMS interprets zero as false and non-zero as true (which is what the programming language C, also lacking a boolean data type, does as well). The results of operations using AND, OR, XOR and NOT are shown in Table 6.4.

Table 6.4:   Operations with AND, OR, XOR and NOT

Operands		*Results*			
a	b	a AND b	a OR b	a XOR b	NOT a
0	0	0	0	0	1
0	non-zero	0	1	1	1
non-zero	0	0	1	1	0
non-zero	non-zero	1	1	0	0

6.4 (b)   The Dollar Operator ∎

With the above mechanisms laid out conceptually, we now turn to the one language feature that everybody has trouble learning to use: the dollar operator. The dollar operator provides powerful and concise exception-handling capability. To describe it, we first revert to simple fragments interspersed with text, and show more useful examples later. The first example illustrates what is often called "dollar on the right" (of the = sign). Consider the following:

```
SCALAR X,Y ;
Y = 2 ; X = 1 ;
X = 2$(Y GT 1.5) ;
```

The meaning of the last statement is, in words: if the value of Y is larger than 1.5, assign the value 2 to X but if not, assign the value zero. Therefore an if-then-else type of construct is implied, but the else operation is predefined and never made explicit. An assignment is *always* made after this type of expression has been evaluated. In the above case the value assigned to X will be 2. Notice that we can construct an explicit if-then-else with

```
X = 2$(Y GT 1.5) + 0$(Y LE 1.5) ;
```

whose meaning is exactly the same. This use of logical opposites has been found to be not particularly useful in practice, however. As always, we can make a term with a dollar operator part of a more complicated expression. More examples will be given as we proceed. Now we look at an example with a similar appearance but different logic. This one is familiarly known as "dollar on the left":

```
SCALAR X,Y ;
Y = 2 ; X = 1 ;
X$(Y GT 1.5) = 2 ;
```

This means: if the value of Y is larger than 1.5, assign the value 2 to X; if not, do not make an assignment at all. More generally, this is a *conditional* assignment: if the logical relationship is true, the assignment is made; if it is not, however, the existing value is retained, zero being used if no previous value has been given. An extension of this idea is the use of the dollar to control SUMs or PRODs, discussed below.

In practice, the dollar operator is almost always used in indexed assignments (discussed in this chapter), or in indexed equations, which will be dealt with in Chapter 8. Here are a few examples. The first is from [CHENERY]. We have already defined the parameter SIG(I) and we use the results to calculate RHO(I) as follows:

```
RHO(I)$(SIG(I) NE 0) = (1./SIG(I)) - 1. ;
```

In this example we are protecting ourselves against dividing by zero. If any of the values associated with SIG(I) turn out to be zero, no assignment is made, and the previous values of RHO(I) remain. As it happens, RHO was previously uninitialized, and zeroes will be used for any label for which the assignment was suppressed.

Now recall the convention that non-zero implies true and zero implies false. This means that the assignment above could also be written as

```
RHO(I)$SIG(I) = (1./SIG(I)) - 1. ;
```

This concise style has been adopted by many experienced GAMS users, and the models in the Library use this convention almost exclusively, although new users may not find it immediately clear. A last point about this example: the "dollar on the right" form happens to be equivalent (by chance) in this case, and indeed is more meaningful as there is no ambiguity about what happens if SIG(I) is zero:

```
RHO(I) = ( (1./SIG(I)) - 1.)$(SIG(I) NE 0) ;
```

Notice also that we can again do if-else assignments. Suppose we truly want a division by zero to result in INF, but wish to suppress an execution error:

```
R(I) = INF $ (S(I) EQ 0) + (1/S(I)) $ (S(I) NE 0) ;
```

Many would write, equivalently but not as clearly,

```
R(I) = INF ; R(I)$S(I) = 1/S(I) ;
```

We suggest that in any modeling work you will have to explain to others that you use the form that shows your intent as clearly as possible. In the case above the more long-winded form is preferable.

The next example is from [FERTD]. The set I is the set of plants, and the parameter IED contains distance data for various ways of importing raw material. We are calculating MUR(I), the cost of transporting imported raw materials. In some cases a barge trip must be followed by a road trip because the plant is not alongside the river and we must combine the separate costs. The assignment is:

```
MUR(I) =    (1.0 + .0030*IED(I,"BARGE"))$ IED(I,"BARGE")
         + (0.5 + .0144*IED(I,"ROAD" ))$ IED(I,"ROAD") ;
```

This means that if the entry in the distance table is not zero, then calculate and add in the cost of shipping using that link, which has a fixed and a variable component. If there is no distance entry, there is no contribution to the cost, presumably because that mode is not used.

The next segment is from [GTM], with some pruning. The assignment to SUPB looks formidable, but is in fact only a linear interpolation. The set I represents regions that supply natural gas. One of the data values in SDAT(I,'LIMIT') is INF, and we want to assign the value 0 to SUPB for this label, but do the interpolation normally for the others. Afterwards we replace the INF with 100, which is a very large number compared with the other values in SUPC, but leave the other values unchanged.

```
SUPC(I) = SDAT(I,'LIMIT');
SUPB(I) = ( (SDAT(I,'REF-P1')-SDAT(I,'REF-P2'))
                        /
     (1/(SUPC(I)-SDAT(I,'REF-Q1'))-1/(SUPC(I)-SDAT(I,'REF-Q2')))
                                    )$(SUPC(I) NE INF);
SUPC(I)$(SUPC(I) EQ INF) = 100;
```

Now let us move on to controlling index operations with the dollar operator. This is conceptually similar to the "dollar on the left" shown above: if the condition is true, include the term in the SUM; if not, do not. For instance, we may need to write in [GTM] above:

```
TSUBC = SUM(I$(SUPC(I) NE INF), SUPC(I)) ;
```

in order to find the sum of the finite values in SUPC. A small digression is in order here. It is not possible to test directly for the special value UNDF. A function, MAPVAL, provides a classification of real values that may be tested, and the example above could be written as

```
TSUBC = SUM(I$(MAPVAL(SUPC(I)) NE MAPVAL(INF)), SUPC(I)) ;
```

The most common use of dollar controlled index operations is where the control is itself a set. This is a new concept, and one we will develop gradually until we deal with assignment to sets in Chapter 11. We used a set to define the mapping between mines and ports in Chapter 4. Another typical example is a set-to-set mapping defining the relationship between states and regions, used for aggregating data obtained by state to the model's requirements (by region).

```
SETS   R   REGIONS
               / NORTHWEST, SOUTHWEST /
       S   STATES
               / WASHINGTON, OREGON, TEXAS, OKLAHOMA /
       CORR(R,S) CORRESPONDENCE OF REGIONS AND STATES
               / NORTHWEST.(WASHINGTON, OREGON)
                         SOUTHWEST.(TEXAS, OKLAHOMA) /
PARAMETER Y(R)      INCOME OF EACH REGION
          INCOME(S)    INCOME OF EACH STATE
               / WASHINGTON   3.5,   OREGON      3.2
                 TEXAS        6.4,   OKLAHOMA    2.5 /
```

The set CORR provides a correspondence to show which states belong to which regions. The parameter INCOME is the income of each state. Y(R) can be calculated with the assignment statement:

```
Y(R) = SUM(S $ CORR(R,S), INCOME(S));
```

For each region R, the summation over S is only over those pairs of (R,S) for which CORR(R,S) exists. Conceptually, set existence is analogous to the boolean value "true" or the arithmetic value "not zero." The effect is that only the contributions for WASHINGTON and OREGON are included in the total for NORTHWEST, and SOUTHWEST includes only TEXAS and OKLAHOMA. The use of sets to control dollar operations is common and leads to concise and powerful ways of expressing complex logical relationships. We will list a few examples from [RDATA].

```
Q1(UNION,COMPANY)    =
             SUM(PLANT$OWNERSHIP(COMPANY,PLANT),   EMP(PLANT,UNION));

Q2(UNIT,REGION)     =
             SUM((PLANT,CITY,STATE)$GEOGRAPHY(PLANT,CITY,STATE,REGION),
                     K80(UNIT,PLANT));
```

Here is an example of explicit if-else constructs with the dollar on the index. The problem is to find the SUM of the absolute values in X(I). The obvious way to do this is

```
ABSTOT = SUM(I, ABS(X(I) ) ;
```

but we could use

```
ABSTOT = SUM(I$(X(I) GE 0), X(I) ) + SUM(I$(X(I) LT 0), -X(I) );
```

or even

```
ABSTOT = SUM(I$(X(I) GE 0), X(I) ) + SUM(I$(NOT(X(I) GE 0)), -X(I) );
```

A source of possible confusion is when we need to have two independent conditions on the same assignment. With purely numeric values it is possible to write

```
S(I) = V(I) $ (V(I) GE 2 AND V(I) LE 4) ;
```

and obtain the desired result, in this case setting S(I) to zero or to a value in the inclusive interval 2 to 4. This is not possible with sets however, because AND is a numeric operator and is not able to handle set relationships. We have not yet covered how to use sets to rewrite the assignment above, but will show an example. K, S(K), T(K) and I are sets, and U(I), A(I) and B(K) are parameters, and the summation will be over those members of K that are also members of both S and T:

```
U(I) = SUM(K $( S(K) $T(K) ), A(I)*B(K));
```

The entire expression after the first dollar *must* be enclosed in parentheses.

6.5   DATA INTEGRITY AND THE ABORT STATEMENT   ■

A careful modeler should try to make sure that his model contains checks that data relationships that are assumed to hold in fact do hold. This is prudent practice given that data and models are likely to be changed, and that assumptions made when the first version is done may be forgotten later. The ABORT statement provides for the termination of a GAMS task if some logical or numerical condition is found not to hold. This prevents wasting resources by solving incorrect models. The general form for the ABORT statement is similar to the DISPLAY statement, and is:

```
ABORT $ (condition) ident,"text", . . . . . ;
```

The meaning is: if "condition" evaluates to "true" or "non-zero," then display the following identifiers and/or text and terminate processing with an error condition. If not, continue processing with the statement following. As an example, assume that market shares must sum to 1. We would write

```
ABORT $ (SUM(I, SHARE(I)) NE 1) "Error in market share data",SHARE;
DISPLAY "Market shares sum to 1";
```

If the market share numbers do not sum to 1, the first message will be displayed and then the bad data, and the program will stop with an error condition. Otherwise the message following will be displayed and execution will continue. Note that it is preferable to allow for a little rounding error, as shown below.

```
ABORT $ (ABS(SUM(I, SHARE(I)) - 1.0) GT 0.005) . . .
```

6.6 A FINAL EXAMPLE ■

The calculation of great-circle airline distances [GREAT] illustrates the use of trigonometric functions and assignment statements. The problem is to (1) specify the latitude and longitude of each airport, (2) transform this into location in x, y, z coordinates, (3) calculate the straight-line distance through the earth, and (4) find the great-circle distance over the face of the globe.

We show selections of the compiler listing interspersed with comments. First, the sets of coordinates and airports are specified with the statements

```
24  SETS  K    COORDINATES  / X-AXIS, Y-AXIS, Z-AXIS /
25
26        A    AIRPORTS  / SFO   SAN FRANCISCO
27                         MIA   MIAMI
28                         JFK   NEW YORK
29                         IAH   HOUSTON
30                         IAD   WASHINGTON DC
31                         KHI   KARACHI - PAKISTAN
32                         NNN   NORTH POLE
33                         SSS   SOUTH POLE  /
34  ALIAS (A,AP)
35
```

Next, coordinates (in degrees and minutes of latitude and longitude) are shown for each airport in a TABLE statement:

```
36          TABLE  LOC(A,*)  LOCATION ON MAP
37
```

```
38               LAT-DEG  LAT-MIN    LONG-DEG  LONG-MIN
39   SFO          37        37        -122      -23
40   MIA          25        48        - 80      -17
41   JFK          40        38        - 73      -47
42   IAH          29        58        - 95      -20
43   IAD          38        57        - 77      -25
44   KHI          24        40          67       10
45   NNN          90
46   SSS         -90
47
```

Then the value of pi and the radius of the earth are specified with a SCALAR statement, and the latitude and longitude are converted to radians with the assignment statements following:

```
48   SCALAR PI TRIGONOMETRIC CONSTANT  / 3.141592653 /
49          R  RADIUS OF EARTH (MILES) / 3959 /
50
51   PARAMETERS LAT(A)      LATITUDE ANGLE (RADIANS)
52              LONG(A)     LONGITUDE ANGLE (RADIANS)
53              UK(A,K)     POINT IN CARTESIAN COORDINATES (UNIT SPHERE)
54              USEG(A,AP)  STRAIGHT LINE DISTANCE BETWEEN POINTS (UNIT
                                                              SPHERE)
55              UDIS(A,AP)  GREAT CIRCLE DISTANCES (UNIT SPHERE)
56              DIS(A,AP)   GREAT CIRCLE DISTANCES (MILES);
57
58   LAT (A) = (LOC(A,'LAT-DEG')  + LOC(A,'LAT-MIN') /60)*PI/180;
59   LONG(A) = (LOC(A,'LONG-DEG') + LOC(A,'LONG-MIN')/60)*PI/180;
```

Next, the sine and cosine functions SIN and COS are used to compute the Cartesian coordinates in x, y, z space for each airport as follows:

```
60
61   UK(A,'X-AXIS') = COS(LONG(A))*COS(LAT(A));
62   UK(A,'Y-AXIS') = SIN(LONG(A))*COS(LAT(A));
63   UK(A,'Z-AXIS') = SIN(LAT(A));
64
```

The formulae above are easily verified by looking at a geometrical view of the unit sphere, as shown in Figure 6.1. These coordinates are for points on the unit sphere, i.e., a sphere with a radius of one mile. Later the results will be transformed for a sphere the size of the earth. Next, the straight-line distance through the earth between all pairs of airports is computed using the square root (SQRT) and the square (SQR) functions:

```
65   USEG(A,AP) = SQRT(SUM(K, SQR(UK(A,K)-UK(AP,K)) ));
```

Then the angle between lines from each airport to the center of the earth is calculated. The ARCTAN function is used as it is the only inverse trigonometric function we have; the arcsin would have been more convenient. The dollar operation is used because the formula

Figure 6.1: Conversion of Spherical to Cartesian Coordinates

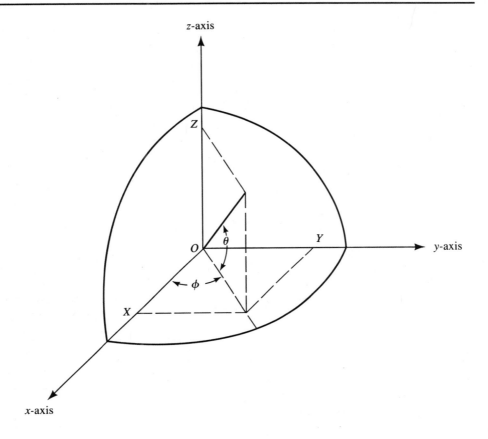

If θ is the latitude (LAT in the program), and ϕ is the longitude (LONG in the program), of a point on the unit sphere, then the Cartesian coordinates (OX, OY and OZ above) are given by:

$$OX = \cos\theta\cos\phi \qquad OY = \cos\theta\sin\phi \qquad OZ = \sin\theta$$

is not valid for two points diametrically opposite each other, but the result in this case is, evidently, PI. The statements on lines 66 and 67 thus represent an if-else assignment.

```
66    UDIS(A,AP) = PI;
67    UDIS(A,AP)$(USEG(A,AP) LT 1.99999) = 2*ARCTAN(USEG(A,AP)/2
68                                         /SQRT(1-SQR(USEG(A,AP)/2)));
```

Then the arc between the airports will be the same as the angle because the calculations have been done on the unit circle. In Figure 6.2 we show the situation graphically.

Finally, the radius of the earth is multiplied by the distance UDIS to scale the calculation up from the unit circle. The OPTION is used to change the default layout of the display. DIS has 0 places of decimals shown, and the other parameters will have 5.

Figure 6.2: Conversion of Straight-Line Distance to Angle

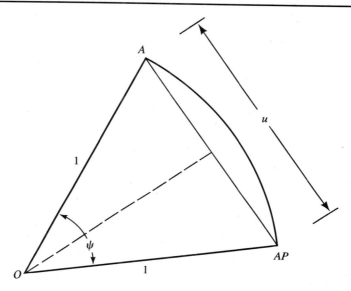

If u is the straight line distance through the unit sphere between points A and AP (corresponds to USEG in the program), then the angle ψ subtended at the center of the unit circle is:

$$\psi = 2\,\tan^{-1}\left(\frac{u/2}{\sqrt{1-(u/2)^2}}\right) \quad \text{for} \quad u \neq 2$$

$$= \pi \quad \text{for} \quad u = 2$$

```
69    DIS(A,AP)  = R*UDIS(A,AP);
70
71  OPTIONS LAT:5, LONG:5, UK:5, USEG:5, UDIS:5, DIS:0;
72
73  DISPLAY LOC, LAT, LONG, UK, USEG, UDIS, DIS;
```

DIS(A,AP) now contains the great-circle route distance between each pair of airports as shown below.

----	73 PARAMETER DIS		GREAT CIRCLE DISTANCES (MILES)			
	SFO	MIA	JFK	IAH	IAD	KHI
SFO		2582	2580	1634	2416	8089
MIA	2582		1091	962	924	8328
JFK	2580	1091		1415	225	7276
IAH	1634	962	1415		1191	8488
IAD	2416	924	225	1191		7482
KHI	8089	8328	7276	8488	7482	
NNN	3620	4436	3411	4148	3527	4514
SSS	8818	8002	9026	8289	8910	7923

	73 PARAMETER DIS	GREAT CIRCLE DISTANCES (MILES)	

+	NNN	SSS
SFO	3620	8818
MIA	4436	8002
JFK	3411	9026
IAH	4148	8289
IAD	3527	8910
KHI	4514	7923
NNN		12438
SSS	12438	

6.7 CONCLUSION ∎

This has been a long and difficult chapter. If you have mastered the material in it, however, you have gone a long way towards mastering GAMS. The next chapter, on VARIABLES, will be short and simple, but we will return in Chapter 8 to one last difficult chapter on EQUATIONS; once you have finished with that chapter, you will know enough to build useful models.

VARIABLES 7

This chapter covers the declaration and manipulation of GAMS VARIABLES. Many of the concepts covered in Chapters 4 to 6 are directly applicable in this one.

A VARIABLE is the GAMS name for what are called by economists "endogenous variables," by linear programming experts "columns" or "activities," and by industrial Operations Research practitioners "decision variables." They are the entities whose values are generally unknown until after a model has been solved. A crucial difference between GAMS variables and columns in traditional mathematical programming terminology is that one GAMS variable is likely to be associated with many columns in the traditional formulation. We will use VARIABLES whenever necessary to distinguish between the GAMS type and to the many individual columns the solution system deals with.

7.1 VARIABLE DECLARATIONS ■

A GAMS variable, like all other identifiers, must be declared before it is referenced. We will start by describing the difference between parameters and variables from the data manipulation point of view. If this distinction is clear, then the rest of the chapter should be easy to follow.

A GAMS parameter has one number associated with each unique label combination. A variable, on the other hand, has four. We were introduced to them in Chapter 2. They represent (1) the lower bound and (2) the upper bound, (both always set by the user either explicitly or through default values) and (3) the activity level and (4) the marginal or dual value, both of which receive new values when a model is solved. The level and the marginal can also be set by the user with assignment statements. The user distinguishes between these four numbers when necessary by appending a suffix to the variable name. We list these suffixes in Table 7.1, but do not show examples until Section 2.

Table 7.1: VARIABLE Name Suffixes

.LO	Lower Bound
.UP	Upper Bound
.L	Activity Level
.M	Marginal or Dual value, or Reduced Cost

The declaration of a variable is similar to a set or parameter declaration, in that domain lists and explanatory text are allowed and recommended, and several variables can be declared in one statement. There are, however, two important differences between variable and parameter declarations. The first is that values can *not* be initialized in a variable declaration. The second is that an additional set of keywords can be used to specify bounds and attributes of variables. We illustrate a typical VARIABLE statement below, adapted from [RAMSEY]:

```
VARIABLES K(T)    Capital stock (trillion rupees)
          C(T)    Consumption (trillion rupees per year)
          I(T)    Investment (trillion rupees per year)
          UTILITY Utility measure ;
```

The declaration of K above implies, as usual, that references to K are restricted to the domain of the set T. A model that includes K will probably have several corresponding variables in the associated mathematical programming problem: most likely one for each member of T. In this way, very large models can be constructed using a small number of VARIABLES. (It is quite unusual for a model to have as many as 50 distinct VARIABLES.) It is still unclear from the declaration whether UTILITY is not domain checked or whether it is a scalar variable, i.e., one without associated sets. Later references will be used to settle the issue.

It is important that variable declarations include explanatory text and that this be as descriptive as possible, since the text is used to annotate the solution output. Note the use of "per" instead of "/" in the text above: slashes are illegal in all unquoted text.

Also note the short names chosen for the variables. There are often naming conventions within a given discipline that allow for concise mathematical representations. Economists will recognize, in addition to those above, E (exports), M (imports), L (labor use), Y (income), etc. In industrial sector analysis there are similar acronyms, as there are in military planning and other fields.

The alternative to short names is long and descriptive ones, which are obviously helpful to readers unfamiliar with the application area. A decided advantage of short names, however, besides the obvious one of minimizing keystrokes, is that equations can be written more concisely and probably understood more readily by those familiar with the abbreviations. The only advice we offer is that you carefully consider the background and experience of those who will look at your work, and choose a naming convention that will help them understand what you have done. Teachers should probably use descriptive names, especially if the equations are not complicated. We repeat our only unqualified piece of advice about naming conventions: labels (set members) should have descriptive names.

The types that may be used in VARIABLE statements are shown in Table 7.2, along with the values that will then be used for lower (.LO) and upper (.UP) bounds.

We will discuss these types in more detail while we are discussing how to modify default bounds in the next section. The default type is FREE, which means that if you don't specify a variable as to type it will not be bounded at all. The most frequently used types are FREE, for cases when there is no logical restriction on the values the variable may assume, and POSITIVE, for descriptions of variables for which negative values are meaning-

Table 7.2: Modifiers for VARIABLES and Default Bounds

Keyword	Bounds	
	.LO	.UP
FREE (default)	-INF	+INF
POSITIVE	0	+INF
NEGATIVE	-INF	0
BINARY	0	1
INTEGER	0	100

less, such as capacities, quantities or prices. If your first solution to a linear model is unbounded, it is probably because you forgot to make a variable POSITIVE.

Two styles are commonly used to declare default bounds. The first is to list all variables with domain specifications and explanatory text as a group, and later to group them separately as to type. The example shown below is from [MEXSS]. The default type is FREE, so PHI, PHIPSI, etc. will be FREE variables in the example below. Note the use of variable names derived from the original mathematical representation.

```
VARIABLES
    Z(P,I)       Process level                         (Mill Tpy)
    X(C,I,J)     Shipment of final products            (Mill Tpy)
    U(C,I)       Purchase of domestic materials (Mill units per year)
    V(C,J)       Imports                               (Mill Tpy)
    E(C,I)       Exports                               (Mill Tpy)
    PHI          Total cost                            (Mill US$)
    PHIPSI       Raw material cost                     (Mill US$)
    PHILAM       Transport cost                        (Mill US$)
    PHIPI        Import cost                           (Mill US$)
    PHIEPS       Export revenue                        (Mill US$) ;
POSITIVE VARIABLES Z, X, U, V, E ;
```

The way to think about this example is to understand that it is possible to declare an identifier more than once, but that the second and any subsequent declarations should only add new information that does not contradict what has already been entered. The commas in the list of POSITIVE VARIABLES are required separators. The second popular way of declaring variables is to list them in groups by type. We rewrite the example above using this second method.

```
FREE VARIABLES
    PHI          Total cost                 (Mill US$)
    PHIPSI       Raw material cost          (Mill US$)
    PHILAM       Transport cost             (Mill US$)
    PHIPI        Import cost                (Mill US$)
    PHIEPS       Export revenue             (Mill US$)
    ;
```

```
POSITIVE VARIABLES
    Z(P,I)      Process level                          (Mill Tpy)
    X(C,I,J)    Shipment of final products             (Mill Tpy)
    U(C,I)      Purchase of domestic materials (Mill units per year)
    V(C,J)      Imports                                (Mill Tpy)
    E(C,I)      Exports                                (Mill Tpy)
    ;
```

How you choose to do it is up to you; we would only once more urge you to follow our often repeated advice to use the presentation that your readers will find clearest and most logical.

7.2 BOUNDS ON VARIABLES ■

Bounds on variables are the reponsibility of the user. After variables have been declared, default bounds have already been assigned: for many purposes, especially in linear models, the default bounds are sufficient. In nonlinear models, on the other hand, it may be necessary to provide bounds to prevent undefined operations, such as division by zero. Unfortunately, it is also often necessary to bound variables to define a "reasonable" solution space for nonlinear problems, and this is likely to be a matter of trial and error. There will be much more on this in Chapter 15. The purpose of this section is to introduce briefly a few aspects of bounds before we learn how to modify them in Section 7.3.

All default bounds set at declaration time can be changed using assignment statements. The one practical restriction is that the lower bound cannot be greater than the upper: if you happen to impose such a condition, GAMS will exit with an error condition. It is common for the lower bound to equal the upper, resulting in what is often called a fixed variable. It is only for types BINARY and INTEGER that the consequences of the type declaration cannot be completely undone. These declarations are for discrete variables appearing in mixed integer or mixed binary models (SOLVE USING MIP, to look ahead to Chapter 9), and there are additional restrictions on their bounds. BINARY variables must have bounds of 0 and 1 or be fixed. INTEGER variables must have non-negative integer bounds or be fixed.

7.3 VARIABLES IN DISPLAY AND ASSIGNMENT STATEMENTS ■

When variables are used in DISPLAY statements you must specify which of the four value fields should be displayed. This is done by appending the appropriate suffix to the variable name. As before, *no* domain specification can appear. As an example we show how to DISPLAY the level of PHI and the level and the marginal values of X from [MEXSS]:

```
DISPLAY PHI.L, X.L, X.M;
```

The output looks exactly similar, except that (of course) the listing shows which of the values is being DISPLAYed. Because zeroes, and especially all zero rows or columns, are suppressed, the patterns seen in the level and marginal displays will be quite different, since non-zero marginal values are often associated with activity levels of zero.

We should mention here a clarification of our previous discussion of displays. It is actually the default values that are suppressed on display output. For parameter and variable levels and marginal values the default is zero, and so zero entries are not shown. For bounds, however, the defaults can be non-zero. The default value for the upper bound of a POSITIVE VARIABLE is +INF, and if above you display X.UP, for example, you will probably see (ALL +INF). If any of the bounds have been changed from the default value, then only the entries for the changed elements will be shown. This sounds confusing, but since few users display bounds it has not proved troublesome in practice.

Assignment statements also operate on one variable attribute at a time, and require the suffix to specify which. Any index list comes after the suffix:

```
X.UP(C, I, J) = 1000 ; PHI.UP = INF ;
```

A very common use is to bound one particular entry individually:

```
X.UP('PELLETS', 'AHMSA', 'MEXICO-DF') = 200;
```

or to put small lower bounds on all variables associated with an identifier for nonlinear programming:

```
C.LO(T) = 0.01 ;
```

or to provide initial values for a nonlinear problem:

```
C.L(T) = 4 * CINIT(T) ;
```

A convenient shorthand in bound assignment is the .FX suffix, which means that both the lower and upper bounds are set to be equal to the expression on the right:

```
C.FX('PERIOD-1') = 1 ;
```

Remember that the order is important in assignments, and notice that the two pairs of statements below produce very different results. In the first case, the lower bound for 1985 will be 0.01, but in the second, 1.

```
C.FX('1985') = 1; C.LO(T) = 0.01;

C.LO(T) = 0.01; C.FX('1985') = 1;
```

We have had to make a small extension to the assignment statement to include the suffix. Otherwise, however, everything works as described in the previous chapter, including the various mechanisms described there of indexed operations, dollar operations, subset assignments and so on. Also we can of course use variable values in expressions, often for generating reports. (It is not permissible to use the .FX suffix as a reference in an expression.) The examples are from [CHENERY]:

```
SCALAR  CVA Total value added at current prices
        RVA Real value added
        FVE Foreign exchange value of exports
        EMP Total employment
        CLI Cost of living index ;
```

```
           CVA = SUM(I, V.L(I)*X.L(I)) ;
           FVE = SUM(T, E.L(T)*H.L(T)) ;
           EMP = SUM(I, L.L(I)*X.L(I)) ;
           CLI = SUM(I, P.L(I)*YNOT(I))/SUM(I, YNOT(I)) ;
           RVA = CVA/CLI ;

    DISPLAY CLI,CVA,RVA,FVE,EMP ;
```

As with parameters, a variable must have some non-default data values associated with it before you can use it in a display or on the left of the = sign in an assignment statement. This condition is true after a SOLVE statement (to be discussed in Chapter 9) has been processed, or if non-default values have been set with an assignment statement.

7.4 SUMMARY   ■

A good way to remember these principles is to realize that wherever a parameter can appear in a display or an assignment statement, a variable can also appear—provided that it is qualified with one of the four suffixes. The only places where a variable name can appear without a suffix is in a variable declaration, as was shown here, or in an equation definition, which is discussed in the next chapter.

EQUATIONS 8

EQUATIONS are the GAMS names for the symbolic algebraic relationships that will be used to generate the constraints in your model. As with VARIABLES, one GAMS EQUATION will map into arbitrarily many individual constraints, depending on the membership of the defining SETS. This chapter will cover the declaration and then the definition of EQUATIONS. There is also another section on the dollar operator, but happily its function is very similar to what we described in Chapter 6 on assignments. We will continue to use the convention established in Chapter 7: EQUATIONS means the GAMS symbolic definition, and is used when necessary to distinguish from the individual constraints generated from the model's logic and the data.

8.1 EQUATION DECLARATIONS ■

EQUATIONS, like all identifiers, must be declared before they can be used. A declaration may be thought of as an assertion of the general form "the following identifiers will be equations and here are a few of the attributes of each". The form of the declaration is, as we have come to expect, a list of names, each probably followed by a domain list and by explanatory text to be associated with each name. The rules are simple: there are no modifying keywords as there are with variables, and no initializing data list as there may be with parameters and sets. The example is adapted from an inventory and production management problem [PRODSCH]. The relevant set definitions are also shown.

```
SETS    Q    Quarters
             /   SUMMER, FALL, WINTER, SPRING /
        S    Shifts
             / FIRST, SECOND /;

EQUATIONS
        COST        Total cost definition
        INVB(Q)     Inventory balance
        SBAL(Q,S)   Shift employment balance
        EB(Q)       Employment balance;
```

The declaration for the first equation follows the keyword equations. This declaration begins with the name of the equation, in this case COST, and is followed by the text, namely "Total cost definition." The rules for equation names are the same as those for other identifiers such as sets and variables, i.e., they are limited to ten characters and cannot include any special characters or embedded blanks. Each name is optionally followed by its domain if it is not a scalar equation, that is, one with no associated sets. The equation COST above is probably a scalar equation since the model is from the library where good practices are followed. A scalar equation will produce at most one equation in the associated optimization problem.

By contrast, the equation SBAL is declared over the sets Q (4 members) and S (2 members), and is thus likely to produce eight individual equations, one for each unique combination of labels. We will later discuss in detail the circumstances under which less than eight equations might be produced: briefly they are that SBAL may later be defined over subsets of Q or of S, or that the dollar operator might be used to restrict the number of equations generated. It is certainly true, however, that no more than eight equations will be produced. The ideas behind domain checking of equations and variables are thus very similar. It is also noteworthy that domain checking of equations and variables catches the common (and otherwise disastrous) error of writing indices in the wrong order if there are more than one.

The rules for text are the same as always: all on one line, not more than 80 characters, no commas or slashes unless the whole text is enclosed in single or double quotes, no starting with a reserved word or two dots, and so on.

There is no reason to avoid using descriptive names for equations. Each name probably appears only twice in your input file, and, as we will see below, does not clutter the algebraic representation.

It is sensible always to end an equation declaration with a semicolon ";". The next statement is probably an equation definition, which will not start with a reserved word.

8.2   SIMPLE EQUATION DEFINITIONS   ∎

The definitions are the mathematical specification of the equations in the GAMS language. Equation writing may therefore be viewed as a translation from mathematical statements to GAMS statements. This section begins with the translations. Following the translation discussion, there are sections on some of the key components of equation definitions, namely indices and function references. Then there is a section on the role of the dollar operator in equations, followed by a brief discussion of the data attributes of equations.

We will start with simple examples, and gradually increase their complexity. Remember that these are definitions, and that it is not until a MODEL is solved that they are used. The very simplest equation is scalar, and contains only scalar variables. [MEXSS] contains a good example. The associated declarations are also included.

```
VARIABLES
    PHI         Total cost              (Mill US$)
    PHIPSI      Raw material cost       (Mill US$)
    PHILAM      Transport cost          (Mill US$)
    PHIPI       Import cost             (Mill US$)
    PHIEPS      Export revenue          (Mill US$)
    ;
EQUATIONS
    OBJ         Accounting: total cost  (Mill US$)
    ;
OBJ ..  PHI    =E=  PHIPSI + PHILAM + PHIPI - PHIEPS ;
```

OBJ is the name of the equation being defined. The two dots "`..`" are always required between the equation name and start of the algebra: they are useful to GAMS in deciding how to interpret your input, and to you when you want to find the first equation definition in your file. The algebra in this case is simple. The `=E=` symbol means that this is an equality (as opposed to an inequality, see below). The semicolon signals the end of the definition. The meaning is: if you evaluate the left and right sides of the expression above, using the level values of the variables, then they must be equal for the constraint to be satisfied. (This is difficult to describe: most readers will intuitively grasp the concept.) It is awkward to keep referring to "the level value of PHI," so from now on we will say "the value of PHI."

Although this example is simple, it has a subtlety that should be mentioned. The arrangement of the terms in the equation is a matter of choice, but often a particular one is chosen because it makes the model easier to understand. In this case, all the identifiers on the right have their values determined in other parts of the model, but the one on the left (PHI) does not. This constraint is therefore an "accounting row" that determines the value (activity level) of PHI given the values of all the others, and the arrangement of the terms is used to illustrate this. It is mathematically equivalent, but less meaningful, to write:

```
OBJ  ..    PHIEPS - PHIPSI =E= PHILAM - PHI + PHIPI ;
```

By now you will know what the point is: you should do all you can to help your reader easily grasp complex logical relationships. Not that the equation above is complex, but it is part of a larger whole that can only be understood by understanding the ways its parts interact. We would also venture to say that many modelers attain a more precise understanding of their own work as a result of explaining it to others. In this spirit we adopt a new convention for the use of mixed upper/lower case. Variable and equation names will be in upper case in all equation definitions, and set and parameter names will be in lower. This makes it clear which symbols represent given data, and which are unknown. If you decide to adopt this convention yourself, you should include the compiler directive "`$OFFUPPER`" (the "`$`" must be in column 1) somewhere near the beginning of your input file. This will cause the listing of your input on the output file to match the case you have used. (A complete description of all the compiler directives is in Appendix B.)

Now we use many illustrations of more complicated EQUATIONS from [CHENERY]. First we show the relevant set, variable, and equation declarations, but not parameters.

```
SETS I     Sectors    / LIGHT-IND, FOOD+AGR, HEAVY-IND, SERVICES /
     T(I)  Tradables  / LIGHT-IND, FOOD+AGR, HEAVY-IND / ;
ALIAS (I,J) ;

VARIABLES
   X(i)    Quantity of output
   V(i)    Value added per unit output at current prices
   Y(i)    Final consumption
   P(i)    Prices
   L(i)    Labor use per unit of output
   K(i)    Capital use per unit of output
   E(i)    Quantity of exports
```

```
    M(i)     Quantity of imports
    G(t)     Foreign exchange cost of imports
    H(t)     Foreign exchange value of exports
    PK       Nominal market price of capital
    PI       Factor price ratio
    TD       Total demand
    PD       Price deflator
    VV(i)    Intermediate result ;
POSITIVE VARIABLES X,Y,E,M,G,H,P,K,L,V ;
EQUATIONS
    DTY      Total demand: definition
    MB(i)    Material balance
    TB       Trade balance
    DG(t)    Definition of imports
    DH(t)    Definition of exports
    DEM(i)   Demand equations
    LC       Labor constraint
    KC       Capital constraint
    SUP(i)   Supply equations
    FPR      Factor price ratio definition
    DVV(i)   Definition of VV
    DL(i)    Definition of labor coefficient
    DK(i)    Definition of capital coefficient
    DV(i)    Value added ;
```

The first example is again a scalar equation, but it contains an index operator.

```
DTY..  TD =E= SUM(i, Y(i)) ;
```

The meaning here is that TD must equal the sum over the SET I (all sectors) of the values of Y (consumption). This is another accounting row, but is written concisely to take advantage of the logical relationship between the sectors. Notice that as Y is a positive variable, TD will be positive or zero in the final solution. In nonlinear models (this is one), it is not wise to rely on this, because it will not always be true in solutions in progress.

It is often necessary to use labels explicitly in equations. The definition of DTY above, for example, could be written as shown below. This is not an example to copy, it just illustrates a point.

```
DTY..  TD =E= Y('LIGHT-IND') + Y('FOOD+AGR') + Y('HEAVY-IND')
              + Y('SERVICES') ;
```

Now we see an inequality. (More particularly a resource constraint, whose general meaning is that you cannot use more of something than is available.)

```
LC..  SUM(i, L(i)*X(i)) =L= lbar ;
```

The expression on the left must evaluate to less than or equal to the term on the right (which is a constant) for the constraint to be satisfied. This is our first example of a nonlinear equation, as it involves multiplication of two variables. Its purpose is to ensure that the use of labor is not greater than the supply. We can see from the texts in the declarations that X(i) is the production in each sector, and L(i) is the labor used per unit of production in each sector. So X(i)*L(i) is the labor used in each sector, and the SUM over sectors is the total usage of labor at the given level of production. In Table 8.1 we show the operators used to relate the right-hand side (rhs) of an EQUATION to the left (lhs).

Table 8.1:   Relational Symbols Used in EQUATIONS

=E=	Equality: rhs must equal lhs
=G=	Greater than: lhs must be greater than or equal to rhs
=L=	Less than: lhs must be less than or equal to rhs
=N=	No relationship enforced between lhs and rhs

One final point before we leave simple equation definitions. An equation, once defined, can not be altered or re-defined. If you need to change the logic you will have to define a new equation with a new name. It is sometimes possible to change the meaning of an equation by changing the data it uses, or by using exception handling mechanisms (dollar operations) built into the definition.

8.3   INDEXED EQUATION DEFINITIONS   ■

All the set references in the previous section were within the scope of SUMS: many variable references have thereby been included in one equation. The next example is of a singly indexed equation, meaning one that produces a separate constraint for each member of the driving (or controlling) set.

```
DG(t)..  G(t) =E= mew(t) + xsi(t)*M(t) ;
```

The domain checking used in the declaration implies that DG *must* be defined over the set T or a subset. As T has three members, three constraints will be generated, each one specifying separately for each traded sector, the dependence of the cost of imports (G) on their quantity (M). Note also that MEW and XSI are parameters: the data associated with them are used in building up the individual constraints. These data do not have to be known when the equation is defined, but do have to be when a model containing the equation is solved.

Each equation in [CHENERY] contains at most one index position. The extension to two or more index positions on the left of the ".." should be obvious. There will be one constraint generated for each label combination that can be constructed using the indices inside the ( ). We sometimes call this (rather ponderously but we can't think of a better way) the "domain of definition" of the equation. Here are two examples from [AIRCRAFT], a scheduling model.

```
BD(j,h)..  B(j,h) =E= dd(j,h) - Y(j,h);

YD(j,h)..  Y(j,h) =L= SUM(i, p(i,j)*X(i,j));
```

The domain of definition of both equations is the Cartesian product of J and H: constraints will be generated for every label pair that can be constructed from the membership of the two sets. The first equation is a simple accounting relationship, the second is a resource constraint.

8.4   FUNCTIONS AND ARITHMETIC OPERATORS IN EQUATION DEFINITIONS   ■

All the mechanisms that may be used to evaluate expressions in assignments are also available in EQUATIONS. As with assignment statements, EQUATION definitions can be carried over as many lines of input as needed. Blanks can be inserted to improve readability, and expressions can be arbitrarily complicated. Here is another highly nonlinear example from [CHENERY] showing parentheses and exponentiation:

```
DEM(i).. Y(i) =E= ynot(i)*(PD*P(i))**thet(i) ;
```

Function references in equation definitions can be classified into two types: those in which the argument(s) do not depend on variable values (often called "known" or "exogenous" arguments), and those that do depend on variable values ("unknown" or "endogenous" arguments). If the argument(s) are known, the expression is evaluated once when the model is being set up, and all functions except the random distribution functions UNIFORM and NORMAL are allowed. The rules are stricter for unknown arguments: in this case the function will be evaluated many times at intermediate points while the model is being solved. First note that the occurrence of *any* function with endogenous arguments implies that the model is not linear. The "smooth" functions (EXP, SIN, LOG and so on) can be used routinely in nonlinear models, but the "nonsmooth" ones (e.g., MAX, MIN and ABS) may cause numerical problems and should be used only if unavoidable, and only in a special type of model called "DNLP." The "discontinuous" functions (CEIL, TRUNC, SIGN, etc.) are not allowed at all with endogenous arguments. A fuller discussion is given in Chapter 9. For convenience the functions are classified in Table 8.2, separately for unknown (endogenous) and known (exogenous) arguments.

Remember that variable bounds are needed to prevent undefined operations, such as division by zero. Here is a function reference from [RAMSEY], preceded by the bounding of the variables:

```
C.LO(t) = 0.01;
UTIL..  UTILITY =E= SUM(t, beta(t)*LOG(C(t)));
```

8.5   DOLLAR OPERATIONS IN EQUATIONS   ■

The dollar operator is also used for exception handling in equations. The three contexts we used in Chapter 6 remain applicable, but there are some extensions to the concept. We discuss dollar control of index operations, dollar operators within the body of an equation, and dollar control of the domain of definition.

8.5 (a)   Dollar Control of Index Operations   ■

The dollar controlled SUM is the most common of the dollar controlled index operations, and works as in assignment statements. There are two good examples in [GTM]. I and J are

Table 8.2: Classification of functions in EQUATIONS

Name	Description	Endogoneous Classification	Endogoneous Model Type	Exogoneous Classification
ABS	Absolute value	Nonsmooth	DNLP	Legal
ARCTAN	Arctangent	Smooth	NLP	Legal
CEIL	Ceiling	Discontinuous	Illegal	Legal
COS	Cosine	Smooth	NLP	Legal
ERRORF	Error function	Smooth	NLP	Legal
EXP	Exponential	Smooth	NLP	Legal
FLOOR	Floor	Discontinuous	Illegal	Legal
LOG	Natural logarithm	Smooth	NLP	Legal
LOG10	Common logarithm	Smooth	NLP	Legal
MAPVAL	Mapping function	Discontinuous	Illegal	Legal
MAX	Largest value	Nonsmooth	DNLP	Legal
MIN	Smallest value	Nonsmooth	DNLP	Legal
MOD	Remainder	Discontinuous	Illegal	Legal
NORMAL	Normal random	Illegal	Illegal	Illegal
POWER	Integer power	Smooth*	NLP	Legal
ROUND	Rounding	Discontinuous	Illegal	Legal
SIGN	Sign	Discontinuous	Illegal	Legal
SIN	Sine	Smooth	NLP	Legal
SQR	Square	Smooth	NLP	Legal
SQRT	Square root	Smooth	NLP	Legal
TRUNC	Truncation	Discontinuous	Illegal	Legal
UNIFORM	Uniform random	Illegal	Illegal	Illegal

*Classification is for the first argument only: the second must be an integer and is normally a constant.

the sets of producing and consuming regions for natural gas. The mapping set IJ(I,J) defines the available pipelines between I and J: not all pairs are possible. X(I,J) is the shipment of gas from I to J, and S(I) and D(J) are the supply and demand, respectively. (These are not constant as in the Tutorial example, because in [GTM] supply and demand both depend on the price.)

```
SB(i)..   SUM(j$ij(i,j), X(i,j)) =L= S(i) ;

DB(j)..   SUM(i$ij(i,j), X(i,j)) =G= D(j) ;
```

The definition of the supply balance, SB, means that the total gas shipped from each supply region must be less than (or equal to) the available supply in that region. However, for each producing region we can only ship gas to a restricted number of consuming regions: those to which there is a pipeline connection. The dollar restriction on the summation ensures that the only links used are those explicitly allowed in the mapping set IJ(I,J), and thus ensures a correct specification.

The demand balance is exactly analogous: the total gas piped into each region using existing pipeline connections must be greater than or equal to the demand in that region. The dollar operator acts here to restrict the number of ways gas can be moved while retaining the concise specification allowed by the SUM. That is the essence of a dollar controlled index operation: to restrict the number of contributions to less than the membership of the SET controlling the operation. As before, the controlling expression can be either "set-valued" as above, or a relational expression. The shorthand that allowed us to write "$A(I)" rather than "$(A(I) NE 0)" is still useful and convenient. The dollar term can not contain any variable references: all dollar operations must depend only on exogenous data or logic.

Notice also the "conservation of indices"; each equation has one controlling index, the second set name appearing only within the scope of the SUM. We will attempt to summarize all the principles we have illustrated in this chapter at the end of this section.

8.5 (b)   Dollar Operators within the Algebra   ■

A dollar operator within an equation is an implied if-else operation as it was with assignments. It is used to exclude parts of the definition from some of the generated constraints. The examples below are again from [CHENERY]. It is useful to recall our example from Chapter 6 to show the relationship between the PARAMETERS RHO and SIG:

```
rho(i) = (1./sig(i) - 1.)$(sig(i) ne 0) ;

DL(i)..  L(i)*efy(i) =E=
              ( (del(i)/VV(i) + (1-del(i)))**(1/rho(i)) )$(sig(i) ne 0)
              + 1$(sig(i) eq 0) ;

MB(i)..  X(i) =G= Y(i) + SUM(j, aio(i,j)*X(j)) + ( E(i) - M(i) )$t(i) ;
```

The definition of DL actually contains an explicit if-else, and is written out in full (SIG(I) NE 0). The situation is that if SIG(I) is 0, then RHO(I) is also zero and the complicated expression involving VV(I) can not be evaluated. The dollar operator protects us against dividing by zero. The desired result in this case is 1, as specified by the second term.

The second definition above, a material balance, is indexed over all sectors (I), but trade (exports and imports, E and M) is only possible in a subset (T). The effect of the dollar operation is to limit the trade term to those constraints where trade is possible. Notice that we have to write E(I) and not E(T) in the equation since it is indexed over I, and that means the original declaration of E was E(I) and not E(T). The meaning of the constraint in words is "for each sector separately, production must be greater than, or equal, consumption, plus use as inputs in other sectors, plus net exports if the sector is traded."

Finally we illustrate that there is more than one way to write most dollar operations. The supply balance (SB) from [GTM] that we discussed above is a good example. Here are two ways of writing it:

```
SB(i)..   SUM(j$ij(i,j), X(i,j)) =L= S(i) ;
```

and

```
SB(i)..   SUM(j, X(i,j)$ij(i,j) ) =L= S(i) ;
```

We prefer the original ("dollar on the index") because the logic seems cleaner.

8.5 (c) Dollar Control of the Domain of Definition of the Equation ∎

The third category of dollar operations is analogous to our "dollar on the left" from Chapter 6, and if you think of "on the left" as meaning on the left of the ".." then the analogy is even closer. The purpose of this construct is to restrict the number of constraints generated to less than that implied by the domain of the defining sets. We revert to [CHENERY]:

```
DVV(i)$(sig(i) ne 0)..
    VV(i) =E= (PI*(1-del(i))/del(i))**(-rho(i)/(1+rho(i))) ;
```

In this case, the individual constraints are generated only for those sectors for which SIG(I) is not zero. Another example is a material balance from [FERTS]:

```
MBD(cf,j) $ demand(cf,j)..  SUM(i, XF(cf,i,j)) =G= demand(cf,j) ;
```

This constraint requires that the shipments XF of final products CF from plant I to market J be greater than or equal to the demand for final product CF at market J. The constraint will not be generated for all (CF,J) pairs, however; the such-that restriction

```
MBD(cf,j) $ demand(cf,j)..
```

means "Generate an equation for each (CF,J) pair for which DEMAND(CF,J) is non-zero". Lastly we demonstrate what is probably the most common of the domain modifying constructs, where the dollar operator is controlled by a SET. From [FERTS]:

```
CC(m,i)$mpos(m,i)..  SUM(p$ppos(p,i), b(m,p)*Z(p,i)) =L= util*k(m,i) ;
```

CC is a capacity constraint defined for all units (M) and locations (I). Not all types of units exist at all locations, however, and the mapping set MPOS(M,I) is used to restrict the number of constraints actually generated. The control of the summation over P with PPOS(P,I) is an additional one, and is required because not all processes (P) are possible at all locations (I).

8.6 DATA HANDLING ASPECTS OF EQUATIONS ∎

We have spent some time on the algebraic nature of equations , but there is another aspect: equations as data. As with variables, four data values are associated with each unique "label-tuple" (unique label combination) of every equation. In practice these are used mainly for reporting purposes after a SOLVE, and so the discussion will be brief. The suffixes associated with the four values are .L, .M, .LO and .UP, as with variables. They may be assigned values in assignments (this is rare), or referenced in expressions or displayed, which is more common, especially for the marginal, .M. We will describe the meanings of the attributes .LO, .L and .UP with respect to an individual constraint rather than the symbolic EQUATION. Think of the constraint with the unknown terms grouped on the left and the known terms combined to give a constant on the right (this is the form used to show individual constraints on the EQUATION LISTING part of the output file):

```
<unknown terms>  <relation symbol>  <rhs (constant)>
```

Table 8.3:   Subfield Definitions for EQUATIONS

Type	.LO	.UP	*(if feasible)* .L
=E=	rhs	rhs	rhs
=L=	-INF	rhs	$\leq$ rhs
=G=	rhs	INF	$\geq$ rhs
=N=	-INF	INF	any

After a solution has been obtained, there is a value associated with the unknown terms on the left, and this is by definition .L. In Table 8.3 we show the meaning of .LO and .UP in terms of the constant right-hand-side (rhs) and the variable left-hand-side (.L) for each of the equation types. The relationship between rhs and .L is satisfied only if the constraint is feasible at the solution point.

The meaning of the marginal value (.M) in terms of the objective value is discussed in detail in most texts on mathematical programming.

8.7   SUMMARY   ■

Here we will summarize the principles of equation definition. Generally, set names mentioned in the domain of definition may appear anywhere in the EQUATION. Other set names can only appear in connection with one of the indexed operations (SUM, PROD, SMIN, SMAX) or with a dollar operation. The scope of any indexed operation cannot include the relational operator, but there can be independent SUMs, for instance, on either side of the operator. Labels can appear anywhere. As always, all appearances of set names and labels must be consistent with the dimensionality and domains of the identifiers.

There is an obvious similarity between EQUATIONS and indexed assignment statements. It may help if we attempt to show the relationship in a general way:

```
"parameter reference(controlling sets)$(modifier)" = "expression"

"equation reference(controlling sets) $(modifier)" .. "algebraic relationship"
```

This completes the discussion of equations. This should be enough for all models except those dealing explicitly with time (lags, leads and ordered sets). After we discuss grouping equations together into a model and obtaining a solution with the SOLVE statement in the next chapter, we will return to discuss these special topics in Chapter 11.

MODEL & SOLVE STATEMENTS 9

This chapter brings together all the concepts discussed in previous chapters by showing how you specify a model and how to solve it.

9.1 THE MODEL STATEMENT ■

The MODEL statement is used to collect equations into groups and to label them so that they can be solved. The simplest form of the MODEL statement uses the keyword ALL: the model consists of all equations *declared* before the MODEL statement is entered. For most simple applications this is all you need to know about the MODEL statement. Here is an example with the general form under it:

```
MODEL       TRANSPORT    A transportation model    / ALL / ;

keyword     model-name            text              /model-list/ ;
```

The model name is a GAMS identifier. It and the (optional) text follow the normal rules. The / ALL / is a particular form of a list enclosed in slashes "/." This list is required. The keyword ALL is a shorthand for all known equations. Several models can be declared (and defined) in one MODEL statement. This is useful if you are experimenting with different ways of writing a model, or if you have different models that draw on the same data. An example says it all. This one is from [PROLOG], in which different groups of the equations are used in alternative versions of the problem. Three versions are solved—the linear, nonlinear, and 'expenditure' versions. The MODEL statement to define all three is

```
MODEL   NORTONL   Linear version        / CB, RC, DFL, BC, OBJ /
        NORTONN   Nonlinear version     / CB, RC, DFN, BC, OBJ /
        NORTONE   Expenditure version   / CB, RC, DFE, BC, OBJ /;
```

where CB, RC, etc. are the names of the equations. We will describe below how to obtain the solution to each of the three models.

9.2 CLASSIFICATION OF MODELS ■

A variety of types of problem can be solved with GAMS. To solve a model you must know which type it is. Here we will briefly describe the model types. GAMS checks that your model is in fact the type you think it is, and issues explanatory error messages if it discovers, for instance, that a supposedly linear model contains nonlinear terms. (Why does GAMS insist that you know this and then complain if you are wrong? Because some problems can be solved in more than one way, and you have to choose which way to use: if you have binary or integer variables, for instance, you can choose MIP or RMIP. We fill in the details below.)

The problem types and their identifiers, which are needed in the SOLVE statement, are listed below.

LP   Linear programming. There are no nonlinear terms or discrete (BINARY or INTEGER) variables in your model.

NLP   Nonlinear programming. There are general nonlinear terms involving only "smooth" functions in your model, but no discrete variables. The functions were classified as to smoothness in Table 8.2

DNLP   Nonlinear programming with discontinuous derivatives. This is the same as NLP, except that "nonsmooth" functions can appear as well. These are more difficult to solve than normal NLP problems.

RMIP   Relaxed mixed integer programming. The model can contain discrete variables but the discrete requirements are relaxed, meaning that the integer and binary variables can assume any values between their bounds.

MIP   Mixed integer programming. Like RMIP but the discrete requirements are enforced: the discrete variables must assume integer values between their bounds.

RMIDNLP   Relaxed mixed integer nonlinear programming with discontinuous derivatives. The model can contain both discrete variables and general nonlinear terms. The discrete requirements are relaxed. This class of problem is the same as DNLP in terms of difficulty of solution.

MIDNLP   Mixed integer nonlinear programming with discontinuous derivatives. Characteristics are the same as for RMIDNLP, but the discrete requirements are enforced. There are no routine methods for solving this class of problem.

It is important to remember that GAMS itself does not solve your problem, but passes the problem definition to one of a number of separate solver programs. More details about some of these are in the OPTION section at the end of the chapter. Because arrangements to use solvers must be made independently of GAMS, you may not have solvers for all classes of problem. If you are using a centrally administered mainframe computer, the contact person listed in the online help file (your GAMS coordinator) can tell you which ones are available. (If you enter the command "GAMS" without any input file specification, the computer's response will tell you how to look at the online help file. There are more details in Appendix A.)

9.3   THE SOLVE STATEMENT ■

The syntax of the SOLVE statement is simple. Again we show a general syntax under the example:

```
SOLVE TRANSPORT USING LP MINIMIZING COST ;
SOLVE "model" USING "model-type" "direction" "objective" ;
```

SOLVE and USING are reserved words. TRANSPORT is the name of the model, LP is the class of problem, MINIMIZING is the direction of optimization, and COST is the objective variable. The opposite of MINIMIZING is MAXIMIZING, both reserved words and both with American spelling ("Z" and not "S"). An objective variable is used instead of the traditional row or function to avoid the ambiguity that can occur because equations can be written with unknowns on either side of the relation symbol. The objective variable must be scalar and type FREE, and must appear in at least one of the equations in the model.

We will describe briefly below what happens when a SOLVE statement is processed, and will give more details on how the resulting output is to be interpreted in the next chapter. The next section discusses sequences of SOLVE statements. The final section in this chapter will be on options that are important in controlling SOLVE statements.

When GAMS encounters a SOLVE statement during compilation (the syntactic check of your input file) or execution (actual execution of your program), it initiates a number of special actions. The purpose is to prevent waste that would be caused by solving a model that has apparently been incorrectly specified. During compilation the following are verified:

- All symbolic equations have been defined and the objective variable is used in at least one of the equations;
- The objective variable must be scalar and of type FREE;
- Each equation fits into the specified problem class (linearity for LP, continuous derivatives for NLP, as we outlined above);
- All sets and parameters in the equations have values assigned.

At execution time the SOLVE statement triggers a sequence of steps that usually look like this:

- The model is translated into the representation required by the solution system to be used (which is chosen by default or by choice: see the OPTION section below);
- The debugging and comprehension aids that the user wishes to see (again by default or by choice) are produced and written to the output file (EQUATION LISTING, etc);
- GAMS verifies that there are no inconsistent bounds or unacceptable values (for example NA or UNDF) in the problem;
- Any errors detected at this stage cause termination with as much explanation as possible, using the GAMS names for the identifiers causing the trouble;
- GAMS designs a solution strategy based on the possible availability of level values or basis information from a previous solution: all available information is used to provide efficiency and robustness of operation. Any specifications provided by the user (iteration limits and so forth) are incorporated. The most suitable solver is chosen unless the user has chosen one;
- GAMS passes control to the solution subsystem and waits while the problem is solved;
- GAMS reports on the status of the solution process and loads solution values back into the GAMS database. This causes new values to be assigned to the .L

and .M fields for all individual equations and variables in the model. A row by row and column by column listing of the solution is provided by default. Any apparent difficulty with the solution process will cause explanatory messages to be displayed. Errors caused by forbidden nonlinear operations, which are caused by required bounds not being specified, are reported at this stage.

The outputs from these steps, including any possible error messages, are discussed in detail in the next chapter.

9.4 PROGRAMS WITH SEVERAL SOLVE STATEMENTS ■

Several SOLVE statements can be processed in the same program. If you have to solve sequences of expensive or difficult models, you should read Chapter 14 on workfiles to find out how to interrupt and continue program execution. There are a variety of reasons for using several solves, and they are described below.

9.4 (a) Several Models ■

If there are different models then the solves may be sequential, as below. Each of the models in [PROLOG] consists of a different set of equations, but the data are identical, so the three solves appear in sequence with no intervening assignments:

```
SOLVE NORTONL USING NLP MAXIMIZING Z;
SOLVE NORTONN USING NLP MAXIMIZING Z;
SOLVE NORTONE USING NLP MAXIMIZING Z;
```

When there is more than one SOLVE statement in your program, GAMS uses as much information as possible from the previous solution to provide a starting point in the search for the the next solution.

9.4 (b) Case and Sensitivity Analysis and Reporting ■

Multiple SOLVE statements can be used not only to solve different models, but also to conduct sensitivity tests, or to perform case analysis of models by changing data or bounds and then solving the same model again.

An example of sensitivity testing is in the simple oil refining model [MARCO]. Because of pollution control, one of the key parameters in oil refining models is an upper bound on the sulfur content of the fuel oil produced in the refinery. In this example, the upper bound on the sulfur content of fuel oil was set at 3.5 percent in the original data for the problem. First the model is solved with this value. Next a slightly lower value of 3.4 percent is used and the model is solved again. Finally, the considerably higher value of 5 percent is used and the model is solved for the last time. After each solve, key solution values (the activity levels associated with Z, the process levels by process P and by crude oil type CR) are saved for later reporting. This is necessary because a following solve replaces any existing values. The complete sequence is:

```
PARAMETER REPORT(*,*,*)  Process level report;
QS('upper','fuel-oil','sulfur') = 3.5;
SOLVE OIL USING LP MAXIMIZING PHI;
REPORT (CR,P,'base') = Z.L(CR,P);
REPORT('sulfur','limit','base') = QS('upper','fuel-oil','sulfur');
```

```
QS('upper','fuel-oil','sulfur') = 3.4;
SOLVE OIL USING LP MAXIMIZING PHI;
REPORT(CR,P,'one') = Z.L(CR,P);
REPORT('sulfur','limit','one') = QS('upper','fuel-oil','sulfur');

QS('upper','fuel-oil','sulfur') = 5.0;
SOLVE OIL USING LP MAXIMIZING PHI;
REPORT(CR,P,'two') = Z.L(CR,P);
REPORT('sulfur','limit','two') = QS('upper','fuel-oil','sulfur');

DISPLAY REPORT;
```

This example shows not only how simple sensitivity analysis can be done, but also how the associated multi-case reporting can be handled. The parameter QS is used to set the upper bound on the sulfur content in the fuel oil, and the value is retrieved for the report.

The output from the display is shown below. Notice that there is no production at all if the permissible sulfur content is lowered. The "case attributes" have been listed in the row SULFUR.LIMIT. The "wild card" domain is useful when generating reports: otherwise it would be necessary to provide special sets containing the labels used in the report. Any mistakes made in spelling labels used only in the report should be immediately apparent, and their effects should be limited to the report. Chapter 13 contains more detail on how to arrange reports in a variety of ways.

```
----    205 PARAMETER REPORT          PROCESS LEVEL REPORT

                         BASE         ONE          TWO

MID-C .A-DIST           89.718                     35.139
MID-C .N-REFORM         20.000                      6.772
MID-C .CC-DIST           7.805                      3.057
W-TEX .CC-GAS-OIL                                   5.902
W-TEX .A-DIST                                      64.861
W-TEX .N-REFORM                                    12.713
W-TEX .CC-DIST                                      4.735
W-TEX .HYDRO                                       28.733
SULFUR.LIMIT             3.500        3.400         5.000
```

GAMS users do not have access to the sensitivity analysis or ranging capabilities provided in the commercial linear systems.

9.4 (c)   Iterative Implementation of Non-standard Algorithms ∎

Another use of multiple solve statements is to permit iterative solution of different blocks of equations, most often using solution values from the first as data in the next.

An example of a problem that is solved in this way is an input-output system with endogenous prices, described in Henaff (1980). The model consists of two groups of equations. The first group uses a given final demand vector to determine the output level in each sector. The second group uses some exogenous prices and input-output data to compute sectoral price levels. Then the resulting prices are used to compute a new vector of final demands, and the two block of equations are solved again. This iterative procedure is repeated until satisfactory convergence is obtained. Henaff has used GAMS statements to perform this kind of calculation. The statements that solve the system for the first time and the next iteration are shown below.

```
MODEL USAIO  / MB, OUTPUT /;
MODEL DUALMODEL / DUAL, TOTP /;

SOLVE USAIO USING LP MAXIMIZING TOTAL;
SOLVE DUALMODEL USING LP MAXIMIZING TOTPRICE;

PBAR(T) = (SUM(I, PD.L(I,T))/4.);
D(I,T) = (DB(I) * G(T)) / (PD.L(I,T) / PBAR(T));

SOLVE USAIO USING LP MAXIMIZING TOTAL;
SOLVE DUALMODEL USING LP MAXIMIZING TOTPRICE;
```

MB is a set of material balance (input-output) equations, and OUTPUT is a total output equation. DUAL is a group of price equations, and TOTP is an equation that sums all the sectoral prices. The domestic prices PD used in the calculation of the average price PBAR are divided by four because there are four sectors in this example. Also the .L is appended to PD to indicate that this is the level of the variable in the solution of the model—namely in DUALMODEL. Thus the iterative procedure uses solution values from one iteration to obtain parameter values for the next one. In particular, both PBAR and PD are used to compute the demand D for the ith product in time period t, D(I,T). Also, the base year demand DB and the growth factor G are used in that calculation. Then when the new final demand vector D is calculated, the two blocks of equations are solved again.

Another application using this type of approach is the work of Paules and Floudas (1988). They solve successively nonlinear then integer problems, using the results of each to modify the next, and in this way are able to find solutions to nonlinear mixed integer problems that have special properties.

9.5 OPTIONS USED WITH SOLVE STATEMENTS ■

We have not discussed OPTION statements until now. They are provided to give flexibility to the user who would like to change the way GAMS would normally do things. GAMS does provide "default" values that are adequate for most purposes, but there are always cases when you would rather, for instance, see less (or more) diagnostic detail. A complete list of options and their meanings is in Appendix C. Here we introduce the concept, and describe the options used to change the default behavior while processing a solve.

The general form of an OPTION statement is

```
OPTION "keyword1" = "value1", "keyword2" = "value2" , . . . ;
```

where the "keywords" are recognized OPTION names (but not reserved words) and the value depends on the context. An OPTION statement is executed by GAMS in sequence with other instructions: therefore if an OPTION statement comes between two SOLVE statements, the new values are assigned between the solves and thus apply only to the second one. The values associated with each keyword can be changed as often as necessary, with the new one replacing the old one each time. As an example, consider limiting the number of iterations made by a solver. This means that if the problem has not been solved to completion after a given number of iterations, the solver is stopped and the intermediate solution is reported to the user, along with the reason for stopping, in this case "ITERATION INTERRUPT." The keyword for this limit is ITERLIM. We alter the excerpt from [MARCO] to illustrate:

```
OPTION ITERLIM = 200 ;
SOLVE OIL USING LP MAXIMIZING PHI ;

QS("UPPER","FUEL-OIL","SULFUR") = 3.4 ;
OPTION ITERLIM = 30 ;
SOLVE OIL USING LP MAXIMIZING PHI ;
```

MARCO is a small and simple model, and the first solve normally needs about 50 iterations and the subsequent ones less than 10. The effect of the sequence above is to limit the first solve to less than 200 iterations and the second to less than 30. The default iteration limit is normally 1000.

With the principle established, we now catalog the available options and briefly describe their effect. There are four general areas where they are useful.

9.5 (a) Control of Output Detail

These options control the amount of diagnostic, explanatory or debug output that is produced during all phases of the SOLVE statement. This output is not described in detail until the next chapter. We use the shorthand notation that ⟨n⟩ means an integer number without a sign and that ⟨r⟩ stands for a real number, also unsigned.

```
OPTION LIMROW = ⟨n⟩ ;
```

This controls the number of rows that are listed in the EQUATION LISTING for each equation. The default value of three is used if the user does not force a change. Specify zero to suppress the EQUATION LISTING altogether.

```
OPTION LIMCOL = ⟨n⟩ ;
```

This means that detail for ⟨n⟩ columns for each variable will be shown in the COLUMN LISTING. Again the default value is three.

```
OPTION SYSOUT = ON;
```

Causes the solver status file to be listed as part of the output. This is useful if you are interested in the behavior of the solver. If it appears that some trouble has occurred, this will happen automatically. The default is not to list the file. You can revert to this by using "OPTION SYSOUT = OFF;"

```
OPTION SOLPRINT = OFF;
```

Using this specification suppresses the list of the solution following a solve. Although this saves paper, we do not recommend it unless you understand your model very well and solve it often. The default, to list the solution, will be restored if you enter "OPTION SOLPRINT = ON;"

9.5 (b) Control of Computer Resources Used by the Solver ■

```
OPTION RESLIM = <r> ;
```

This causes the solver to terminate the solution process after `<r>` units of processor time have been used. The units are minutes on the "wall clock" for personal computers, or CPU seconds for larger machines. The default limit is normally 1000.0. (The SOLUTION SUMMARY part of your output shows what limit was used.)

```
OPTION ITERLIM = <n> ;
```

This causes the solver to terminate the solution process after `<n>` iterations. The default limit is normally 1000.

```
OPTION OPTCR = <r> ;
```

This option (and the next) are only used with problems containing discrete variables, the GAMS model type MIP. General mixed integer problems are often extremely difficult to solve, and proving that a solution found is the best possible can use enormous amounts of resources. This option sets a "relative termination tolerance," which means that GAMS will stop and report on the first solution found whose objective value is within this tolerance of the best possible solution. The default value is 0.1, which means, for instance, that if the problem is a minimization and the solver determines that the smallest objective value possible is 100, then the first solution found with an objective value of less than 110 will cause the solver to stop and GAMS to recover this solution. Chapter 16 on mixed integer models contains more details.

```
OPTION OPTCA = <r> ;
```

This is an absolute termination tolerance, and works in the same way as OPTCR except that the measure is absolute. The value 10 would have the same effect on the example above as the use of OPTCR = 0.1. The default value of OPTCA is 0, which means that it is only effective if you set it yourself.

9.5 (c) Control of Actions Taken by the Solver ■

Most of these options are discussed in separate documents specific to each solver. Consult your GAMS coordinator, or your installation instructions if it is a personal machine. The ones common to many solvers are:

```
OPTION DOMLIM = <n> ;
```

This controls the number of undefined operations (e.g., division by zero) a nonlinear solver will perform before it terminates the run. The default value is zero. Nonlinear solvers have difficulty recovering after attempting an undefined operation.

```
OPTION BRATIO = <r> ;
```

This one is quite specialized. It is used to specify whether or not basis information (probably from an earlier solve) is used. It is meaningful only for solvers that work by doing linear iterations, which currently means all linear systems and MINOS 5. Setting BRATIO to 1 will cause all existing basis information to be discarded, which is sometimes needed with MINOS 5 and nonlinear problems. The default value is 0.25, which almost always causes basis information available from a previous solve to be used, provided that

Table 9.1: Solvers Available with GAMS

Model Solver Type	Solver Subsystems
LP	BDMLP, MINOS 5, ZOOM, MPSX,© SCICONIC,© APEX IV©
NLP	MINOS 5, CONOPT, GRG 2, NLPNETG, NPSOL
MIP	ZOOM, MPSX,© SCICONIC,© APEX IV©

the changes in the problem are minor. Values used for BRATIO must be in the range 0 to 1 to make sense: 0 forces GAMS to construct a basis using whatever information is available. If BRATIO has been set to 0 and there was no previous solve, an "all slack" (sometimes called "all logical") basis will be provided.

This option has no effect on ZOOM.

9.5 (d)   Control of Which Solver is Used ■

An example of the use of this option is shown below, with the general form underneath.

```
OPTION LP = MINOS5 ;
OPTION "model-type" = "solver-name";
```

Check with your GAMS coodinator for a list of available solvers and their local names and capabilities. GAMS will not allow you to specify a solver for an incompatible model type. The default solver has been set by your GAMS coodinator, or by licensing arrangements. On GAMS systems numbered version 2.05 or later you can specify "OPTION NLP = DEFAULT;" to revert, for example, to the default nonlinear solver.

A partial list of solvers available with GAMS and the problem class they were designed for is shown in Table 9.1. More details are given in Table 9.2. Many of the commercial systems (marked with a © symbol) are only available on specific machines. Solvers for nonlinear mixed integer problems (MIDNLP) will soon become available: they are starting to emerge from pure research environments.

Table 9.2: Details About Solvers

Solver	Availability, References
APEX IV©	CDC NOS and NOS/BE; Control Data Corp (1982).
BDMLP	Portable*; distributed with GAMS. No reference. No license needed.
CONOPT	Portable*; Drud (1985).
GRG 2	Portable*; Lasdon et al. (1978).
MINOS 5	Portable*; Murtagh and Saunders (1987).
MPSX©	Large IBM; IBM Corp. (1978).
NLPNETG	Portable*; Ahlfeld et al. (1988).
NPSOL	Portable*; Gill et al. (1986).
SCICONIC©	VMS VAX, Prime, Data General, CDC NOS/VE, large IBM, others; Scicon Ltd. (1986).
ZOOM	Portable*; includes the linear programming package XMP; Marsten (1981), Singhal et al. (1987).

*"Portable" means that the solver design does not restrict it to a particular set of machines.

Special programming is needed to link solvers with GAMS. The work has already been done for those listed above, but it still means that you must get the GAMS compatible version or (in the case of commercial systems) the interface routines. The installation instructions for each GAMS system contain full details of solver availability, licensing and contact people.

9.6 MAKING NEW SOLVERS AVAILABLE WITH GAMS ■

This short section is to encourage those of you who have a favorite solver not mentioned in the list above. Linking a solver program with GAMS is a straightforward task, and we can provide documents that describe what is necessary and provide the source code (most often FORTRAN) that has been used for existing links. The benefits of a link with GAMS to the developer of a solver are several. They include:

- Immediate access to a wide variety of test problems.
- An easy way of making performance comparisons between solvers.
- The guarantee that a user has not somehow provided an illegal input specification.
- Elaborate documentation, particularly of input formats, is not needed.
- Access to the existing community of GAMS users, for marketing or testing.

This completes the discussion of the MODEL and SOLVE statements. In the next chapter we describe the components of GAMS output in some detail.

GAMS OUTPUT 10

The output from GAMS contains many aids for checking and comprehending a model. In this chapter we will discuss what is in the output file and how to use its various features to understand and check your work or that of others. We will also describe in passing many of the ways in which you can control the amount of diagnostic output produced, although complete lists of all these controls are not given until Appendices B and C. We use [PORTFOL], a small nonlinear model by Alan S. Manne to illustrate what is in the output, and list it piece by piece as we discuss the various components. The possibilities for extension to large models with voluminous output (which is when the diagnostics are really useful) should be apparent.

The output from GAMS is produced on one file, which is designed to be read by humans. It can of course be printed, erased or archived like any other file. The output file is the only place where GAMS can write results for inspection or for use by other programs. In Appendix A you can find out how to specify the name of this file. In the near future GAMS will be able to write results to other files, but for now the output file is all that is available. Chapter 14 on work files shows how you can write an output file containing just a report: you should read it and Chapter 13 on the DISPLAY statement if you need to export data from GAMS to, for example, a spreadsheet program.

10.1 COMPILATION OUTPUT ■

This is the output produced during the initial check of your program, often referred to as compilation. It contains two or three parts: the echo print of your program, an explanation of any errors detected, and the maps.

10.1 (a) Echo Print of the Input File ■

The echo print of your program is always the first part of the output file: it cannot be suppressed. It is just a listing of your input (by default converted to upper case: see the subsection (c) on dollar directives) with line numbers and header lines added. We show this part of the output from [PORTFOL], interspersed with comments to illustrate some other details. [PORTFOL] is a portfolio selection model whose object is to choose a portfolio of investments whose expected return meets a target while minimizing the variance. Before we start explaining the output we list the entire input file for reference.

```
$TITLE   A QUADRATIC PROGRAMMING MODEL FOR PORTFOLIO ANALYSIS
$OFFUPPER
$ONTEXT
   This formulation is described in 'GAMS/MINOS: Three examples'
   by Alan S. Manne, Department of Operations Research, Stanford
   University, May 1986.
$OFFTEXT
* Alterations by A Brooke to include a DISPLAY statement and some comments
 SETS
      I  Securities   /HARDWARE, SOFTWARE, SHOW-BIZ, T-BILLS/

 ALIAS (I,J)

 SCALAR  TARGET    Target mean annual return on portfolio (%)   /10/

 PARAMETERS  MEAN(I)  Mean annual returns on individual securities (%)

      /HARDWARE   8
       SOFTWARE   9
       SHOW-BIZ  12
       T-BILLS    7 /

 TABLE V(I,J)  Variance-covariance array (%-squared annual return)

                   HARDWARE  SOFTWARE  SHOW-BIZ  T-BILLS

      HARDWARE        4         3        -1         0
      SOFTWARE        3         6         1         0
      SHOW-BIZ       -1         1        10         0
      T-BILLS         0         0         0         0

 SCALARS    LOWYIELD Yield of lowest yielding security
            HIGHRISK Variance of the highest risk security;

 LOWYIELD = SMIN(I, MEAN(I));
 HIGHRISK = SMAX(I, V(I,I));
 DISPLAY LOWYIELD, HIGHRISK;

* In GAMS the default VARIABLE type is FREE

 VARIABLES  X(I)      Fraction of portfolio invested in asset I
            VARIANCE  Variance of portfolio

 POSITIVE VARIABLE X;

 EQUATIONS  FSUM    Fractions must add to 1.0
            DMEAN   Definition of mean return on portfolio
            DVAR    Definition of variance;

 FSUM..   SUM(I, X(I))                     =E=  1.0  ;
 DMEAN..  SUM(I, MEAN(I)*X(I))             =G=  TARGET;
 DVAR..   SUM(I, X(I)*SUM(J,V(I,J)*X(J)))  =E=  VARIANCE;

 MODEL PORTFOLIO  /ALL/ ;

 SOLVE PORTFOLIO USING NLP MINIMIZING VARIANCE;
```

Now starts the output.

```
GAMS 2.04 PC AT/XT                    87/11/29 16:23:49  PAGE     1
A QUADRATIC PROGRAMMING MODEL FOR PORTFOLIO ANALYSIS
            This formulation is described in 'GAMS/MINOS: Three examples'
            by Alan S. Manne, Department of Operations Research, Stanford
            University, May 1986.
   8  * Alterations by A Brooke to include a DISPLAY statement and some
                                                              comments
   9
```

The first point to notice is that the first line number shown is 8, and if you count lines on the input you will see that in fact line 8 is the comment shown above: it appears after 7 lines of dollar directives and comments. The line starting $TITLE has caused text of the user's choice to be put on the page header, replacing the default title, which just announces GAMS. The $OFFUPPER directive causes the case of the output to match the input. Dollar directives are only listed if you enable a directive to list them, or if they contain errors. The text within the $ONTEXT-$OFFTEXT pair is listed without line numbers, whereas comments starting with asterisks have line numbers shown. Line numbers always refer to the physical line number in your input file.

```
  10   SETS
  11          I  Securities    /HARDWARE, SOFTWARE, SHOW-BIZ, T-BILLS/
  12
  13
  14   ALIAS (I,J)
  15
  16
  17   SCALAR  TARGET     Target mean annual return on portfolio (%)
                                                                  /10/
  18
```

Here we see what happens if an input line is too long to go onto a line of output. The line is broken at a separator and the remainder is pushed to the end of the next line *without* a line number. This results in readable output except for TABLES, which are likely to become unreadable. If you are using a personal computer and have inherited a mainframe model you may be forced to rewrite the table. The easy thing to do is to ask GAMS to write long lines onto the output file with the PW command line option. See Appendix A.

```
  19
  20   PARAMETERS  MEAN(I)  Mean annual returns on individual
                                                     securities (%)
  21
  22        /HARDWARE   8
  23         SOFTWARE   9
  24         SHOW-BIZ  12
  25         T-BILLS    7 /
  26
```

```
27   TABLE V(I,J)  Variance-covariance array (%-squared annual return)
28
29                    HARDWARE  SOFTWARE  SHOW-BIZ  T-BILLS
30
31        HARDWARE      4         3         -1        0
32        SOFTWARE      3         6          1        0
33        SHOW-BIZ     -1         1         10        0
34        T-BILLS       0         0          0        0
35
36   SCALARS   LOWYIELD Yield of lowest yielding security
37             HIGHRISK Variance of the highest risk security;
38
39   LOWYIELD = SMIN(I, MEAN(I));
40   HIGHRISK = SMAX(I, V(I,I));
41   DISPLAY LOWYIELD, HIGHRISK;
42
43   * In GAMS the default VARIABLE type is FREE
44
45   VARIABLES  X(I)      Fraction of portfolio invested in asset I
46              VARIANCE  Variance of portfolio
47
48   POSITIVE VARIABLE X;
49
50   EQUATIONS  FSUM   Fractions must add to 1.0
51              DMEAN  Definition of mean return on portfolio
52              DVAR   Definition of variance;
53
54   FSUM..   SUM(I, X(I))                    =E=  1.0  ;
55   DMEAN..  SUM(I, MEAN(I)*X(I))            =G=  TARGET;
56   DVAR..   SUM(I, X(I)*SUM(J,V(I,J)*X(J))) =E=  VARIANCE;
```

GAMS 2.04 PC AT/XT   87/11/29 16:23:49 PAGE   2
A QUADRATIC PROGRAMMING MODEL FOR PORTFOLIO ANALYSIS

```
57
58   MODEL PORTFOLIO  /ALL/ ;
59
60   SOLVE PORTFOLIO USING NLP MINIMIZING VARIANCE;
61
```

That is the end of the echo of the input file. If errors had been detected, the explanatory messages would come here. (We have grouped all discussion of error messages in section 10.4.) Next come the maps.

10.1 (b) Maps Produced ■

The maps are extremely useful if you are looking into someone else's model, or if you are trying to make some changes in one of your own after a time away from it. All maps can be turned off by entering a line containing $OFFSYMXREF OFFSYMLIST at the start of your program. See the next section for details.

The first map is the symbol cross reference, which lists all your identifiers (symbols) in alphabetical order, identifies them as to type, shows the line numbers where the symbols appear, and classifies each appearance. First we show the map, then explain it below.

```
GAMS 2.04 PC AT/XT                        87/11/29 16:23:49  PAGE      3
A QUADRATIC PROGRAMMING MODEL FOR PORTFOLIO ANALYSIS
SYMBOL LISTING

SYMBOL      TYPE    REFERENCES

DMEAN       EQU     DECLARED     51  DEFINED      55  IMPL-ASN       60
                    REF          58
DVAR        EQU     DECLARED     52  DEFINED      56  IMPL-ASN       60
                    REF          58
FSUM        EQU     DECLARED     50  DEFINED      54  IMPL-ASN       60
                    REF          58
HIGHRISK    PARAM   DECLARED     37  ASSIGNED     40  REF            41
I           SET     DECLARED     11  DEFINED      11  REF            14
                    20           27       39  2*40       45          54
                    2*55         2*56 CONTROL     39       40         54
                    55           56
J           SET     DECLARED     14       REF     27  2*56
                    CONTROL      56
LOWYIELD    PARAM   DECLARED     36  ASSIGNED     39  REF            41
MEAN        PARAM   DECLARED     20  DEFINED      22  REF            39
                    55
PORTFOLIO   MODEL   DECLARED     58  DEFINED      58  REF            60
TARGET      PARAM   DECLARED     17  DEFINED      17  REF            55
V           PARAM   DECLARED     27  DEFINED      27  REF            40
                    56
VARIANCE    VAR     DECLARED     46  IMPL-ASN     60  REF            56
                    60
X           VAR     DECLARED     45  IMPL-ASN     60  REF            48
                    54           55       2*56
```

The symbol name and type are self-explanatory. Then comes a list of references to the symbol, grouped by reference type and identified by the line number in the input file. The actual reference can then be found by referring to the echo print of your program, which has line numbers on it. The entry "2*56" shown for X just above means that there are two "REF" references to X on line 56 of the input file. The types of reference and their meanings are:

DECLARED   This is where the identifier is declared as to type. This must be the first appearance of the identifier.

DEFINED   This is the line number where an initialization (a table or a data list between slashes) or symbolic definition (equation) starts for the symbol.

ASSIGNED   This is when values are replaced because the identifier appears on the left of an assignment statement.

IMPL-ASN   This is an "implicit assignment": an equation or variable will be updated as a result of being referred to implicitly in a solve statement.

CONTROL   This refers to the use of a set as the driving index in an assignment, equation, loop or other indexed operation (SUM, PROD, SMIN or SMAX)

REF   This is a reference: the symbol has been referenced on the right of an assignment, in a display, in an equation, or in a model or solve statement.

The next map is the "symbol listing." All identifiers are grouped alphabetically by type and listed with their explanatory texts. This is another very useful aid to have handy when first looking into a large model prepared by someone else.

```
SETS

I            SECURITIES J          ALIASED WITH I

PARAMETERS

HIGHRISK     VARIANCE OF THE HIGHEST RISK SECURITY
LOWYIELD     YIELD OF LOWEST YIELDING SECURITY
MEAN         MEAN ANNUAL RETURNS ON INDIVIDUAL SECURITIES (%)
TARGET       TARGET MEAN ANNUAL RETURN ON PORTFOLIO (%)
V            VARIANCE-COVARIANCE ARRAY (%-SQUARED ANNUAL RETURN)

VARIABLES

VARIANCE     VARIANCE OF PORTFOLIO
X            FRACTION OF PORTFOLIO INVESTED IN ASSET I

EQUATIONS

DMEAN        DEFINITION OF MEAN RETURN ON PORTFOLIO
DVAR         DEFINITION OF VARIANCE
FSUM         FRACTIONS MUST ADD TO 1.0

GAMS 2.04 PC AT/XT                    87/11/29 16:23:49  PAGE      4
A QUADRATIC PROGRAMMING MODEL FOR PORTFOLIO ANALYSIS
SYMBOL LISTING

MODELS

PORTFOLIO

COMPILATION TIME    =      0.082 MINUTES
```

10.1 (c)   Useful Dollar Control Directives   ■

We conclude our discussion of the output of the GAMS compiler by reviewing the most useful of the Dollar Control Directives. These must not be confused with the dollar exception handling operators we dealt with in Chapters 6 and 8: the similarity of terminology is unfortunate. What we discuss here are the directives you can put into your input file to control the appearance and amount of detail in the output produced by the GAMS compiler. A complete list is in Appendix B. In all cases the $ symbol *must* be in the first character position on the line. These directives are dynamic: they affect only what happens after they are encountered, and they can be set and reset whenever appropriate. They are remembered in "continued compilations" started from work files (see Chapter 14). The directives that do not have following text can be entered many to a line, as shown below for the map controls.

$TITLE followed by up to 80 characters of text.

> This causes every page of your output to have the title you have specified. The title can be reset later by using another $TITLE line.

$ONTEXT
$OFFTEXT

> $ONTEXT-$OFFTEXT pairs are used to create "block comments" that are ignored by GAMS. Every $ONTEXT must have a matching $OFFTEXT in the same file. The $OFFTEXT must be on a line by itself.

$OFFUPPER

> This directive causes the echo print of the portion of your GAMS program following the directive to appear on the output file in the case you have used to enter it. This is necessary if you have used case conventions in your program, for example to distinguish between variables and parameter in equations. The effect can be undone, and the default restored, with $ONUPPER, which causes all echo print to be in upper case.

$ONSYMXREF ONSYMLIST ONUELLIST ONUELXREF
$OFFSYMXREF OFFSYMLIST OFFUELLIST OFFUELXREF

> These eight directives are used to control the production of maps. Maps are most often turned ON or OFF at the beginning of your program and left as initially set, but it is possible to produce maps of parts of your program by using a "on-map" directive followed later by an "off-map." There are four types of maps that can be produced. The first two are the symbol cross reference and symbol listing (both produced by default and which have been discussed in detail above). The other two are the unique element maps, which show set membership labels. These label maps are suppressed by default. The "UELLIST" lists all labels in both GAMS entry and alphabetical order. The "UELXREF" shows a complete cross reference list by line number.
>
> The default setting for map production/suppression would therefore be produced by the directive:
>
> $ONSYMXREF ONSYMLIST OFFUELLIST OFFUELXREF

$OFFDIGIT

> GAMS has been designed to run on different machines. There is a danger that numbers specified very precisely in your program will have trailing digits ignored on machines that use less precision, and GAMS reports an error if this happens. You can use this directive to tell GAMS to ignore the meaningless trailing digits without protesting. $ONDIGIT restores the default, which is to issue an error message. The personal computer version of GAMS allows 10 digits, and other machines more, if you do not use $ONDIGIT.

The line length of the output file cannot be set with a compiler directive. It must be specified on the GAMS call, and is almost always referred to as "PW" (print width). Details are in Appendix A and in the user help file accessible on your computer by entering "GAMS" (without any filenames) on the command line.

10.2 EXECUTION OUTPUT ■

The only output that appears while GAMS is executing (performing data manipulations) is from the DISPLAY statement. The form of this output was discussed briefly in Chapter 6, and all the user controls available to change the format will be discussed in detail in Chapter 13. The output from the DISPLAY statement on line 41 of [PORTFOL] is shown below. Note the wrap of the explanatory text.

```
GAMS 2.04 PC AT/XT                    87/11/29 16:23:49  PAGE      5
A QUADRATIC PROGRAMMING MODEL FOR PORTFOLIO ANALYSIS
E X E C U T I N G

----    41 PARAMETER LOWYIELD      =        7.000 YIELD OF LOWEST
                                                  YIELDING SECURITY

           PARAMETER HIGHRISK      =       10.000 VARIANCE OF THE
                                                  HIGHEST RISK
                                                  SECURITY
```

If errors are detected because of illegal data operations, a brief message indicating the cause and the line number of the offending statement will appear.

10.3 OUTPUT PRODUCED BY A SOLVE STATEMENT ■

Here we will explain the content of all the output produced when a SOLVE statement is executed. In Chapter 9 we listed all the actions that are triggered by a solve and saw how to control the amount of output produced (OPTIONS LIMROW, LIMCOL, SYSOUT and SOLPRINT). All output produced as a result of a solve is labeled with a subtitle identifying the model, its type, and the line number of the SOLVE statement.

10.3 (a)   The Equation Listing ■

The first output is the EQUATION LISTING, which is marked with that subtitle on the output file. By default the first three equations in every block are listed (or all if there are three or fewer). [PORTFOL] has three blocks, each producing one equation. We will explain following the listing.

```
GAMS 2.04 PC AT/XT                    87/11/29 16:23:49  PAGE      6
A QUADRATIC PROGRAMMING MODEL FOR PORTFOLIO ANALYSIS
EQUATION LISTING    SOLVE PORTFOLIO USING NLP FROM LINE 60

---- FSUM      =E=  FRACTIONS MUST ADD TO 1.0

FSUM..  X(HARDWARE) + X(SOFTWARE) + X(SHOW-BIZ) + X(T-BILLS) =E= 1 ;

        (LHS = 0 ***)

---- DMEAN     =G=  DEFINITION OF MEAN RETURN ON PORTFOLIO

DMEAN..  8*X(HARDWARE) + 9*X(SOFTWARE) + 12*X(SHOW-BIZ) + 7*X(T-BILLS)

        =G= 10 ; (LHS = 0 ***)
```

```
---- DVAR        =E=  DEFINITION OF VARIANCE

DVAR..  (0)*X(HARDWARE) + (0)*X(SOFTWARE) + (0)*X(SHOW-BIZ) - VARIANCE

        =E= 0 ; (LHS = 0)
```

The EQUATION LISTING is an extremely useful debugging aid. It shows which variables appear in which constraints, and what the individual coefficients and right-hand-side values evaluate to after all the data manipulations have been done.

Most of the listing is self-explanatory. The name, text, and type of constraint are shown. The four dashes are useful for mechanical searching. All the terms depending on VARIABLES are collected on the left, and all the constant terms are combined into one number on the right, any necessary sign changes being made. Four places of decimals are shown if necessary, but trailing zeroes following the decimal point are suppressed. E-format is used to prevent small numbers being displayed as zero.

One possibility for confusion comes with nonlinear equations. If the multiplier of a variable is enclosed in parentheses, as they all are in DVAR, then that term is nonlinear, and the value of the coefficient depends on the activity levels of one or more of the variables. The listing is not algebraic, but shows the partial derivative of each variable evaluated at the initial point. In DVAR above, all the derivatives are zero because all the X variables have their default level values, namely zero. Another example will help to clarify the point. Suppose we have an EQUATION and associated level values:

```
EQ1..  2*SQR(X)*POWER(Y,3) + 5*X - 1.5/Y =E= 2; X.L = 2; Y.L = 3;
```

then the EQUATION LISTING is

```
EQ1..  (221)*X + (216.1667)*Y =E= 2 ; (LHS = 225.5 ***)
```

The coefficient of X is determined by first differentiating the equation above with respect to X. The result is $2*(2*X.L)*POWER(Y.L,3) + 5$, which evaluates to 221. Similarly the coefficient of Y is obtained by evaluating $2*(SQR(X.L)*3*SQR(Y.L) + 1.5/SQR(Y.L)$, giving 216.1667. Notice that we could not have found the coefficient of Y if its level had been left at zero: the attempted division by zero would have produced an error and premature termination.

Also shown (but only for nonlinear models) is the result of evaluating the unknown terms in the equation at the initial point. In the example above it is 225.5, and the three asterisks are a warning that the constraint is infeasible at the initial point.

The order in which the equations are listed depends on how the model was defined. If it was defined with a list of equation names, then the listing will be in the order in that list. If it was defined as / ALL /, then the list will be in the order of *declaration* of the equations. The order of the entries for the individual constraints is determined by the label entry order. We will give full details in Chapter 13 on the DISPLAY statement.

10.3 (b)   The Column Listing   ∎

This comes next, and is a list of the individual coefficients sorted by column rather than by row. Once again the default is to show first three entries for each variable, along with their bound and level values. The format for the coefficients is exactly as in the EQUATION LISTING, with the nonlinear ones enclosed in parentheses, trailing zeroes dropped and so on. The order in which the VARIABLES appear is the order in which they were declared.

```
GAMS 2.04 PC AT/XT                      87/11/29 16:23:49  PAGE      7
A QUADRATIC PROGRAMMING MODEL FOR PORTFOLIO ANALYSIS
COLUMN LISTING      SOLVE PORTFOLIO USING NLP FROM LINE 60

---- X          FRACTION OF PORTFOLIO INVESTED IN ASSET I

X(HARDWARE)
                (.LO, .L, .UP = 0, 0,  +INF)
        1       FSUM
        8       DMEAN
       (0)      DVAR

X(SOFTWARE)
                (.LO, .L, .UP = 0, 0,  +INF)
        1       FSUM
        9       DMEAN
       (0)      DVAR

X(SHOW-BIZ)
                (.LO, .L, .UP = 0, 0,  +INF)
        1       FSUM
       12       DMEAN
       (0)      DVAR

REMAINING ENTRY SKIPPED

---- VARIANCE   VARIANCE OF PORTFOLIO

VARIANCE
                (.LO, .L, .UP =  -INF, 0,  +INF)
       -1       DVAR
```

10.3 (c)   The Model Statistics

The final information generated while a model is being prepared for solution is the
statistics block, shown below. Its most obvious use is to find out quickly how big and how
nonlinear a model is. The BLOCK counts refer to GAMS equations and variables, the SINGLE
counts to individual rows and columns in the problem generated. For nonlinear models the
count of nonlinear matrix entries is also shown, and there are a few extra counts, which
give more information about the nonlinearities. In general, the more nonlinear a problem
is, the more difficult it is to solve. The times that follow statistics are also useful. The
GENERATION TIME is the time spent preparing the model for solution, while the EXECUTION
TIME is all the time used since the syntactic check finished, including the time spent
generating the model. The measurement units are given, and represent ordinary clock time
on personal computers, or central processor usage on larger machines.

```
GAMS 2.04 PC AT/XT                      87/11/29 16:23:49  PAGE      8
A QUADRATIC PROGRAMMING MODEL FOR PORTFOLIO ANALYSIS
MODEL STATISTICS    SOLVE PORTFOLIO USING NLP FROM LINE 60

MODEL STATISTICS

BLOCKS OF EQUATIONS     3      SINGLE EQUATIONS      3
BLOCKS OF VARIABLES     2      SINGLE VARIABLES      5
```

NON ZERO ELEMENTS	12	NON LINEAR N-Z	3
DERIVATIVE POOL	10	CONSTANT POOL	4
CODE LENGTH	88		

| GENERATION TIME | = | 0.045 MINUTES |
| EXECUTION TIME | = | 0.104 MINUTES |

10.3 (d)   The Solve Summary   ■

This is the point (chronologically speaking) where the model is solved, and the next piece of output contains detail about the solution process. It is divided into two parts, the first being common to all solvers, and the second being specific to a particular one. We will explain them at the bottom of each.

```
GAMS 2.04 PC AT/XT                    87/11/29 16:24:16  PAGE    9
A QUADRATIC PROGRAMMING MODEL FOR PORTFOLIO ANALYSIS
SOLUTION REPORT     SOLVE PORTFOLIO USING NLP FROM LINE 60

                  S O L V E     S U M M A R Y

         MODEL   PORTFOLIO        OBJECTIVE  VARIANCE
         TYPE    NLP              DIRECTION  MINIMIZE
         SOLVER  MINOS5           FROM LINE  60

**** SOLVER STATUS     1 NORMAL COMPLETION
**** MODEL STATUS      2 LOCALLY OPTIMAL
**** OBJECTIVE VALUE          2.8990

    RESOURCE USAGE, LIMIT      0.081    1000.000
    ITERATION COUNT, LIMIT     4        1000
    EVALUATION ERRORS          0        0
```

The common part of the solve summary is shown above. It can be found mechanically by searching for four asterisks. There is some recap detail from the SOLVE statement, followed by a terse characterization of the outcome, and then a few key indicators about resource usage and errors (corresponding to RESLIM, ITERLIM and DOMLIM). The error count is suppressed for linear models since evaluation errors are not applicable.

The SOLVER STATUS and MODEL STATUS require special explanation. Each possible outcome for the solver (the state of the program) and the model (what the solution looks like) have been characterized, and we list all these outcomes below, with comments.

A. List of possible MODEL STATUS messages:

1 OPTIMAL

This means that the solution is optimal. It only applies to linear problems or relaxed mixed integer problems (RMIP).

2 LOCALLY OPTIMAL

This message means that a local optimum has been found. This is the message to look for if your problem is nonlinear, since all we can guarantee for general nonlinear problems is a local optimum.

3 UNBOUNDED

This means that the solution is unbounded. This message is reliable if your problem is linear, but occasionally it appears for difficult nonlinear problems that are not truly unbounded, but that lack some strategically placed bounds to limit the variables to sensible values.

4 INFEASIBLE

This means that your linear problem is infeasible. Something is probably mis-specified in the logic or the data.

5 LOCALLY INFEASIBLE

This message means that no feasible point could be found for your nonlinear problem from the given starting point. It does not necessarily mean that no feasible point exists. Check the hints on nonlinear problems (Chapter 15) for ideas on how to proceed.

6 INTERMEDIATE INFEASIBLE

This means that the current solution is not feasible, but that the solver program stopped, either because of a limit (iteration or resource), or because of some sort of difficulty. Check the solver status for more information.

7 INTERMEDIATE NONOPTIMAL

This is again an incomplete solution, but it appears to be feasible.

8 INTEGER SOLUTION

An integer solution has been found to a MIP (mixed integer problem). There is more detail following about whether this solution satisfies the termination criteria (set by options OPTCR or OPTCA, and discussed in Chapters 9 and 16).

9 INTERMEDIATE NON-INTEGER

This is an incomplete solution to a MIP. An integer solution has not yet been found.

10 INTEGER INFEASIBLE

There is no integer solution to a MIP. This message should be reliable.

ERROR UNKNOWN
ERROR NO SOLUTION

There is no solution in either of these cases. Look carefully for more detail about what might have happened.

B. List of possible SOLVER STATUS messages:

1 NORMAL COMPLETION

This means that the solver terminated in a normal way: i.e., it was not interrupted by limits or internal difficulties. The model status describes the characteristics of the accompanying solution. (The possibilities are: one of the two optimal outcomes, one of the three infeasible ones, really or apparently unbounded, or an integer solution that is within tolerances.)

2 ITERATION INTERRUPT

This means that the solver was interrupted because it used too many iterations. Use option ITERLIM to increase the iteration limit if everything seems normal.

3 RESOURCE INTERRUPT

This means that the solver was interrupted because it used too much time. Use option RESLIM to increase the time limit if everything seems normal.

4 TERMINATED BY SOLVER

This means that the solver encountered difficulty and was unable to continue. More detail will appear following this message.

5 EVALUATION ERROR LIMIT

Too many evaluations of nonlinear terms at undefined values. You should use bounds to prevent forbidden operations, such as division by zero. The rows in which the errors occur are listed just before the solution. An example showing this type of outcome is in the section on errors below.

6 UNKNOWN

ERROR PREPROCESSOR ERROR(S)

ERROR SETUP FAILURE

ERROR SOLVER FAILURE

ERROR INTERNAL SOLVER ERROR

ERROR POST-PROCESSOR ERROR(S)

ERROR SYSTEM FAILURE

All these messages announce some sort of unanticipated failure of GAMS, a solver, or the interface between the two. Check the output thoroughly for hints as to what might have gone wrong.

Now comes part of the solve summary that is particular to the solver program that has been used. This section normally begins with a message identifying the solver and its authors: MINOS 5.1 was used in the example here. One common piece of information relates the work space used by the program to that available, and this is helpful if you are using a personal computer and plan to make your model larger. There will also be diagnostic messages in plain language if anything unusual was detected, and specific performance details as well, some of them probably technical. The user manual for the solver will help explain these. (There is a short explanation of the details shown below for MINOS 5.1 in Section 15.2 (a).) In case of serious trouble GAMS will always show you everything printed by the solver: the cause of the difficulty may then be obvious. If it is not, we suggest that you look at the solver documentation or seek help from a more experienced user.

```
M I N O S  ---  VERSION 5.1  Jun  1987
= = = = =

B. A. Murtagh, University of New South Wales
   and
P. E. Gill,  W. Murray,  M. A. Saunders and M. H. Wright
Systems Optimization Laboratory, Stanford University.

WORK SPACE NEEDED (ESTIMATE)  --    580 WORDS.
WORK SPACE AVAILABLE          --  31232 WORDS.

EXIT -- OPTIMAL SOLUTION FOUND
MAJOR ITNS, SUPERBASICS        1      2
FUNOBJ, FUNCON CALLS           7      0
INTERPRETER USAGE            .00
NORM RG / NORM PI    1.635E-16
```

10.3 (e)   The Solution Listing   ■

This is a row-by-row then column-by-column listing of the solution returned to GAMS by the solver program. The format detail in the listing is that which best fits the context, and the whole listing can be suppressed by confident users (OPTION SOLPRINT=OFF;).

The columns headed LOWER, LEVEL, UPPER and MARGINAL correspond to the LO, .L, .UP and .M subfields of the equation and variable identifiers. For variables the values in the LOWER and UPPER columns refer to the bounds. For equations they are obtained from the (constant) right-hand-side value and from the relational type of the equation. These relationships were illustrated in Table 8.3.

The LEVEL and MARGINAL values have been determined by the solver, and the values shown are used to update the GAMS values. In the list they are shown with fixed precision, but the values are returned to GAMS with full machine accuracy. The single dots "." on the list represent zero, and will be familiar to users of traditional commercial linear programming systems.

"EPS" is the GAMS extended value that means very close to but different from zero. It is common to see a marginal value given as EPS, since GAMS uses the convention that marginals are zero for basic variables, and not zero for others. EPS is used with nonbasic variables whose marginal values are very close to, or actually, zero, or (in nonlinear problems) with superbasic variables whose marginals are zero or very close to it. (A superbasic variable is one between its bounds at the final point but not in the basis. There are brief explanations of technical terms used in this section in the Glossary.)

The order of the equations and variables and the individual entries are as on the LISTINGS we saw earlier, and as will be described in Chapter 13. Any row or column for which the LEVEL is not feasible (i.e., not between LOWER and UPPER) is marked with the characters INFES. Similarly, any nonbasic entries for which the marginal sign is incorrect, or superbasic ones for which the marginal value is too large, are marked NOPT, meaning 'nonoptimal.' If the problem is unbounded, the column (or row) that appears to cause the trouble is marked UNBND.

There is one more small (but important) part to the solution report, and it is discussed below.

```
                        LOWER       LEVEL       UPPER     MARGINAL

    ---- EQU FSUM       1.000       1.000       1.000      -13.529
    ---- EQU DMEAN     10.000      10.000       +INF         1.933
    ---- EQU DVAR         .           .           .         -1.000

       FSUM      FRACTIONS MUST ADD TO 1.0
       DMEAN     DEFINITION OF MEAN RETURN ON PORTFOLIO
       DVAR      DEFINITION OF VARIANCE

    ---- VAR X          FRACTION OF PORTFOLIO INVESTED IN ASSET I

                  LOWER       LEVEL       UPPER     MARGINAL

    HARDWARE        .         0.303       +INF          .
    SOFTWARE        .         0.087       +INF         EPS
    SHOW-BIZ        .         0.505       +INF          .
    T-BILLS         .         0.106       +INF         EPS
```

```
GAMS 2.04 PC AT/XT                     87/11/29 12:24:16  PAGE    10
A QUADRATIC PROGRAMMING MODEL FOR PORTFOLIO ANALTSIS
SOLUTION REPORT     SOLVE PORTFOLIO USING NLP FROM LINE 60

                       LOWER     LEVEL    UPPER    MARGINAL

---- VAR VARIANCE       -INF     2.889    +INF

    VARIANCE   VARIANCE OF PORTFOLIO
```

Here is the report summary, marked with four asterisks (as are all important components of the output). It shows the count of rows or columns that have been marked INFES, NOPT, or UNBND in the solution. The sum of infeasibilities will be shown if it the reported solution is infeasible. The error count is only shown if the problem is nonlinear.

```
**** REPORT SUMMARY :      0     NONOPT
                           0  INFEASIBLE
                           0   UNBOUNDED
                           0     ERRORS
```

If [PORTFOL] had display output for reporting, it would come here. The last piece of the output file is important: it gives the names of the input and output disk files. If work files (save or restart) have been used, they will be named here as well.

```
**** FILE SUMMARY

INPUT    C:\K-MINTRO\PORTFOL.GMS
OUTPUT   C:\K-MINTRO\PORTFOL.LST

EXECUTION TIME    =       0.090 MINUTES
```

10.4   ERROR REPORTING ■

We have collected all comments and description about errors into one section because in our experience it is comforting to have one place to refer to when disaster strikes.

Effective error detection and recovery are important parts of any modeling system. GAMS is designed around the assumption that the "error state" is the normal state of modeling. Experience shows that most compilations during the early stages of development will produce errors. Not to worry! The computer is much better at checking details than the human mind and should be able to provide positive feedback and suggestions about how to correct errors or avoid ambiguities. Developing a model is like writing a paper or an essay: many drafts and rewrites are required until the argument is presented in the most efficient way for the reader and meets all the requirements of proper English. GAMS acts like a personal assistant with knowledge of mathematical modeling and of the syntactic and semantic details of the language.

Errors are detected at various stages in the modeling process. Most of them are caught at the compilation stage, the proofreading stage of the modeling process. Once a problem has passed through the rigorous test of this stage, the error rate drops almost to zero. Most of the execution runs, which are much more expensive than compilation, proceed without difficulties because GAMS "knows" about modeling and has anticipated problems. Many of the typical errors made with conventional programming languages are associated with concepts that do not exist in GAMS. Those error sources—such as address calculations, storage assignment, subroutine linkages, input-output and flow control—create problems at execution time, are difficult to locate, often lead to long and frustrating searches, and leave the computer user intimidated. GAMS takes a radically different approach. Errors must be spotted as early as possible, must be reported in a way understandable to the user, must include clear suggestions for how to correct the problem, and must present the source of the error in terms of the user's problem.

Errors are grouped into the three phases of GAMS modeling: compilation, execution and model generation (which includes the following solution). All error messages have two common characteristics. First, they are marked with four asterisks "****" at the beginning of a line in the output listing. Second, they are all fatal: there is no such thing as a warning message in GAMS. Processing will be stopped at the next convenient opportunity and work files will not be saved. A model will never be solved after an error has been detected. The only remedy is to fix the error and repeat the run.

10.4 (a) Compilation Errors   ■

Compilation errors were discussed in some detail in Chapter 2 and briefly in Section 5.6. There is some overlap between the material there and here. Several hundred different types of errors can be detected during compilation and can often be traced back to just one specific symbol in the GAMS input. Most of the errors will be caused by simple mistakes: forgetting to declare an identifier, putting indices in the wrong order, leaving out a necessary semicolon, or misspelling a label. For errors that are not caused by mistakes, the explanatory error message text will help you diagnose the problem and correct it.

When a compilation error is discovered, a $-symbol and error number are printed below the offending symbol (usually to the right) on a separate line that begins with the four asterisks. If more than one error is encountered on a line (possibly because the first error caused a series of other spurious errors) the $-signs may be suppressed and error numbers squeezed. GAMS will not list more than 10 errors on any one line. At the end of the echo print of your program, a list of all error numbers encountered, together with a description of the probable cause of each error, will be printed. The error messages are self-explanatory and will not be listed here. (It is worth noting that it is easy to produce a model that does not do what you want it to do, but does not contain errors in the sense we are using the term here. The best precaution is to check your work carefully and build in as many automatic consistency checks as possible.)

One mistake that may cause confusion (because for technical reasons it is impossible to provide helpful messages) occurs if you use a GAMS reserved word for a label or an identifier. Another common problem is that an error may not be detected until the statement following its occurrence, where it may produce a number of error conditions whose explanations seem quite silly. Always check carefully for the cause of the *first* error in such a group, and look at the previous statement (and especially for missing semicolons) if nothing seems obvious.

The following example illustrates the general reporting format for compiler errors.

```
     1    SET C CROPS / WHEAT, CORN, WHEAT, TOOLONGANAME /
****                                     $172         $109
     2
     3    PARAMETER PRICE(C) / WHEAT 200, COTTON 700 /
****                                          $170
```

```
ERROR MESSAGES
 109   ELEMENT TOO LONG - ONLY 10 CHARACTERS ARE ALLOWED
 170   DOMAIN VIOLATION FOR ELEMENT - THIS LABEL DOES NOT BELONG TO THE
       SET USED AS DOMAIN IN THIS INDEX POSITION
 172   ELEMENT IS REDEFINED - THIS LABEL OR N-TUPLE HAS BEEN REPEATED

**** USER ERROR(S) ENCOUNTERED
```

The reporting format for errors found while analyzing SOLVE statements is more complicated than for normal compilation errors, mainly because many things must be checked. All identifiers referenced must be defined or assigned, the mathematics in the equations must match the model class, and so on. More elaborate reporting is required to accurately describe any problems found. The SOLVE statement is only checked if the model has been found to be error free up to this point. This is not only because the check is comparatively expensive, but also because many erroneous and confusing messages can be produced while checking a solve in a program containing other errors.

Solve error messages are reported in two places and in two formats. First, they are shown immediately below the SOLVE statement with a short text that includes the name of any offending identifier and the type of model involved. This will be sufficient in most cases. Second, a longer message with some hints appears with the rest of the error messages at the end of the compilation. The example below illustrates how the reports look:

```
   1   VARIABLES X, Y, Z; EQUATIONS EQ1, EQ2;
   2
   3   EQ1.. X**2 - Y =E= Z ;
   4
   5   EQ2.. MIN(X,Y) =L= 20;
   6
   7   MODEL SILLY / ALL / ; SOLVE SILLY USING LP MAXIMIZING Z;
 ****                                              $54,51,256
 ****      THE FOLLOWING LP ERRORS WERE DETECTED IN MODEL SILLY:
 ****      54 IN EQUATION EQ1        .. ENDOG OPERANDS FOR **
 ****      51 IN EQUATION EQ2        .. ENDOG ARGUMENT(S) IN FUNCTION
   8                        SOLVE SILLY USING NLP MAXIMIZING Z;
 ****                                              $257

ERROR MESSAGES
  51   ENDOGONEOUS FUNCTION ARGUMENT(S) NOT ALLOWED IN LINEAR MODELS
  54   ENDOGONEOUS OPERANDS FOR ** NOT ALLOWED IN LINEAR MODELS
 256   ERROR(S) IN ANALYZING SOLVE STATEMENT.  MORE DETAIL APPEARS
       BELOW THE SOLVE STATEMENT ABOVE
 257   SOLVE STATEMENT NOT CHECKED BECAUSE OF PREVIOUS ERRORS

 ****      USER ERROR(S) ENCOUNTERED
```

10.4 (b)   Execution Errors ■

Execution time errors are usually caused by illegal arithmetic operations such as division by zero or taking the log of a negative number. GAMS prints a message on the output file with the line number of the offending statement and continues execution. A GAMS program should never abort with an unintelligible message from the computer's operating system if an invalid operation is attempted. GAMS has rigorously defined an extended algebra that contains all operations including illegal ones. The library problem [CRAZY] contains all non-standard operations and should be executed to study its exceptions. Recall that GAMS arithmetic is defined over the closed interval [-INF,+INF] and contains the special values EPS (small but not zero), NA (not available), and UNDF (the result of an illegal operation). The results of illegal operations are propagated through the entire system and can be displayed with standard display statements. However remember that you cannot solve a model or save a work file if errors have been detected previously.

10.4 (c)   Solve Errors   ∎

The execution of a SOLVE statement can trigger additional errors called MATRIX errors, which report on problems encountered during transformation of the model into a format required by the solver. Problems are most often caused by illegal or inconsistent bounds, or an extended range value being used as a matrix coefficient. The example below shows the general format of these errors:

```
1    VARIABLE X; EQUATION EQ1; SCALAR BAD;
2
3    EQ1.. X*BAD =E= NA;
4
5    BAD = 20 / 0;
6
7    MODEL WRONG / EQ1 /; SOLVE WRONG USING LP MAXIMIZING X;

          COMPILATION TIME     =       0.087 MINUTES

****  EXECUTION ERROR AT LINE 5 .. DIVISION BY ZERO

****  MATRIX ERROR - VALUE OF RHS BELOW IS NA
      EQ1

****  MATRIX ERROR - COEFFICIENT IN VARIABLE BELOW IS UNDF
      X

****  USER ERROR(S) ENCOUNTERED
```

Some SOLVE statements require the evaluation of nonlinear functions and the computation of derivatives. Since these calculations are not carried out by GAMS but by other subsystems not under its direct control, errors associated with these calculations are reported in the solution report. Unless reset with the DOMLIM OPTION, the subsystem will interrupt the solution process if arithmetic exceptions are encountered. They are then reported on the listing as shown in the following example:

```
1    VARIABLE X, Y; EQUATION ONE;
2
3    ONE..  Y =E= SQRT(10/X);  X.L = 10; X.LO = 0;
4
5    MODEL DIVIDE / ALL /; SOLVE DIVIDE MAXIMIZING Y USING NLP;
```

```
            S O L V E          S U M M A R Y

      MODEL    DIVIDE           OBJECTIVE  Y
      TYPE     NLP              DIRECTION MAXIMIZE
      SOLVER   MINOS5           FROM LINE 5

 **** SOLVER STATUS     5 EVALUATION ERROR LIMIT
 **** MODEL STATUS      7 INTERMEDIATE NONOPTIMAL
 **** OBJECTIVE VALUE              1.7025

 RESOURCE USAGE, LIMIT         0.067     1000.000
 ITERATION COUNT, LIMIT          1       1000
 EVALUATION ERRORS               1          0

            < other output >

 **** ERRORS(S) IN EQUATION ONE
      1 INSTANCE OF - UNDEFINED SQUARE ROOT (RETURNED .0 )

            < other output >

 **** REPORT SUMMARY :       1    NONOPT ****
                             0 INFEASIBLE ****
                             0  UNBOUNDED ****
                             1     ERRORS ****
```

Note that the solver status returned with code number 5, meaning that the solver has been interrupted because more than DOMLIM evaluation errors have been encountered. The type of evaluation error and the equation causing the error are also reported. This is (perhaps confusingly) not a true GAMS error, in the sense that a following SOLVE will still be attempted. The only fatal GAMS error that can be caused by a solver program is the failure to return any solution at all. If this happens then, as we mentioned above, all possible information is listed on the GAMS output file and any SOLVEs following will not be attempted.

10.5 CONCLUSION ■

This is the end of our sequential discussion of the GAMS language. The material in the next two chapters will be needed by those who want to use dynamic models involving linkages between time periods, but for most applications we have covered all necessary topics. Chapters 13 to 19 cover particular points, and can be studied in any order.

DYNAMIC SETS 11

In this chapter we will discuss changing the membership of SETS. This is a topic we have avoided until now because of a potential confusion for new users (which we explain here). This material is useful for advanced work, however.

All readers should read Section 11.1. The remaining sections can be skipped by a first-time or casual reader: the treatment assumes a thorough understanding of Chapters 4 through 8, and the topic is comparatively esoteric for many.

11.1 STATIC AND DYNAMIC SETS ◼

All the sets we have seen until now had their membership declared as the SET itself was declared, and the membership was never changed. We will call such a set a static set to contrast it with a dynamic set, which is one whose membership changes because of assignments. The reason to make the distinction is important. We will state it in a general way now, but will illustrate the principle throughout this chapter.

- All the domain checks made by GAMS are made during the initial syntactic check, or, in our jargon, at compilation time. (The reason is to detect errors as soon as possible, a deliberate choice to avoid wasting resources.) This means that the membership of sets that are used for domain checking *must* be known at compilation time and assumed not to change later— which in turn implies that such sets are initialized with a list of labels when the set is declared, and are never changed afterwards.

GAMS keeps track of which sets must retain their static property, and issues an error message if you try to alter the membership. A rule of thumb is that a set is static until it becomes dynamic because of an assignment.

11.2 SET ASSIGNMENTS ◼

Sets can be assigned in a similar way to other data types. One difference is that arithmetic cannot be done on sets in the same way that it can on "value typed" identifiers (parameters, or variable and equation subtypes). A dynamic set is most often used as a "controlling index" in an assignment or an equation definition, or as the controlling entity in a dollar-controlled indexed operation. We will introduce and illustrate the concepts with simple artificial examples. (We use the same sets as in [ZLOOF] but different examples. [ZLOOF] will repay study if you want to see different types of dynamic set operations.)

Consider the following declarations:

```
SET ITEM           All items
                            / DISH, INK, LIPSTICK, PEN, PENCIL, PERFUME /
         SUBITEM1(ITEM) First subset of item
                            / PEN, PENCIL /
         SUBITEM2(ITEM) Second subset of item;
```

Then the following assignments:

```
SUBITEM1('INK') = YES;
SUBITEM1('LIPSTICK') = YES;
SUBITEM2(ITEM) = YES;
SUBITEM2('PERFUME') = NO;
DISPLAY 'After the first series of assignments', SUBITEM1, SUBITEM2;
```

The first thing to notice is that even though SUBITEM1 and SUBITEM2 become dynamic because of assignments, they are also domain checked: the only members they will ever be able to have must also be members of ITEM. And ITEM is a static set and henceforth its membership is frozen. The first two statements each add one new element to SUBITEM1. The third is an example of the familiar indexed assignment: SUBITEM2 is assigned all the members of ITEM. The last removes a member of SUBITEM2. The effect of the keywords YES (or NO) is to add (or remove) one or more members to (or from) a set. The display will show (at execution time) what the effect of the assignments has been. We include the output here so you can verify what happened.

```
GAMS 2.04 PC AT/XT
G E N E R A L   A L G E B R A I C   M O D E L I N G   S Y S T E M
E X E C U T I N G

----     11 AFTER THE FIRST SERIES OF ASSIGNMENTS

----     11 SET       SUBITEM1      FIRST SUBSET OF ITEM

INK    ,    LIPSTICK,    PEN    ,     PENCIL

----     11 SET       SUBITEM2      SECOND SUBSET OF ITEM

DISH   ,    INK    ,    LIPSTICK,    PEN    ,     PENCIL
```

A detail to which we will return in the chapter on the display is that the elements are displayed in the internal order, which in this case is the order specified in the declaration of ITEM.

The next example illustrates an important distinction:

```
SUBITEM1(ITEM) = NO;
SUBITEM1(SUBITEM2) = YES;
```

The first assignment ensures that SUBITEM1 is empty. The next assigns all the current members of SUBITEM2 to SUBITEM1. Notice that we can make an assignment over the domain of a dynamic set, which is not the same as doing domain checking using a dynamic set. It all works because both the dynamic sets are known to be proper subsets of ITEM. All the dollar control machinery is available, so the two statements above could be written as

```
SUBITEM1(ITEM) = YES$SUBITEM2(ITEM) ;
```

which is shorthand for

```
SUBITEM1(ITEM) = YES$SUBITEM2(ITEM) + NO$(NOT SUBITEM2(ITEM)) ;
```

which in turn means: "Run the assignment over all the elements in ITEM. For each element, if found to be a member of SUBITEM2, add it to SUBITEM1. If not, remove it from SUBITEM1." This has the effect of replacing all members of SUBITEM1. The value used in the implied "else" that goes with "dollar on the right" is NO in a set assignment, rather than zero (which is used with normal data).

It is when we look at dynamic sets with more than one label position that the full power of the indexed operators becomes apparent. We will illustrate with a fragment from [ZLOOF]. This is not a trivial example.

```
SET     DEP       Departments
                  / cosmetics, hardware, household, stationery, toy /

        SUP       Suppliers
                  / bic, dupont, parker, revlon /

        ITEM      Items sold
                  / disk, ink, lipstick, pen, pencil, perfume  /

        SUPPLY(ITEMS, SUP)  Items and suppliers      /
            dish.           (bic, dupont)
            ink.            (bic, parker)
            lipstick.       revlon
            pen.            (parker, revlon)
            pencil.         (bic, parker)
            perfume.        revlon                   /

        SALES(DEP, ITEM)    Department and items sold /
            cosmetics.      (lipstick, perfume)
            hardware.       ink
            household.      (dish, pen)
            stationery.     (dish, ink, pen, pencil)
            toy.            (ink, pen, pencil)       / ;

SET     GO3(DEP)    Departments selling items supplied by Parker;

        GO3(DEP) =
                SUM(ITEM $ SUPPLY(ITEM,'PARKER'), SALES(DEP, ITEM));
```

The assignment above is used to create the set of departments that sell items supplied by Parker. The summation is over all the items sold, provided the supplier is Parker. Given the declaration of SUPPLY, this means (ink, pencil). The associated departments are thus (hardware, household, stationery, toy). The assignment is run over the domain of DEP, and the SUM is made over ITEM with the control provided by SUPPLY, for each member of DEP.

One warning before we pass on: data types are either "value" or "set" typed, and assignments must be of one type or the other. All the components used in evaluating the expression on the right must match the type of the identifier on the left. Relational expressions and the arguments of dollar operands cannot be mixed either. In many cases a choice is possible: you can control a dollar operation with a set (dynamic or static) or with, for example, a parameter containing values of 0 and 1. The choice is often a matter of taste, but if you understand the principles you will be able to decide out of concern for your readers rather than using the construct that "seems to work." The purpose of set assignments is to make calculations based on given data (the static sets) for use in exception handling. It is one more example of the principle of entering a small amount of data and building a model up from the most elemental information.

It is of course possible to use dynamic sets that are not domain checked, and this provides additional power, flexibility, lack of intelligibility, and danger. Any label is legal as long as the dimensionality, once established, is preserved.

11.3 SET OPERATIONS: UNIONS, INTERSECTIONS AND COMPLEMENTS ■

We continue our discussion of set valued assignments with a brief look at various symbolic set operations. The symbols +, -, *, and the NOT operator provide the set operations union, set difference, intersection and complement, respectively. Once again let us use ITEM, SUBITEM1 and SUBITEM2, and introduce a new one, SUBITEM3(ITEM). Then we can write in turn expressions involving a union, difference, intersection and complement.

```
SUBITEM3(ITEM) = SUBITEM1(ITEM) + SUBITEM2(ITEM) ;
SUBITEM3(ITEM) = SUBITEM1(ITEM) - SUBITEM2(ITEM) ;
SUBITEM3(ITEM) = SUBITEM1(ITEM) * SUBITEM2(ITEM) ;
SUBITEM3(ITEM) = NOT SUBITEM1(ITEM) ;
```

The membership of SUBITEM3 is successively set equal to (1) all the elements of SUBITEM1 and all the elements of SUBITEM2, then (2) all elements that are members of the first but not of the second, then (3) only those present in both, and finally (4) all those in ITEM but not in SUBITEM1. For a final illustration, we write the same four assignments in different (but longer) ways.

```
SUBITEM3(ITEM) = NO; SUBITEM3(SUBITEM2) = YES; SUBITEM3(SUBITEM1) = YES;
SUBITEM3(ITEM) = YES$(SUBITEM1(ITEM)); SUBITEM3(SUBITEM2) = NO;
SUBITEM3(ITEM) = YES$(SUBITEM1(ITEM)$SUBITEM2(ITEM));
SUBITEM3(ITEM) = YES; SUBITEM3(SUBITEM1) = NO;
```

11.4 DOMAIN CHECKING WITH DYNAMIC SETS ■

We finish our discussion of dynamic sets with a brief look at how we can continue to use domain checking while maintaining the flexibility of dynamic sets. The most important principle to follow is that a dynamic set should always be domain checked at declaration time to be a subset of a static set (or sets). If the dynamic set is used, for example, to dollar control index operations, everything is easy. We list fragments from [FERTS] to illustrate the point.

The meanings of the static sets referenced below are: M is the set of process types; I the SET of plant locations; C the set of all commodities (including raw materials and intermediates); and P the processes. CR and CS are subsets of C (raw materials and intermediate products), and IP is an ALIAS for I. The declarations of these sets are lengthy, which is why we have ñot shown them.

All the sets declared in this fragment are dynamic, and the assignments (using previously established data and the static sets) are shown beneath them. Then we show some equation definitions where either the domain of definition or an indexed operation is modified by one of the dynamic sets.

```
    SETS

        MPOS(M,I)       Productive units possibilities
        PPOS(P,I)       Process possibilities
        CPOS(C,I)       Commodity possibilities
        CPOSP(C,I)      Commodity production possibilities
        CPOSN(C,I)      Commodity consumption possibilities
        CPOSI(C,I,I)    Interplant consumption and production possibilities
        CPOSD(C,I)      Domestic raw material purchase possibilities
        CPOSR(C,I)      Imported input commodity possibilities
        ;

MPOS  (M,I)        = YES$K(M,I);
PPOS  (P,I)        = YES$(SUM(M$(NOT MPOS(M,I)), B(M,P) NE 0) EQ 0) ;
PPOS  ('CAN-310','HELWAN') = NO;
PPOS  ('CAN-335','ASWAN')  = NO;
CPOSP(C,I)         = YES$SUM(P$PPOS(P,I), A(C,P) GT 0) ;
CPOSN(C,I)         = YES$SUM(P$PPOS(P,I), A(C,P) LT 0) ;
CPOSI(CS,I,IP)     = CPOSP(CS,I)*CPOSN(CS,IP);
CPOSD(CR,I)        = YES$(CPOSN(CR,I)$PD(I,CR));
CPOSR(CR,I)        = YES$(CPOSN(CR,I)$PV(CR));
CPOS(C,I)          = CPOSP(C,I) + CPOSN(C,I) ;

DISPLAY MPOS, PPOS, CPOSP, CPOSN, CPOS , CPOSI, CPOSD, CPOSR;

MB(c,i)..  SUM(p$ppos(p,i), a(c,p)*Z(p,i))
            + SUM(ip, XI(c,ip,i)$cposi(c,ip,i) - XI(c,i,ip)$cposi(c,i,ip))
            + VR(c,i)$cposr(c,i) + U(c,i)$cposd(c,i)
            - SUM(j$cposp(c,i), XF(c,i,j))$cf(c) =G= 0 ;

CC(m,i)$mpos(m,i)..
                SUM(p$ppos(p,i), b(m,p)*Z(p,i)) =L= util*k(m,i) ;

AP.. PSIP =E= SUM((cr,i)$cposd(cr,i), pd(i,cr)*U(cr,i)) ;
```

On the other hand it is sometimes necessary to define an equation over a dynamic set. The trick then is to declare it over the entire domain but define it over the dynamic set. This is often necessary in models that will be solved for arbitrary groupings of regions simultaneously, for example. We assume there are no explicit links between regions, but that we have a number of independent models with a common data definition and common logic. Perhaps a small number of them can be solved one after another on a personal computer, but a mainframe can make a simultaneous solution of the whole system. We illustrate with an artificial symbolic example, leaving out lots of details.

```
SET ALLR All regions / N, S, W, E, N-E, S-W /
    R(ALLR)  Region subset for particular solution
  ;
TABLE DATA (ALLR,type) All the data . . .
  ;
EQUATIONS RESOURCE1(ALLR) First resource constraint,
          PRODBAL1(ALLR)  First production balance . . .
  ;
VARIABLES ACTIVITY1(ALLR) First activity
          ACTIVITY2(ALLR) Second activity
          REVENUE(ALLR)   Revenue . . .
  ;
RESOURCE1(R).. ACTIVITY1(R) =L= DATA(R,'resource-1');
PRODBAL1(R)..  ACTIVITY2(R)*PRICE =E= REVENUE(R);

MODEL REGMODEL Flexible multi-region model / ALL/ ;
R(ALLR) = assignment to R;
SOLVE REGMODEL USING LP MINIMIZING OBJECTIVE;
R(ALLR) = another assignment to R;
SOLVE REGMODEL USING LP MINIMIZING OBJECTIVE;
```

To repeat the important point: the equations are *declared* over ALLR but *defined* over R, a subset. The variables and data are *declared* over ALLR but *referenced* over R. Then we can make arbitrary assignments to R (within the membership of ALLR) and solve the model any number of times for the chosen groupings of regions.

SETS AS SEQUENCES: DYNAMIC MODELS 12

In our original discussion of sets in Chapter 4, we said that unless there is a special need to do things differently, a one-dimensional set should be regarded as a collection of labels in no particular order. In this chapter we will discuss special features that can be used when you do need to do things differently: when you need to regard a set as representing some entity that is inherently consecutive, or, to put it another way, when you need to be able to deal with a set as if it were a sequence.

In economic models that explicitly represent conditions in different time periods, it is necessary to refer to the "next" or "previous" time period, because there must be links between the periods. For example, stocks of capital are normally tracked through such models by equations of the form "stocks at the end of period n are equal to stocks at the end of period $n - 1$ plus net gains during period n." Location and scheduling problems, where the formulation may require a representation of contiguous areas, as in a grid representation of a city, are another class of problem in which sets must also have the properties of sequences.

We will use examples from models involving sequences of time periods, which are often called dynamic models, because they describe how conditions change over time. This use of the word "dynamic" unfortunately has a different meaning from that used in connection with sets in Chapter 11, but this is unavoidable.

12.1 ORDERED AND UNORDERED SETS ■

As with sets used in domain checking, restrictions are imposed when you need to refer to a set as if it were a sequence. The set must be *static*, and it must also be *ordered*. We introduced the notion of a static set in Chapter 11: the set must be initialized with a list of labels enclosed in slashes at the time the set is declared, and never changed afterwards. What ordered means is more difficult to explain, but since most sets used as sequences are naturally ordered, it is not often a concern.

- Ordered means that the order of the labels in the initialization list is the same as the GAMS entry order.

- The GAMS entry order is the order in which the individual labels first appear in your program, either explicitly or as a result of using the shorthand asterisk notation.

You can see a map of your labels in the GAMS order by putting the compiler directive $ONUELLIST in column 1 of your program somewhere before the first set declaration. The map is shown with the other compiler maps after the listing of your program. A good rule of thumb is that if the labels in a set you want to be ordered have not been used already, then they will be ordered. In the example below we show ordered and unordered SETS and the map showing the order. The input is:

```
$ONUELLIST
  SET T1  / 1987, 1988, 1989, 1990, 1991 /
      T2  / 1983, 1984, 1985, 1986, 1987 /
      T3  / 1987, 1989, 1991, 1983, 1985 /
```

We could have used the asterisk form in T1 and T2, but the lists are more revealing. The first point to notice is that the label "1987" is the first label seen by GAMS. Its appearance again as the last label in the initialization list for T2 means that T2 is not ordered, and any attempt to use T2 in a context implying order (lags or ORD, to anticipate) will cause error messages. Secondly, T3 is ordered! Not in the normal way, but in the sense we are using the term here, i.e. the GAMS definition of label order. All the members of T3 have appeared before, and in the same order that they are listed in the definition of T3.

The map below shows the entry order (the important one) and the sorted order, obtained by sorting the labels into dictionary order. The single digits on the left are the sequence numbers of the first label on that line.

```
GAMS 2.04 PC AT/XT
G E N E R A L   A L G E B R A I C   M O D E L I N G   S Y S T E M
UNIQUE ELEMENT LISTING

UNIQUE ELEMENTS IN ENTRY ORDER

    1   1987        1988        1989        1990        1991
    6   1983        1984        1985        1986

UNIQUE ELEMENTS IN SORTED ORDER

    1   1983        1984        1985        1986        1987
    6   1988        1989        1990        1991
```

These restrictions are more of a nuisance and source of confusion than they are a practical problem. A set can always be made ordered by moving its declaration closer to the beginning of the program. With these restrictions in mind, we move on to operations that are used in dealing with sets as sequences.

12.2 ORD AND CARD ■

ORD and CARD are transfer functions that return integer values. CARD returns the number of elements in a set, whereas ORD returns the relative position of a member. CARD can be used with any set, even dynamic or unordered ones. We have waited until now to introduce it because its only real use is in connection with sequences. ORD can be used only with a one-dimensional, static, ordered SET. Some examples show the usage.

```
SET T Time periods / 1985*1995 /
PARAMETER VAL(T), S;
S = CARD(T);
VAL(T) = ORD(T);
```

As a result of the statements above, S will be assigned the value 11, and the value of VAL("1985") will be 1, VAL("1986") will be 2 and so on. A common use of ORD is in setting up vectors that represent quantities growing in some analytically specified way. For example, suppose a country has 56 million people in the base period and population is growing at the rate of 1.5 percent per year. Then we could calculate the population in succeeding years by using:

```
POPULATION(T) = 56 * (1.015**(ORD(T)-1)) ;
```

A common use of CARD is to specify some condition only for the final period, for example to fix a variable. An artificial example is:

```
C.FX(T)$(ORD(T) EQ CARD(T)) = DEMAND(T) ;
```

which fixes the variable for the last member only: no assignment is made for other members of T. The advantage of this way of fixing C is that the membership of T can be changed safely and this statement will always fix C for the last one.

It is often useful to simulate general matrix operations in GAMS. The first index on a two dimensional parameter can conveniently represent the rows, and the second the columns, and order is necessary. The example below shows how to set the upper triangle of a matrix equal to the row index plus the column index, and the diagonal and lower triangle to zero:

```
SET I Row and Column labels / X1*X10 /;
ALIAS (I,J);
PARAMETER A(I,J) A general square matrix;
A(I,J) = (ORD(I) + ORD(J)) $ (ORD(I) LT ORD(J));
```

12.3   LAG AND LEAD OPERATIONS   ■

The lag and lead operators are used to relate the "current" to the "next" or "previous" member of a set. Obviously the set in question must be ordered. The most troublesome feature of lags and leads is the question of what happens at the end of a sequence. What is the value previous to the first, or after the last? GAMS provides some built in facilities to deal with this problem, but in any work involving sequences the user must think carefully about the treatment of endpoints, and all models will need special exception handling logic to deal with them.

12.3 (a)   Lags and Leads in Assignments   ■

GAMS provides both "end-off" and "circular" lag and lead operators. We will deal with the "end-off" ones first, because they are the more common. The "end-off" lag and lead operators are + and -. GAMS is able to distinguish these from the arithmetic operators by context: the general form of a lag (or lead) operation is "index set-lag (or lead) operator-integer valued expression." As is our standard practice, we invoke examples and start simple.

```
SET T Time sequence / Y-1987*Y-1991 /;
PARAMETER A(T), B(T), C(T);
A(T) = 1986 + ORD(T);
B(T) = -1; B(T) = A(T-1);
C(T) = -1; C(T+2) = A(T);
OPTION DECIMALS=0; DISPLAY A, B, C;
```

The OPTION statement suppresses the decimal places from the display (see Chapter 13). The results are shown below.

```
GAMS 2.04 PC AT/XT
G E N E R A L   A L G E B R A I C   M O D E L I N G   S Y S T E M
E X E C U T I N G

----      6 PARAMETER A

Y-1987 1987,    Y-1988 1988,    Y-1989 1989,    Y-1990 1990,    Y-1991 1991

----      6 PARAMETER B

Y-1988 1987,    Y-1989 1988,    Y-1990 1989,    Y-1991 1990

----      6 PARAMETER C

Y-1987   -1,    Y-1988   -1,    Y-1989 1987,    Y-1990 1988,    Y-1991 1989
```

For A we get, as expected, the values 1987, 1988 up to 1991 corresponding to the labels "Y-1987", "Y-1988" and so on. B and C were assigned the values -1 so that the results of the following assignments could be seen clearly.

For B, the assignment is done over all members of T, and for each, the value of A from the previous period is assigned to the current member of B. If no previous period, as with "Y-1987", zero is used, and B("Y-1987") becomes zero, replacing the previous value of -1.

The assignment to C is different. It is best to spell it out in words. "For each member of T in sequence, find the member of C associated with T+2. If it exists, replace its value with that of A(T). If not (as with "Y-1990" and "Y+1991") make no assignment." The first member of T is "Y+1987", and therefore the first assignment is to C("Y-1989") which takes the value of A("Y-1987"), viz, 1987. No assignments at all are made to C("Y-1987") or C("Y-1988"): these two retain their previous values of -1.

Another way to distinguish between these two cases is to realize that the first is a reference, the second is the definition of a domain of assignment. A *reference* to a non-existent element causes the default value (zero in this case) to be used, whereas an attempt to *assign* to a non-existent element results in no assignment being made.

The lag (or lead) value does not have to be an explicit constant: it can be an arbitrary expression, provided that it evaluates to an integer. If it does not, error messages will be produced. A negative result causes a switch in sense (from lag to lead, for example). The following is guaranteed to set D(T) to all zero:

```
D(T) = D(T - ORD(T));
```

The "circular" lag and lead operators are for modeling time periods that repeat, such as months of the year or hours in the day. It is quite natural to think of January as the month following December. Agricultural farm budget models and workforce scheduling models are examples of applications where circular leads occur naturally. The notion is that "first − 1" is a reference to "last" and "last + 2" is the same as "first + 1" and so on. All references and assignments are defined. The operators are ++ and --. An example says it all.

```
SET S Seasons / SPRING, SUMMER, AUTUMN, WINTER /;
PARAMETER VAL(S)
                   / SPRING 10, SUMMER 15, AUTUMN 12, WINTER 8 /
          LAGVAL2(S)
          LEADVAL(S);
LAGVAL2(S) = VAL(S--2); LEADVAL(S++1) = VAL(S);
OPTION DECIMALS=0; DISPLAY VAL,LAGVAL2,LEADVAL;
```

The output is

```
GAMS 2.04 PC AT/XT
G E N E R A L  A L G E B R A I C  M O D E L I N G  S Y S T E M
E X E C U T I N G

----      7 PARAMETER VAL

SPRING 10,     SUMMER 15,     AUTUMN 12,     WINTER  8

----      7 PARAMETER LAGVAL2

SPRING 12,     SUMMER  8,     AUTUMN 10,     WINTER 15

----      7 PARAMETER LEADVAL

SPRING  8,     SUMMER 10,     AUTUMN 15,     WINTER 12
```

12.3 (b)   Lags and Leads in Equations   ∎

The principles established above follow quite naturally into equation definitions. A lag or lead operation in the body of an equation (to the right of the ".." symbol) is a reference, and if the associated label is not defined, the term vanishes. An "end-off" lag or lead to the left of the ".." is a modification to the domain of definition of the equation, causing one or more individual equations to be suppressed. All lag operands must be exogenous. It is common to see a lag on the left and the right. Here is an example constructed by taking excerpts from [RAMSEY]. The declaration of T is included, as are a couple of dynamic sets that are used to handle the first and last periods ("terminal conditions" is the jargon) in a clean way.

```
SETS    T         Time periods    /1990*2000/
        TFIRST(T) First period
        TLAST(T)  Last period;
TFIRST(T) = YES$(ORD(T) EQ 1);
TLAST(T) = YES$(ORD(T) EQ CARD(T));
DISPLAY TFIRST, TLAST;
```

```
VARIABLES K(T)   Capital stock (trillion rupees)
          I(T)   Investment (trillion rupees per year) ;
EQUATIONS KK(T)  Capital balance (trillion rupees)
          TC(T)  Terminal condition (provides for post-terminal growth) ;

KK(t+1)..         K(t+1) =E= K(t) + I(t);

TC(tlast)..       g*K(tlast) =L= I(tlast);
```

The interesting EQUATION is KK, the capital balance. The set T contains members "1990" to "2000", and so there will be a capital stock constraint for "1991" to "2000". The constraint for "1991" will be, spelled out:

```
K("1991") =E= K("1990") + I("1990") ;
```

The lead operator on the domain of definition has restricted the number of constraints generated so that there are no references to non-existent variables: the generated problem will have 10 KK constraints defining the relationship between the 11 K capital values. There are other ways to write this EQUATION, most of them clumsier. A common alternative is

```
KK(t)$(ORD(t) GT 1).. K(t+1) =E= K(t) + I(t) ;
```

The other interesting point in the [RAMSEY] excerpt is that the constraint TC is explicitly defined only for the final period because of the assignment to the set TLAST. This construct is also often replaced with a dollar control on the domain of definition, as in

```
TC(t)$(ORD(t) EQ CARD(t)).. g*K(t) =L= I(t) ;
```

The set TFIRST is used in other parts of the model to set initial conditions, particularly the capital stock in the first period, K("1990").

This is the end of our discussion of lags and leads. If you understood the examples and keep the principles in mind, you should be able to use lags and leads in a natural way to write powerful models concisely.

12.4   THE LOOP STATEMENT ■

The LOOP statement is provided for the rare cases when parallel assignments are not sufficient. This happens most often when there is no analytic relationship between, for example, the values to be assigned to a parameter. Consider a hypothetical case when a growth rate is empirical:

```
SET T Time periods / 1985*1990 /
PARAMETER POP(T) Population at start of time period T / 1985 3456 /
          GROWTH(T) Growth in period T
    / 1985 25.3, 1986 27.3, 1987 26.2, 1988 27.1, 1989 26.6, 1990 26.6 /;
```

We can use the LOOP statement to calculate the cumulative sums

```
LOOP(T, POP(T+1) = POP(T) + GROWTH(T) );
```

in a recursive rather than a parallel way.

The LOOP statement causes GAMS to execute the statements within the scope of the loop for each member of the driving set(s) in turn. In the example above there is one statement in the scope of the loop, and one driving, or controlling, set. The order of evaluation is the entry order of the labels. A loop is thus another, more general, type of indexed operation. The loop set may be dollar-controlled and does not need to be static or ordered, and there may be several statements inside the body of a loop. Loops may be nested, and they may be controlled by more than one set. It is illegal to modify any controlling set inside the body of the loop. The following statements are legal inside loops: assignments, OPTION, DISPLAY, LOOP and ABORT. Remember that loops should only be used when parallel operations are not possible.

A loop is often used to perform iterative calculations. Here is an example of how to use Newton's method of square root evaluation to find square roots. (This is to illustrate: in practice you should use the function SQRT.) Newton's method is the assertion that if X is an approximation to the square root of V, then $(X + V/X)/2$ is a better one.

```
SET
      ITER         Set to drive iterations / IT-1*IT-100 /;
PARAMETER
      VALUE(ITER)  Used to hold successive approximations;
SCALAR
      TARGET       Number whose square root is needed / 23.456 /
      SQRTVAL      Final approximation to SQRT(TARGET)
      CURACC       Accuracy of current approximation
      RELTOL       Required relative accuracy        / 1.0E-06 /;
ABORT $ (TARGET LE 0) "Argument to NEWTON must be positive", TARGET;
VALUE("IT-1") = TARGET/2 ; CURACC = 1 ;
LOOP(ITER $ (CURACC GT RELTOL),
      VALUE(ITER+1) = 0.5*(VALUE(ITER) + TARGET/VALUE(ITER));
      SQRTVAL = VALUE(ITER+1);
      CURACC = ABS(VALUE(ITER+1)-VALUE(ITER)) / (1+ABS(VALUE(ITER+1))) );
ABORT $ (CURACC GT RELTOL) "Square root not found to desired precision";
OPTION DECIMALS=8;
DISPLAY "Square root found within tolerance", SQRTVAL, VALUE;
```

Notice that there is no semicolon between the final statement in the LOOP and the parenthesis that closes it. Two observations should be made about the content of this example. First, it is not necessary to use an indexed parameter to store the successive approximations: the scheme works just as well if you use a scalar to remember only the previous approximation. The loop index would then not appear in any of the statements in the body of the loop. Second, the expression defining CURACC above is a general one for finding the "closeness" of two arbitrary real values. The ABS in the denominator is not strictly necessary because all values calculated in this example must be positive. The output is:

```
----   20 SQUARE ROOT FOUND WITHIN TOLERANCE

----   20 PARAMETER SQRTVAL    =   4.84313948 FINAL APPROXIMATION
                                              TO SQRT(TARGET)
```

```
----     20 PARAMETER VALUE          USED TO HOLD SUCCESSIVE
                                     APPROXIMATIONS

IT-1 11.72800000,    IT-2  6.86400000,    IT-3  5.14062471
IT-4  4.85174713,    IT-5  4.84314711,    IT-6  4.84313948
IT-7  4.84313948
```

12.5 CONCLUSION   ■

That completes Part 2 of this book, which has dealt with the features and syntax of the GAMS language in an ordered way. We suggest that you now select a model from the Library that deals with your subject of interest, and look through it in detail to see how all the component pieces fit together.

The remaining chapters deal with specialized topics, and may be read in any order. The Appendices contain complete lists of OPTIONS and dollar directives, and a glossary follows the Appendices.

PART 3

Special Topics

THE DISPLAY STATEMENT 13

In this chapter we will provide more detail about DISPLAY statements, including the controls that a user has over the layout and appearance of the output. These controls are a compromise to provide some flexibility. We have deliberately chosen not to try to provide a publication quality reporting function, but instead have aimed for functionality that is easy to use, and provides graceful defaults. There is limited capability to "export" results to reporting systems, and this will be improved in the near future.

We introduced the DISPLAY statement in Section 6.2, and there will be some repetition of that material here. The general form of the DISPLAY statement is:

```
DISPLAY ident-ref,"quoted text",ident-ref, . . . ;
```

where "ident-ref" means the name *without* domain lists or driving indices of a set or parameter, or a subfield of an equation or variable. The identifier references and the text can be mixed and matched in any order, and the whole statement can be continued over several lines. It is best to give an example.

```
SET S / X1K * X12K /;
PARAMETER P(S) ;
VARIABLE V(S);
      < statements to define and solve a model >
DISPLAY "First a SET",S,"Then a PARAMETER",P,
        "Then the activity level of a VARIABLE",V.L ;
```

The output produced by a display consists of labels and data: there are illustrations below. For sets, the character string YES (indicating existence) is used instead of values. For the other data types, only the non-default values are displayed. The default value is generally zero, except for the .LO and .UP subtypes of variables and equations. The default values for these are shown in Table 13.1.

Table 13.1: Default Values for .LO and .UP Subtypes

Variable	Equation	.LO	.UP
Positive	=G=	0	+INF
Free	=N=	-INF	+INF
Negative	=L=	-INF	0
Integer	n/a	0	100
Binary	n/a	0	1
n/a	=E=	0	0

Next we summarize in a table the default layout of a display for identifiers of different dimensionality. The figures in the Table 13.2 refer to the index position in the domain list of the identifier. As an example, if we display C, where C has been declared as C(I,J,K,L), then the I labels (the first index) will be associated with the planes or individual subtables, the J and K with the row labels, and the K (the fourth and last index) with the column headings. The first example of DISPLAY output below will help to clarify the point.

Table 13.2: Default Layout of Display Output

Number of Indices	Plane	Index Position(s) on the Row	Column
1		*List Format*	
2	—	1	2
3	—	1,2	3
4	1	2,3	4
5	1,2	3,4	5
6	1,2,3	4,5	6

For the uncommon cases of 7 to 10 indices, the natural progression is followed.

13.1 THE LABEL ORDER IN DISPLAYS ■

Here we will show the default layout for a simple display, and later use the same example to show how the various layout controls work. X has four dimensions or index positions. It is initialized using parameter format and then displayed as shown below:

```
SET   I  FIRST INDEX    /FIRST,SECOND /
      J  SECOND INDEX   /ONE,   TWO,   THREE /
      K  THIRD INDEX    /A,   B /
      L  FOURTH INDEX   /I,   II /;

PARAMETER X(I,J,K,L)  A four dimensional structure
                                                          /
SECOND.ONE  .A.I      +INF,   FIRST .THREE.B.I   -6.31612,
FIRST .ONE  .B.I     5.63559, SECOND.TWO  .B.I   19.83502,
SECOND.ONE  .B.II  -17.29948, FIRST .TWO  .B.II  10.34573,
FIRST .TWO  .A.II    0.02873, SECOND.ONE  .A.II   1.00370,
SECOND.TWO  .A.II     +INF,   FIRST .TWO  .A.I   -2.93926,
FIRST .ONE  .A.II    0.00000
                                                          /;

DISPLAY X;
```

This code fragment produces the following output:

```
----      17 PARAMETER X              A FOUR DIMENSIONAL STRUCTURE

INDEX 1 = FIRST

                      I          II

ONE   .B        5.636
TWO   .A       -2.939        0.029
TWO   .B                    10.346
THREE.B        -6.316

INDEX 1 = SECOND

                      I          II

ONE.A          +INF          1.004
ONE.B                      -17.299
TWO.A                        +INF
TWO.B          19.835
```

Notice that there are two subtables, one for each label in the first index position. The zero in the list for X("FIRST","ONE","A","II") has vanished, since zeroes are not shown for parameters. Similarly, rows and columns containing only zero values are suppressed in each subtable separately. The order of the labels is not the same as in the input data list. Notice that the labels vary slowest for the first index position, and quickest for the third. Within each index position the order is the GAMS entry order of the labels, which we discussed in Chapter 12 in connection with ordered sets. Some users need to manipulate the order, especially when doing reports that involve aggregation.

- The only way to change the order in which the labels for each index position appear on display output is to change the order of appearance of the labels in your GAMS program.

This is most easily done by declaring a set whose only purpose is to list all your labels in the order you want to see them. Make this set the very first declaration in your GAMS program.

The order of the indices is always as in the declaration statement for the symbol. You can declare them in the order you find appealing, or make an assignment to a new identifier with a different order. If you have large models, you may want to read the section on execution efficiency in Chapter 17 and keep the guidelines there in mind when deciding on an ordering of indices.

13.2   OPTION STATEMENTS THAT CONTROL DISPLAYS ■

The simplest of these options is the one controlling the number of digits shown after the decimal point. It affects numbers appearing in all display output following the OPTION statement, unless changed for a specific identifier as shown below. The general form of the statement is OPTION DECIMAL="value"; where "value" is an integer between 0 and 8. If you use 0, the decimal point is suppressed as well. The width of the number field does not change, just the number of decimals, but this may cause numbers which would normally be displayed in fixed format to appear in E-format, i.e., with the exponent represented explicitly. Here is an example. GAMS has rounded or converted numbers to E-format where necessary. The input is:

```
OPTION DECIMALS=1; DISPLAY X;
```

and the output:

```
----      18 PARAMETER X              A FOUR DIMENSIONAL STRUCTURE

INDEX 1 = FIRST

                       I          II

ONE  .B          5.6
TWO  .A         -2.9    2.8730E-2
TWO  .B                    10.3
THREE.B         -6.3

INDEX 1 = SECOND

                       I          II

ONE.A          +INF        1.0
ONE.B                    -17.3
TWO.A                     +INF
TWO.B          19.8
```

It is probably more useful is to control the number of decimals for specific identifiers separately. This can be done by using a statement whose general form is:

```
OPTION:"ident":"d-value";
```

"Ident" represents the name of a parameter, variable or equation, and "d-value" must be (as before) in the range 0 to 8. Exactly "d-value" places of decimals will be shown on all displays of "ident" that follow. This form can be extended to control layout of the data. The general form is:

```
OPTION:"ident":"d-value":"r-value":"c-value";
```

Here "r-value" means the number of index positions that are combined to form the row label and "c-value" means the number on the column headers. We illustrate with an example and then explain. The input is (continuing our example):

```
OPTION X:5:3:1; DISPLAY X;
```

and the output:

```
----      19 PARAMETER X              A FOUR DIMENSIONAL STRUCTURE

                              I          II

FIRST .ONE  .B        5.63559
FIRST .TWO  .A       -2.93926     0.02873
```

```
FIRST .TWO   .B                    10.34573
FIRST .THREE.B        -6.31612
SECOND.ONE   .A           +INF     1.00370
SECOND.ONE   .B                   -17.29948
SECOND.TWO   .A                      +INF
SECOND.TWO   .B       19.83502
```

Five places of decimals are shown, and three labels are used to mark the rows and one on the column. Since this is a four-dimensional structure, there are no remaining indices to be used as subtable labels (on the plane), and we now have the results in one piece. The OPTION statement is checked for consistency against the dimensionality of the identifier, and error messages issued if necessary. Here is an example that puts two indices on each of the row and column labels, and retains five decimal places:

```
OPTION X:5:2:2; DISPLAY X;
```

The output is:

```
----   20 PARAMETER X              A FOUR DIMENSIONAL STRUCTURE

                   A.I        A.II       B.I        B.II

FIRST .ONE                              5.63559
FIRST .TWO      -2.93926    0.02873                10.34573
FIRST .THREE                           -6.31612
SECOND.ONE         +INF     1.00370               -17.29948
SECOND.TWO                     +INF    19.83502
```

Lastly there is what is often known as "list" format. This is when all the labels are spelled out for each value as in the PARAMETER style of data initialization. The format of the OPTION is OPTION:"d-value":0:"c-value"; and in this case the "c-value" specifies the maximum number of items displayed on a line. The actual number will depend on the page width and the number and length of your labels. An example is:

```
OPTION X:5:0:1; DISPLAY X;
```

which gives:

```
----   21 PARAMETER X              A FOUR DIMENSIONAL STRUCTURE

FIRST .ONE   .B.I     5.63559
FIRST .TWO   .A.I    -2.93926
FIRST .TWO   .A.II    0.02873
FIRST .TWO   .B.II   10.34573
FIRST .THREE.B.I     -6.31612
SECOND.ONE   .A.I        +INF
SECOND.ONE   .A.II    1.00370
SECOND.ONE   .B.II  -17.29948
SECOND.TWO   .A.II       +INF
SECOND.TWO   .B.I    19.83502
```

This output nicely illustrates the label order used. The first index varies the slowest, the last fastest, and each one runs from beginning to end before the next one to the left advances. This ordering scheme is also used on equation and column lists and on the solution report, all produced by the solve statement.

13.3   DATA EXPORT TO OTHER PROGRAMS ■

The example above is immediately useful in producing output files that can easily be read by other programs. The simplest approach is to break up the output file with a text editor. Another, slightly more elaborate, is as follows. Run GAMS and save the work files (see the next chapter for details). Then use the restart facility to run a program whose only purpose is to display the identifiers of interest in list format with one entry per line. It is easy to write a program to read this type of output. Use very long pages (PS=9999 on the GAMS command line call for personal computers, and similar on other machines) to minimize the number of page breaks your program has to skip over and to make sure that the data for each identifier are in a contiguous block. The four dashes "----" at the beginning of each make it easy for your program to find its way around. You may like to filter out extended range values by using something similar to the fragment below. We introduced MAPVAL in Chapter 6: it returns 0 for ordinary numbers and positive integers for the extended range values.

```
PARAMETER XCOPY(I,J,K,L) Filtered copy of X;
XCOPY(I,J,K,L) = X(I,J,K,L) $ (MAPVAL( X(I,J,K,L) ) EQ 0)
                 - 777.7777 $ (MAPVAL( X(I,J,K,L) ) GT 0) ;
OPTION  XCOPY:4:0:1;
DISPLAY XCOPY;
```

In this example a copy is made of X in which all extended range values have been replaced by one number that is easy to check for in your program: you may need to do something different. Some experimentation will be needed to get a scheme like this working, but it is worth it if you have to produce reports several times.

SAVING & RESTARTING: THE WORK FILE 14

This chapter will be about saving GAMS runs and how saved runs can be restarted later. First we will explain the concept, then give a short discussion of the ways in which this capability is useful.

14.1 THE WORK FILE CONCEPT ◼

We often refer to "work files" or "restart files": these are names that have become associated with saving and restarting GAMS runs. The idea is quite simple, but for reasons we do not understand often causes trouble for new users. You can specify on the command entered to start GAMS that the run is to be "saved" at the end. We will show exactly how this is done later. If the run proceeds normally, i.e., without errors being detected, then work files are saved when GAMS stops. This is the save part of the operation. Later it is possible to "restart" the run. This involves specifying on the GAMS call (again details come later) that this is a restarted run, giving the generic name of the files previously saved, and supplying a GAMS program that continues where the previous one stopped.

It may be clearer if we describe the process in a different way. Imagine taking a large GAMS program and running it, producing one output file. Then think of splitting the program into two pieces. We can run the first piece and ask that work files be saved, producing an output file and the work files. Then we can run the second piece by requiring a restart and giving the names of the saved files, producing yet another output file. The two processes, running the large program and running the two component pieces sequentially, are equivalent. The outputs are rearranged slightly, and in two files, but their content is the same. We were able to interrupt the GAMS task and restart it later. Furthermore, the work files remain. We can repeat the second part, perhaps with changes. If the second part contains errors, we have a chance to correct them. As an example before we go into the details of how we do this, consider the program that illustrates the concept and is distributed with the personal computer version. The entire file is shown below:

```
$TITLE CONTINUATION OF MODEL TRNSPORT

* SAVE ORIGINAL SOLUTION VALUES FOR REPORT

  PARAMETER REPORT(I,J,*) REPORT ON SHIPMENTS;
  REPORT(I,J,'original') = X.L(I,J);
```

```
* NOW CLOSE DOWN SEATTLE --> CHICAGO ARC AND SOLVE AGAIN

X.FX('seattle','chicago') = 0.0;
SOLVE TRANSPORT USING LP MINIMIZING TRCOST;
REPORT(I,J,'scen-1') = X.L(I,J);
OPTION REPORT:0; DISPLAY REPORT;
```

Notice that there is no declaration for I, J, X, TRANSPORT or for TRCOST: these were declared and initialized in the original run, but we refer to them and access their data here because the restarting has made all previous declarations and values available. At the risk of laboring the point, we show the first few lines of the output obtained by restarting, using this input file:

```
GAMS 2.04 PC AT/XT                      87/12/10 18:05:41    PAGE 11
CONTINUATION OF MODEL TRNSPORT

110
111  * SAVE ORIGINAL SOLUTION VALUES FOR REPORT
112
113    PARAMETER REPORT(I,J,*) REPORT ON SHIPMENTS;
114    REPORT(I,J,'original') = X.L(I,J);
115
116  * NOW CLOSE DOWN SEATTLE --> CHICAGO ARC AND SOLVE AGAIN
117
118    X.FX('seattle','chicago') = 0.0;
119    SOLVE TRANSPORT USING LP MINIMIZING TRCOST;
120    REPORT(I,J,'scen-1') = X.L(I,J);
121    OPTION REPORT:0; DISPLAY REPORT;
```

The line and page numbers do not start at 1: the count is continued from the previous output.

14.2 SAVING WORK FILES ■

The only way to save work files is for the user to call GAMS with a request to save them. The GAMS call is most often issued from the operating system prompt, but is sometimes put into "command" files for batch processing, especially on large computers. The details of the call differ from machine to machine, but they can always be found in a document distributed with your GAMS system. The easiest way to find this document is to enter the command "GAMS" with no file names: the diagnostic output will then tell you how to access the instruction or user help file. On the personal computer it is called "GAMS.DOC" and should be kept in the GAMS system directory. We show full details of command line calls for popular machines in Appendix A, but you should always consult the online document: it is certain to contain the correct details. We have tried to make the calls as similar as possible on different machines within the limitations imposed by different operating systems.

In this chapter, we use the personal computer call as an example. The differences on other systems are mainly caused by differences in file-naming conventions and the use of separators, the "=" sign in this example. The general form is shown beneath the particular.

```
GAMS    TRNSPORT       SAVE = SAVTRPT
GAMS "input-name-stem" SAVE = "save-name-stem"
```

This command, entered at the DOS prompt, requests GAMS to process the file "TRNSPORT." If there is no file with this name, GAMS looks instead for a file called "TRNSPORT.GMS." The output will be written to the file "TRNSPORT.LST." If no errors are detected, GAMS saves restart files called "SAVTRPT.G01" to "SAVTRPT.G08" (eight files in all) at the end of the run. Any existing files with these names will be overwritten and their original contents lost. The keyword "SAVE" may be abbreviated to "S" (but not to "SA" or "SAV") and the blanks around the "=" are optional. It is illegal for the name-stem provided for SAVE to contain a dot or a name extension. The name used for the restart files is also shown on the "FILE SUMMARY" at the end of the output file. Here is what is produced for the call shown above:

```
**** FILE SUMMARY

INPUT    C:\K-MINTRO\TRNSPORT.GMS
OUTPUT   C:\K-MINTRO\TRNSPORT.LST
SAVE     C:\K-MINTRO\SAVTRPT.G0?

EXECUTION TIME      =      0.191 MINUTES
```

The "?" is the DOS convention for a single "wild card" character, in this case meaning 1 to 8.

14.3 RESTARTING ■

Restarting uses a very similar procedure. Here is the command (again on DOS machines) to continue the run above using the files saved.

```
GAMS    CTRNSPRT       RESTART = SAVTRPT
GAMS "input-name-stem" RESTART = "name-stem-of-saved-files"
```

This time the input file does not contain a complete program, but a continued one. The files containing the restart information are those we saved above, viz., "SAVTRPT.G01" to "SAVTRPT.G08." It is obviously an error for any of these files not to exist, or not to have been created by GAMS. As before, "RESTART" may be shortened to "R." The output from this command will be, as expected, on the file "CTRNSPRT.LST."

To finish this short section, let us list a few pertinent facts about work files.

- They are created only when the user requests them. How the request is made is machine specific. See the online help file on your computer.

- Work files can be used only by GAMS tasks requesting a restarted run. Again, the details are machine specific, but there are always eight files. They can, of course, be removed using the normal system command for destroying files, or copied for archival or backup purposes.

- Work files created on one type of computer can *not* be used on a different type of computer.

- A restarted run also requires a continuation input file. It is your responsibility to ensure that the contents of the input file matches that of the work files, although the compiler will issue errors if it detects any inconsistencies, such as references to symbols not previously declared.

- The restart does not alter work files. They can be used repeatedly to continue a particular run many times, possibly with many different continuation input files.

- Work files preserve all information (including declarations, values, option settings and compiler dollar directives) known to GAMS at the end of the run that created them.

- Files can be saved following a restarted run, thus producing another set of work files that reflects the state of the job following completion of the statements in the continuation input file.

14.4   WAYS IN WHICH WORK FILES ARE USEFUL ■

The basic function of work files is to preserve information that has been expensive to produce. There are several reasons for wanting to do this, which we briefly discuss below.

14.4 (a)   Incremental Program Development ■

GAMS programs are often developed in stages. (We will have more to say about this in Chapter 17 on large models.) Normally the sets come first, followed by tables and data manipulations, then equations, and finally the assignments used to generate reports. As each piece of the model is built, it should be run and checked for errors by inserting diagnostic DISPLAY and ABORT statements. As confidence mounts in the correctness of what has been done, it is useful to save the completed parts in work files. Then by restarting it is possible to work only on the piece under active development, thereby minimizing computer costs and the amount of output produced in each of the developmental runs. This approach is especially useful when entering the statements needed for reporting. The solution is much more expensive than the report, but the report is likely to involve many details of content and layout that have to be tried several times before they are satisfactory. It is a great help not to have to solve the model every time.

14.4 (b)   Tackling Sequences of Difficult Solves ■

In many cases where solves are known to be difficult and expensive, it may be too risky to ask GAMS to process a job containing many solve statements. The risk is that if one solve does not proceed to normal completion, then the following one will be started from a bad initial point, and much time or money will be wasted. As yet there is no direct way for the user to influence what GAMS does following an unsuccessful solve, although one should be available very soon.

For the moment therefore, the cautious alternative is to request one solve at a time and save the work files. Then the output is carefully inspected before proceeding. If everything is normal, the job is restarted with the next solve requested. If not, the previous solve can be repeated, probably with a different initial point, or continued if the cause of the trouble was an iteration limit, for example.

This approach is common when doing repeated solves of a model that successively represents several consecutive time periods. It uses work files in a sequential rather than a tree-structured way. It also produces many files, which can be difficult to manage; if the solves are especially difficult, it is possible to lose track of exactly what was done. Great care is needed to avoid losing control of this process. Two suggestions on file handling may be useful for personal computer users. The first: always set the time and date correctly when you turn on your machine. Nothing is more daunting than looking at a directory full of files all created on "01/01/80." Second, useful file compression and archiving utilities are available on many bulletin boards; these make handling large numbers of files easier and more economical. A popular one is "ARC."

14.4 (c)   Multiple Scenarios   ■

The majority of modeling exercises involve a "base case," and the point of the study is to see how the system changes when circumstances change, either naturally or by design. This is often done by making many different changes to the base case and separately considering the effects: it is sometimes called "what if" analysis.

The point is that the base case can be saved using work files, and as many different scenarios as may be interesting can then be run separately by restarting. Each scenario probably involves only making a change in data or in bounds, solving the changed model (the base solution is automatically used as a starting point), and reporting. This procedure will be cheap compared to the cost of establishing the base case. This is an example of how work files are used in a tree-structured way: one set of work files is used with many different (but probably very small) input files to produce many different output files. File handling is less likely to be a problem than in the sequential case above.

14.5   SUMMARY   ■

This is all we have to say about work files. If you will be using GAMS extensively, you should learn how to use them. Many users with large models *always* save work files in case they need to run a cheap display to check something. The files should be destroyed after the run has been inspected, unless there is some other reason to save them.

You should be aware that the file handling necessary if you create many work files can be a burden, and that discipline is needed to keep track of the contents and purpose of each set. We have many ideas for changing this situation, and hope to make improvements soon.

NONLINEAR PROGRAMMING 15

This chapter will be devoted to nonlinear programming. The first section contains a general discussion, and the second has details of particular considerations that apply to MINOS 5, the most widely used of the nonlinear solvers.

15.1 GENERAL POINTS ABOUT NONLINEAR PROGRAMMING ■

It is generally more difficult to find solutions to nonlinear problems than to linear ones, and users with difficult nonlinear problems will find that they have to pay much more attention to apparently inconsequential details than they would like. There are two areas of concern. It may be difficult to find a solution to a problem, and when it is found it may not be unique: other solutions, perhaps better, may exist. Here we will deal mainly with the first issue: how to find a solution that is locally optimal, or the best in the vicinity. The second is an unsolved research topic, although analysis of a particular problem may show that it has only one solution.

Some general points before we start on the details. With nonlinear models it is important to keep the formulation as simple as possible and the model as small as possible. Development should be incremental: start small and simple with key relationships and test that these behave as expected. Add size and complexity only when you are confident that what you have done already is working properly. Chapter 17 on large models gives more detailed advice, and should be read carefully by users interested in nonlinear models.

A good case could be made that many of the details we discuss here should be taken care of automatically, and not have to concern a user. We agree, and look forward to the day when nonlinear programming will be more robust, less tedious, and more automatic. GAMS will take more responsibility in handling many of these details, and there will be continual improvements in the performance of solvers as well. Perhaps a newcomer to nonlinear programming will be comforted to know that it is much more reliable and efficient than it used to be, and that progress is still being made.

It is worth noting that problems in which the nonlinear terms are restricted to the objective function are generally easier to solve than those in which nonlinearities appear in constraints. We will discuss in Section 15.1 (d) how GAMS users can take advantage of this fact.

Three different types of details should be kept in mind while you are writing your model: initial values, bounds, and scaling, probably in that order of importance. How much effort you will have to spend depends on the size and complexity of your model. If you start small and simple, it will be much easier to keep these details under control. We will discuss them in turn.

15.1 (a)   Initial Values   ■

Most nonlinear problems can be solved more easily if a guess is provided for the value of important variables. With GAMS at present this has to be done by the user making assignments to the activity level (.L) subfields of variables.

If the user does not provide any initial values, GAMS uses zero or, if the variable is bounded away from zero, the bound that is closest to zero. For many functions zero is a very bad initial value, because the derivatives are also zero. This means that no improvement appears to be possible by changing the value. In extreme cases the so-called "corner point" (all zero) may really be a locally optimal point! You should use assignment statements to provide reasonable initial values, as in

    X.L(I,J) = "value"; or X.L(I,J) = INITVALX(I,J);

A more elaborate method for providing initially feasible points for important equations is as follows. Suppose your model contains the equation:

    PF(i).. Q(i) =E= q0(i) * (K(i)**alpha(i)) * (L(i)**(1-alpha(i))) ;

where Q, K and L are GAMS VARIABLES. The following assignments will make equation PF initially feasible:

    K.L(i) = kap0(i) ; L.L(i) = lab0(i) ;

    Q.L(i) = q0(i) * (K.L(i)**alpha(i)) * (L.L(i)**(1-alpha(i))) ;

The equation PF is a definition, and we have used the same algebra to provide a feasible point using guesses for K and L. In whatever way you decide to specify initial values, the better they are the easier, cheaper and quicker the solution. In many cases of bad or missing initial values there will be no useful solution. (It is normally more important to supply initial values for variables that appear *nonlinearly* in the problem.)

The feasibility of the initial point can be inspected with a complete EQUATION LISTING (OPTION LIMROW=10000;). We discussed how to interpret this information in some detail in Chapter 10.

If your input file contains more than one solve then, unless you specify otherwise, the initial values for second and subsequent solves are the final values returned from the previous one. It is normally not necessary to set initial values for solves after the first one.

15.1 (b)   Bounds   ■

There are two reasons why bounds are important in nonlinear models. The first is to prevent undefined operations, such as division by zero, from being attempted. We will give several examples, starting with the one from [RAMSEY].

    UTIL.. UTILITY =E= SUM(t, beta(t)*LOG(C(t)));

    C.LO(t) = 0.02;

The bounds on C will prevent trouble due to undefined LOGs. Here is an example where bounds are required to generate the model:

        EQ1 .. Z =E= X/Y;

Here it would be appropriate to use Y.LO = 0.01, since otherwise GAMS would stop with an error message during model generation, because the derivative with respect to X would be undefined in the initial point. Note that if you use the expression

        X/(Y + Z)   then   the   constraint   Y + Z =G= 0.01;

is not sufficient protection since the constraint may be violated in intermediate points. It should be safe to write the following, however:

        X/V   together   with   V =E= Y + Z;   and   V.LO = 0.01;

This is because nonlinear functions are evaluated only at points that satisfy the bounds.

Do not forget our earlier warnings on exponentiation. X**Y implies a real valued exponent Y, and hence it is sensible to use something like X.LO = 0.01. If you want integer powers, for instance to minimize the sums of squares, the usage

        SUM(I, SQR(X(I)))

allows X to take negative values. (For larger exponents use the function POWER(X,N), which means X raised to the integer power N.)

The second reason why bounds are useful is that they can ensure that the VARIABLES stay in a region that makes sense. Sometimes values in partial solutions get outrageously large, and considerable resources can be wasted. If you know that an income of 500 is plausible but one of 5000 is not, then perhaps you should specify (using economists' notation) Y.UP=2000. The safest strategy is to bound *all* variables (except the objective) above and below, and to check all solutions to make sure that none of the "safety" bounds are active at the final point.

15.1 (c)   Scaling   ∎

Nonlinear solvers are not as tolerant of wide ranges of values in the problem as are linear ones. A good general rule is that variable values and their derivatives should be not too different from 1. "Too different" is vague. Five orders of magnitude will almost certainly cause trouble, while three are often tolerated. If you keep scaling requirements in mind while writing your model, and express population in units of millions, for example, you may find that your problem is naturally scaled without effort.

To overcome difficulties caused by wide ranges of values, MINOS users should first try the "Scale all variables" option as outlined in Appendix D. This may require a fairly good initial point to produce benefits; if so, you should try instead multiplying selected rows or columns by appropriate scaling factors. (You have to change the GAMS statement of the problem to do this. It is more flexible to use scalars than explicit constants as the multipliers.)

If your problem is badly scaled, then one or other of these remedies is likely to cause a dramatic improvement in the cost and reliability of the solution process.

15.1 (d)   Objective Function Reformulation   ∎

From the point of view of ease of solution, there are two classes of nonlinear problems. The first is when the nonlinear terms are only in the objective function (or in the GAMS equation that defines the objective variable). These problems are generally much easier to solve than the second, which have nonlinear terms throughout the model. It is often worthwhile to write your model in the way that puts as many of the nonlinearities as possible into the objective. There is a special way you can write your model that guarantees the benefits of packing all the nonlinearities into the objective. Three conditions must be fulfilled.

- The GAMS objective variable must be a FREE variable, and the original bounds of [-INF,+INF] must not have been reset.
- It must appear in only one equation, which must be a scalar equality (=E=)
- It must appear alone on the left or right of the =E= symbol (Z =E= f(x); or f(x) =E= Z;).

GAMS/MINOS users can check that this has been successful by looking at the counts of calls to FUNOBJ and FUNCON on their SOLUTION SUMMARY: the count for FUNOBJ should be positive. If your constraints are linear, the count for FUNCON should be zero as well.

15.1 (e)   Discontinuous Derivatives and Multiple Optima   ■

This short section is about some of the most difficult types of nonlinear models: those containing non-smooth functions, and those with multiple solutions.

You should avoid using non-smooth functions (model type DNLP) if at all possible. Use formulation tricks, such as replacing a reference to ABS(X) with the difference of two positive variables, in an effort to eliminate discontinuities. If you are unable to eliminate them, however, it is wise to test the robustness of any solutions by repeating the run with different starting points. For example, if you have an equation that contains the term MAX(X,Y), then see what happens if you start with X larger than Y, and subsequently with Y larger than X.

This type of strategy is also useful if you suspect that your smooth model has multiple local optima. Make a number of runs from different starting points (how different? you will have to experiment), and see if you find more than one solution.

15.2   PARTICULAR POINTS ABOUT GAMS/MINOS   ■

One of the design goals of GAMS was to make mathematical programming available to users without requiring an investment in learning the details of a specific solver. Examples of such details are tolerance settings, the command language, input file formats and (in extreme cases) descriptions of the attributes of necessary scratch files. We have been broadly successful in attaining this goal, especially for the large commercial linear systems, by providing suitable internal "intelligence" in manipulating settings and options. Nonlinear programming is, as we have discussed, more difficult than linear programming. We have tried to provide default settings that minimize the possibility that the solution will not be found. Many users need to evaluate and influence performance by adjusting tolerances and methods. In this section we discuss performance evaluation at the language level. In Appendix D there is an overview of the methods used to solve your problem, and a complete description of defaults and how settings may be changed.

MINOS 5.2 (Murtagh and Saunders 1987) is the nonlinear solver most widely used with GAMS. It has been specially adapted to interface efficiently and automatically. We will refer to the adapted program as GAMS/MINOS whenever the possibility for ambiguity exists. It is important to note that it is *only* the adapted version that will interface correctly with GAMS.

You should study Appendix D as well as this section if you plan to do an extensive nonlinear application, or if you have difficulty finding solutions to your models. In the first four subsections, (a) to (d), we discuss general points about GAMS/MINOS. In the last, (e), there is brief discussion of the use of the "options file," which is a prelude to the complete treatment in Appendix D.

15.2 (a) The GAMS/MINOS Solve Summary ■

In this section we explain briefly the GAMS/MINOS statistics that appear as part of the SOLVE SUMMARY, and before the solution listing. The relevant part of the [PORTFOL] output from Chapter 10 is reproduced again here, and explained below.

```
EXIT -- OPTIMAL SOLUTION FOUND
MAJOR ITNS, SUPERBASICS       1      2
FUNOBJ, FUNCON CALLS          7      0
INTERPRETER USAGE           .00
NORM RG / NORM PI     1.635E-16
```

- All messages containing two dashes "--" are messages from GAMS/MINOS. Any messages that contain the string "XXX" are warnings.

- GAMS/MINOS uses "major iterations" and "minor iterations," which are explained in Appendix D. You should be aware that GAMS/MINOS separately limits the number of major iterations. In all but exceptional situations the default limit of 50 is ample. It can be changed by using an options file. The count of major iterations is labeled "MAJOR ITNS" on the summary.

- "SUPERBASICS" is the count of superbasic variables in the final solution.

- The numbers labeled "FUNOBJ" and "FUNCON" are the number of times the nonlinearities in the objective and constraints, respectively, have been evaluated.

- "INTERPRETER USAGE" contains the time spent evaluating nonlinearities. It is measured in the same units as the resource limit.

- If the number labeled "NORM RG / NORM PI" is larger than $1.0E-06$, and if the solution is "LOCALLY OPTIMAL," then MINOS has had difficulty, and the accompanying solution should be regarded as "not quite optimal."

15.2 (b) Tackling Nonlinear Infeasibility ■

If, in spite of all your efforts with initial values, bounds and scaling, MINOS persists in declaring your nonlinear model to be infeasible, there are two emergency remedies that may help.

The first is simply to duplicate the SOLVE statement, so that the second solve starts from the point at which the first terminated. This is an-easy-to-use procedure that sometimes works.

The second is more elaborate, but also likely to produce useful information. It involves rewriting some (or all) of the equations so that they contain explicit "slack" variables, and so can easily be made feasible. For example, if your model contains the constraints

```
DEM(i).. Y(i) =E= ynot(i)*(PD*P(i))**thet(i);
MB(i)..  X(i) =G= Y(i) + SUM(j, aio(i,j)*X(j));
```

and you want to treat them specially, you would rewrite them as

```
DEM(i).. Y(i) + DEMP(i) - DEMM(i) =E= ynot(i)*(PD*P(i))**thet(i);
MB(i)..  X(i) + MBP(i) =G= Y(i) + SUM(j, aio(i,j)*X(j));
```

where DEMP, DEMM and MBP are positive variables that do not occur elsewhere.

Then set up and solve a model that minimizes the sums of these slacks. A new equation is needed:

```
PHAS1.. SUM(i, DEMP(i) + DEMM(i) + MBP(i)) =E= Z;
```

and a new model

```
MODEL FIXINFES / DEM, MB, PHAS1, . . . /
```

and then

```
SOLVE FIXINFES USING NLP MINIMIZING Z;
```

If a point is found at which Z is zero, a second model should be solved that has the same constraints, the real objective and the slacks fixed at zero. There are several variants of this procedure: the description above is an outline of one approach. Others involve composite objective functions with weights, or minimizing the squares of unbounded slack variables. As in all cases of difficulties with nonlinear programming, care and patience are needed to resolve the situation.

We should mention here our experience that most infeasible models are infeasible because they contain errors in the algebra or in the data. Often such mistakes can be found by looking carefully at display output of transformed data, and at full equation and column listings.

15.2 (c) The Screen Summary ■

There is one aspect of the personal computer version of MINOS that may prove confusing. It concerns the objective value shown on the screen summary that appears while MINOS is solving your problem. The value may *not* be the same as the one GAMS reports because of implementation details. The sign may be reversed, and, if there are constant terms in equation in which the objective variable appears, then the two values will differ by that constant.

15.2 (d) Disregarding the Basis ■

Very occasionally MINOS has trouble with the basis that GAMS provides for a second or subsequent solve. This most often happens if there are new equations or previously unused variables in the model. The symptoms are either that the solution cannot be found, or that it takes far too long to find. A SYSOUT print will probably show messages like

```
"LU6CHK WARNING. Matrix appears to be singular"
```

near the beginning. One possible remedy is to force MINOS to disregard the GAMS basis and use only the level values of the nonlinear variables. This can be done by using OPTION BRATIO=1; (discussed in Chapter 9). Sometimes decreasing the "major damping parameter" (see Appendix D) from its default value of 2.0 to something like 0.2 will prevent the model from going 'wild', but for well behaved problems the solution time will increase. In either case, both careful experimentation and patience are necessary.

15.2 (e)   The Use of the GAMS/MINOS Options File   ∎

If you have a model that is expensive to solve, and must be solved many times, then it may pay you to change the standard GAMS/MINOS settings by using an "options file." The options file is *not* required unless you need to change these settings. It is not recommended for casual use: it is time consuming and tedious to do the experimentation needed to find out which adjustments are useful, and there is abundant opportunity to make the situation worse rather than better.

The content and format of the options file, together with suggestions for useful changes for various classes of models (almost linear, or very nonlinear, and so on), are given in Appendix D. Here we will briefly discuss *how* the options file should be made available and mention a couple of warnings pertaining to its use.

The options file is a file with a particular name, and it must be in the current directory (if you have a directory structured file system). The file's name is made up of two pieces. The first part is the name that you would specify to ask GAMS to use GAMS/MINOS for a particular problem, as we discussed in Chapter 10. If the appropriate statement is OPTION NLP=MINOS5;, then this part of the name will be MINOS5. (This is in fact the most probable name. The uncertainty is because individual installations can change the name, as is needed when testing new versions.) The second part is a machine specific suffix or type, which must fit file-naming conventions. On a personal computer it is OPT while on IBM/CMS it is OPTIONS, resulting in file names "MINOS5.OPT" and "MINOS5 OPTIONS A" on these two machines. Please be sure to study the online "help" documents that were supplied with your GAMS system. They are certain to contain accurate information about the name to be used.

Two warnings are necessary as a consequence of using this file access method.

If a file with appropriate name is found (in the current directory if your computer has a directory-based file system), then its contents are used to modify the GAMS/MINOS default settings. If someone else (or even you) has inadvertently left a file designed for another problem and your task finds it, then your model may misbehave in a disastrous way. If an options file is used (whether you provided it intentionally or not), then its contents will be listed as part of your output immediately below the SOLVE SUMMARY. This piece of output starts with the keyword BEGIN and ends with END.

The second warning is that an options file for the first solve in a series will most probably require settings different from subsequent ones. This means that you will have to save work files and rename option files between the first and second solves. This is a clumsy procedure, which will be changed in future releases.

You should also be aware that under very rare circumstances GAMS/MINOS will stop because of a limit that can only be reset by using an options file. The Major iterations limit is one such limit.

MIXED INTEGER PROGRAMMING 16

16.1 GENERAL POINTS ABOUT MIXED INTEGER PROGRAMMING ■

Integer and mixed integer programming, like nonlinear programming, can be extremely demanding of computing resources. In this chapter we will discuss mixed integer programming, and provide hints on how to avoid spending too much while still producing useful results.

The number of discrete variables (type BINARY or INTEGER) is an important indicator of how difficult a mixed integer problem (model type MIP) will be to solve. Unfortunately, however, there is a very wide range of difficulty for problems with any given number. It is probably true that mixed integer work is not as inherently difficult as nonlinear, but that it is likely to be more expensive. Many users find that they can investigate the properties of their model by fixing as many of the discrete variables as possible and then inspecting the marginal values of the fixed variables at the final point. It is then necessary to make adjustments to the set of fixed variables and try again. Strategies such as this make it possible to gain an understanding of the behavior of the problem comparatively cheaply.

A few hints on formulation may be useful. Always specify the tightest reasonable bounds on integer variables, and bound continuous variables when possible. If, for instance, a continuous variable can never take on negative values, declare it to be a POSITIVE VARIABLE.

While a mixed integer model is under development, you should solve it without the integer restrictions by specifying RMIP ("Relaxed" MIP) instead of MIP in your SOLVE statement. This means that all discrete variables will be treated as continuous variables, i.e., they will be allowed to take on any value between their bounds. These problems are equivalent to ordinary linear ones and are easy to solve. Solving the RMIP is not only useful for quickly checking out the model, but also vital for understanding the characteristics of the discrete model.

16.1 (a) GAMS Termination Tolerances ■

When the model behaves correctly in the relaxed case, it is time to find integer solutions. Often it takes too long to find a proven optimal solution, and then it might be reasonable to settle for one that is known to be within a specified distance from the optimal. This is done using the options OPTCR and OPTCA. OPTCR is a relative measure: if for instance you have specified

    OPTION OPTCR = 0.05;

then GAMS will instruct the solver to continue until an integer solution, guaranteed to be not more than 5 percent from the best one possible, is found. (Unless another limit, such as the iteration limit, intervenes. If no such solution is found the best one will be returned, and the "gap" between it and the best will be reported.) OPTCA is an absolute measure, which is useful when the objective value is close to zero: if OPTCA = 5.0 has been issued, for instance, an integer solution not more than 5.0 from the best one possible is returned. A solution is returned when either the relative or the absolute termination tolerance is satisfied. When starting with a new model, it is obviously best to use wide tolerances, and to decrease them as confidence grows that the model is correct and behaving as expected. Specifying even a small tolerance, e.g., OPTCR = 0.005; is almost always dramatically better than not using any, since a major part of the effort in finding the best solution is proving that it is the best.

Please note that the default settings of these options are

    OPTION OPTCR = 0.10; OPTION OPTCA = 0.0;

corresponding to a 10 percent relative termination tolerance. To get a proven optimal solution, specify OPTION OPTCR = 0.0;.

It must also be mentioned that because different solution systems have different characteristics, the precise definition of OPTCR and OPTCA will depend on the solver being used. For example the tolerances in both ZOOM and MPSX (IBM's large mainframe math programming system) are based on the "estimated best" integer solution. With SCICONIC from SCICON (available on a variety of machines) the tolerance is measured with respect to the solution of the relaxed problem.

16.1 (b)   Restarting MIP Runs ∎

Unfortunately, there is at present no general way of restarting the solve process for a mixed integer problem using knowledge about previously found integer solutions. We are working on this. GAMS/ZOOM users may find it worthwhile to specify an INCUMBENT.

16.2   PARTICULAR POINTS ABOUT GAMS/ZOOM ∎

ZOOM (Singhal et al, 1987; Marsten, 1981) is the only portable solver available for mixed integer work using GAMS. ZOOM is a FORTRAN based system, and has been specially modified to work efficiently with GAMS. We will call the modified version GAMS/ZOOM to distinguish it from the original. We will try to keep the distinction clear where it is important. One very important distinction is that if you have a copy of ZOOM that was not obtained from your GAMS distributor, that program will not work with GAMS.

The other mixed integer solvers that have been interfaced with GAMS (MPSX, SCICONIC, and APEX) are all expensive commercial systems whose availability is restricted to particular types of machines. Details can be seen in the help files available on machines where these programs have been installed.

In this section we will discuss some of the more important features that apply only to GAMS/ZOOM. There are a great many more details in Appendix E, including an overview of the methods used and a discussion of the performance oriented settings that may be modified by a user.

INTEGER variables are not implemented directly in ZOOM. GAMS arranges to provide hidden constraints that relate your INTEGER variables to sums of BINARY variables. Our advice about limiting the range of INTEGER variables is therefore even more important with GAMS/ZOOM. Users with personal computers, in particular, may have troubles with insufficient memory available for GAMS/ZOOM if their models have large numbers of integer variables whose bounded ranges are large.

GAMS/ZOOM users are able to manipulate tolerances, branching order, and other settings by using a non-default "options file" containing GAMS/ZOOM directives. Complete details about the format and meaning of these are given in Appendix E. The use of the options file is not recommended for the casual user. Care and patience are needed to analyze the effects of changing any settings, and there is ample opportunity to make things worse rather than better.

There is one particular additional warning. The options file is a file with a particular name. (On the personal computer this name is likely to be "ZOOM.OPT": details about the naming convention adopted can be found in Appendix E in Section E.3.) If a file with the magic name is found in the current directory, then its contents are used to modify the GAMS/ZOOM default settings. If someone else (or even you) has inadvertently left a file designed for another problem and your task finds it, then your model may take a lot longer to solve than you expect. If an options file is used (whether you provided it intentionally or not), then its contents will be listed as part of your output immediately below the SOLVE SUMMARY. This piece of output starts with the keyword BEGIN and ends with END.

LARGE MODELS 17

In this chapter we will discuss the special circumstances of large models, why they should be avoided, and how you should deal with a large model if you are unable to avoid it.

We should distinguish between what we might call production and strategic models. In many industrial applications, large well-understood models are run in environments where many people and lots of machine power are dedicated to the effort. It is expected that the benefits of such efforts will outweigh the costs. These are production models. They are used in oil refineries, by airlines, and in the financial and military communities. They will normally use specially designed programs or systems designed to operate efficiently.

The GAMS user is more often dealing with strategic models. These are models designed to look into policy or investment decisions rather than day to day operational problems. They are run a comparatively few times between changes, and typically do not have on-going data gathering efforts associated with them. A considerable proportion of the total effort spent in an exercise like this is in getting the formulation right. GAMS has been designed for just this type of work. It is easy and cheap to change the GAMS statement of a model, even to change a linear formulation to a nonlinear one. But there is a cost to be paid for this generality, which is that more computer resources are needed to generate a model in GAMS than in a production system. Most GAMS users are willing to pay this price since it is the total cost of the effort that counts, and the cost of computer resources is steadily declining compared with the cost of the people that use them.

In the discussion that follows of large models and their drawbacks, we are assuming that the modeling is being done in a strategic and not a production environment.

17.1 WHY LARGE MODELS SHOULD BE AVOIDED ■

What is a large model? The answer varies. It is one that takes a lot of time (or money) to solve. It is one that "just fits" into the memory available on your machine. It is one that has more than a few hundred lines of assignments and EQUATIONS when written in GAMS. Briefly, any model that is expensive to solve or difficult to manage, or whose details are so overwhelming that it hard to keep track of them, is large.

We can easily write down four good reasons to avoid large models, and you can probably think of more.

- They are expensive to implement and to solve.

- It is difficult to debug them, and more difficult to verify that they are behaving as designed.
- It is likely to be difficult and unsafe to change them, because of all the "side effects" that must be remembered.
- They are likely not to be credible to policy makers because they are difficult to understand.

Sometimes a model starts its life small and manageable, and grows because "we must treat the rest-of-the-world in more detail" or "now we have data for 1964." The only advice we can give is that you weigh carefully the benefits of increased size and complexity against the costs of more data, more logic, and less understanding. Models designed by committees often fail before they start, whereas many successful efforts are headed by one person who carefully considers the issues to be addressed and resists attempts to broaden the model's size or scope unnecessarily.

17.2 HOW TO DEAL WITH LARGE MODELS ■

The best way to deal with large models is to develop and debug them in small, easily understood pieces. Exactly how to do this depends on the structure: you may want to limit the number of sectors, or of time periods, or of geographical regions during the implementation phase. Or, following our advice in the chapter on nonlinear models, you may find it most productive to start with the key relationships that "drive" the model, and develop these cleanly and thoroughly before adding any details.

If you are developing a farm model, for example, it would be natural to start with cropping activities constrained only by the availability of land within each period in the cropping calendar. Then you could successively add constraints on labor and machinery availability, associate costs with the inputs and revenue with the outputs, and so on. In essence, the incremental approach has the effect of isolating each part of the model, because you can observe the change in solution characteristics as each part is added.

You should use work files as much as possible when developing models that are expensive to run. An expensive solution can be saved and then the repeated runs that may be necessary to develop the reporting part of the model can each be made cheaply.

17.2 SIZE LIMITATIONS IN GAMS AND IN SOLVERS ■

GAMS has been designed to use machine resources in a flexible way. There are some fixed limits, and we will list some representative ones below, but we have tried to make each of these large enough that they will not interfere with the user.

The limit that users are most likely to see is the one caused by limited amounts of memory. On IBM personal computers running DOS, for example, the machine size is limited to 640K bytes. If your job needs more memory than this it will fail, and you will have to make your model smaller or move it to a more powerful machine. Similar limits exist on all machines, but on some the limit is so large that it has never caused trouble. (The limit may be determined by the size of the machine or by administrative decisions by the computer center.) But the overall effect is the same: GAMS needs memory for your data structures, and acquires it as necessary. All data are stored "sparse," meaning that only non-default values are kept. When all available memory has been used, no more progress is possible, and GAMS stops, normally in a most ungraceful way. Because memory is acquired as needed for different types of data structure, we cannot give precise estimates for "what will fit." We have considered various schemes to overcome this problem, but have not adopted one because they are all expensive to implement and not portable across machines.

But there is another, perhaps more important, drawback. Similar limitations exist for the solver programs, most of which need to keep all their data in main memory, and which will fail if there is not enough memory to accomodate them. And it is again the case that this workspace is used for different purposes, making it impossible to state the largest possible problem that can run in workspace of a given size. "Largest" is not a well defined concept: with GAMS/MINOS it depends in a complicated way on at least six different attributes of the model.

In Table 17.1 we list sizes and attributes of representative models that are "large" in the sense that they are near the limit of what is practical on a personal computer, along with the model generation time (GAMS) and solution time (solver), both in minutes. These examples were run on an 8 MHz AT with an 80287 coprocessor and 640K of RAM. The times shown are to give you a rough idea of what is possible: these are not precisely controlled benchmarks, and we have a host of performance improvements in mind for the near future.

Table 17.1: Problem Characteristics

Name	Number of Rows	Number of Columns	Number of Nonzeroes	Generation Time[a]	Solution Time[a]	Iterations	Solver
DINAMICO	318	425	4156	3.0	30.1	628	MINOS
SARF	532	542	3949	37.7	115.8	2775	MINOS
FERTD[b]	458	2968	7252	11.4	28.3	1368	ZOOM
CAMCGE[c]	243	280	1356	0.8	7.0	189	MINOS
GANGES[d]	274	357	1405	1.8	7.3	187	MINOS
YEMCEM[e]	168	258	953	0.9	7.6	600	ZOOM
EGYPT[f]	281	618	3168	4.0	25.3	1551	ZOOM

[a]Measured in minutes.
[b]The problem is too big for MINOS. ZOOM was used instead.
[c]A nonlinear problem. 63% of the non-zeroes are nonlinear.
[d]A nonlinear problem. 58% of the non-zeroes are nonlinear.
[e]A mixed binary problem, with 55 binary variables (solved with a relative termination criterion of 10%).
[f]A linear problem, solved using XMP which is contained within ZOOM.

On DOS machines the GAMS limit and the solver (MINOS or ZOOM) limit are about equally troublesome, so both would need to be fixed to provide relief. We all expect that OS/2 (the new operating system from IBM/Microsoft) will allow much larger models to run on AT compatible machines without requiring a large investment in additional hardware.

There are a few other situations in which users see messages like "GAMS INTERNAL LIMIT." Most of these limits have been relaxed in version 2.05 of GAMS, and there is now only one that may cause trouble. If you have a LOOP statement containing many other statements it might be too big for an internal array. You will see a message like "TERMINATING FROM PROCEDURE PRESCAN." (The allowable size is different on different machines.) The only way to work around this difficulty is to break the LOOP into two or more LOOPS, if possible.

We have listed some GAMS limits in Table 17.2, so that you will have some idea of the sizes. We cannot define the terms precisely, but you should be aware that "instructions" are internal symbolic directives, and that a complicated GAMS assignment is represented internally by a large number of instructions.

Table 17.2: Limits in GAMS

	IBM DOS	*IBM CMS*
Number of instructions in a loop	1,000	5,000
Number of indices per identifier	10	10
Number of identifiers	16,383	16,383
Number of labels	16,383	16,383
Number of instructions compiled at one time	8,000	25,000
Nonlinear instructions per GAMS equation	32,767	1,048,576
Total nonlinear instructions generated	32,767	2,147,483,647

Table 17.3 lists limits in GAMS/MINOS and GAMS/BDMLP. These are limits that we have imposed because of implementation choices, *not* limits established by the original authors of the programs, and apply to all machines that allow the FORTRAN data type INTEGER*2. There are corresponding limits in ZOOM, but they are all so large that they are irrelevant.

Table 17.3: Limits in GAMS/MINOS and GAMS/BDMLP

	MINOS	*BDMLP*
Number of rows	32,767	32,767
Number of columns	32,767	32,767
Number of nonzero elements	2,147,483,647	32,767
Number of nonlinear nonzero elements	32,767	na

17.3   EFFICIENCY CONSIDERATIONS   ■

GAMS has been designed for generality and portability, and these twin goals often directly prevent efficient implementations. We will make some comments relevant to level 2.05 of GAMS, but warn readers that the situation will change as improvements are introduced. It is always wise to consider carefully whether to write things differently in an effort to speed them up. Our advice is to write things in the clearest and most natural way unless there are compelling reasons to do it differently.

The first comment has to do with assignments. Although data are stored sparse, GAMS has to loop over the product of the membership of the controlling sets when doing assignments. For instance, if you have an assignment whose left-hand side looks like:

```
X(A,B,C,D,E,F) = . . . . . ;
```

and if each set has 100 members, then GAMS has to do some multiple of 100^6 (i.e., $1.0E+12$) operations, which is quite simply impossible. (This number is larger than the age of the earth in years.) So the number and cardinality of the driving indices is very important, and clearly justifies changing the way things are done. Quite innocent-looking operations can be overwhelmingly expensive.

In many cases dollar controls can be used to limit the domain of an assignment or of an equation definition to logically allowable combinations of indices. (The [GTM] example from Chapter 8 is applicable. Instead of allowing *all* origin-destination pairs, the dollar restricts variables generated to pairs with pipeline links.) The gains from the use of such controls depends on the sparsity of the data, but improvements can be in both execution efficiency and economical use of memory.

The next comment concerns index order. Data structures are kept in lists in the internal label order, and assignments and equation generation are done by moving through these lists in order. It is easy and cheap to move forwards, but more expensive and difficult to move backwards. Consider the assignment below:

```
X(A,B,C) = 2 * Y(A,B,C) + 3 ;
```

After one particular value, let us say X("A1","B2","C3") has been set, we move on to the next, which is probably X("A1","B2","C4"), and this is an easy and cheap move. What is more important is that it is easy and cheap for Y as well: we remember where we are and take advantage of the natural order. Now imagine we had written (assuming a different declaration for Y):

```
X(A,B,C) = 2 * Y(C,B,A) + 3 ;
```

It is not easy or cheap to move from Y("C3","B2","A1") to Y("C4","B2","A1"): this involves "backing up" and then "moving forward." We have not given enough detail for you to understand exactly how this works: the important point is that if you are able to keep the indices in the same partial order within each identifier assignment and reference, things will go faster.

These warnings are irrelevant for small data structures. It is often worthwhile to compute mentally the product of the cardinality of the driving sets. This number is the most important determinant of how expensive an assignment or equation generation will be.

RELAXED PUNCTUATION 18

Punctuation makes a text written in any language easier to read and understand. GAMS is no exception. It makes liberal use of three main punctuation symbols: (1) semicolons, (2) commas, and (3) end-of-line (EOL). The most important of the three is the semicolon. Since it separates GAMS statements or units, a missing or misplaced semicolon can trigger difficult-to-understand error messages. A basic understanding of the way GAMS uses punctuation is therefore essential.

18.1 SEMICOLON ■

The semicolon is the strongest syntactic symbol in the language. It signals the completion or beginning of a unit or statement. Depending on one's personal taste and style, one of the following rules should be selected. All of them are complete and consistent.

- Every statement or unit in GAMS must end with a semicolon. The only exception is the last in a series of statements inside a LOOP.

- Every statement or unit must start with a semicolon. The only two exceptions are the first statement in a GAMS program and the first statement inside a LOOP.

- No semicolon is needed to separate statements or units. The only exceptions are statements not starting with a reserved symbol or word. These two statements are the assignment and the EQUATION definition statements, which have to be separated from the previous statement with a semicolon. The first assignment statement in a program or LOOP is excluded.

All three statements say the same thing. A syntactically required semicolon can be omitted if the next statement starts with a reserved word. The preferred style is to drop semicolons only at the end or beginning of a line and, of course, followed by a reserved word. The next three program fragments illustrate this style.

```
        Scalar X Parameter Y Positive Variable Z

or      Scalar X; Parameter Y; Positive Variable Z;

or      Scalar      X
        Parameter   Y
        Positive
        Variable    Z
```

A list of reserved words starting new units or statements is given below.

```
ABORT        ASSIGN     EQUATION[S]      INTEGER   OPTION[S]      SET[S]   SOS2
ACRONYM[S]   BINARY     FREE             LOOP      PARAMETER[S]   SOLVE    TABLE
ALIAS        DISPLAY    <identifier>     MODEL[S]  POSITIVE       SOS1     VARIABLE[S]
                                         NEGATIVE  SCALAR[S]
```

18.2   COMMA   ■

When a comma is used as a list separator, it can be omitted at the end or beginning of a line. The commas used to separate index positions should not be omitted, however. The following example illustrates this point:

```
SET  i with commas    / wheat, rice this is text that goes with rice ,
                        cotton ,
                        apples /
           j without commas / wheat
                        rice some text
                        cotton
                        apples /
```

18.3   END OF LINE   ■

An end-of-line can be used in place of a comma to terminate explanatory text or a data element, but not a data list (which requires a slash "/"). It may also be convenient to think of an end-of-line as a statement terminator that can replace a semicolon ";" if the following statement begins with a reserved word.

18.4   QUOTES   ■

Quotes can be single (') or double ("), but the ending quote must be the same as the starting quote. (A quote can therefore be included in a label or in text by using the other quote symbol as a delimiter.) Labels and text associated with symbol definitions can be quoted or unquoted. Most meaningful texts can be written without the use of quotes.

Unquoted labels can only contain letters, digits and the symbols "+" and "-." Unquoted text cannot start with ".." or "=" , must be separated by at least one space from the preceding symbol, and must be on the same line (otherwise the comma implied by end of the line will end the definition). Text is terminated by comma, slash, semicolon, or end-of-line. The following example illustrates these rules:

```
SET i "this is funny text set(i,j) ; "
      / 'single==' ,
        " d/ " /
```

Many users new to GAMS are confused by the fact that labels in set statements are not normally quoted, whereas labels appearing in assignments or equation definitions must be. It may help to realize that the difference is a natural consequence of relaxed punctuation. A program in which all labels and all explanatory text are quoted is not only legal input, but does not need to conform to the special rules that distinguish quoted and unquoted labels and text.

THE MODEL LIBRARY 19

19.1 INTRODUCTION ■

Professor Paul Samuelson is fond of saying that he hopes each generation of economists will be able to "stand on the shoulders" of the previous generation. The library of models included with the GAMS system is a reflection of this desire. We believe that the quality of modeling will be greatly improved and the productivity of modelers enhanced if each generation can stand on the shoulders of the previous generation by beginning with the previous models and enhancing and improving them. Thus the GAMS system includes a large library of 100 models, collectively called GAMSLIB.

The models included have been selected not only because they collectively provide strong shoulders for new users to stand on, but also because they represent interesting and sometimes classic problems. For example the trade-off between consumption and investment is richly illustrated in the Ramsey problem, which can be solved using nonlinear programming methods. Examples of other problems included in the library are production and shipment by firms, investment planning in time and space, cropping patterns in agriculture, operation of oil refineries and petrochemical plants, macroeconomic stabilization, applied general equilibrium, international trade in aluminum and in copper, water distribution networks, and relational databases.

Another criterion for including models in the library is that they illustrate the modeling capabilities that GAMS offers. For example, the mathematical specification of cropping patterns can be represented handily in GAMS. Another example of the system's capability is the style for specifying initial solutions as starting points in the search for the optimal solution of dynamic nonlinear optimization problems.

Finally, some models have been selected for inclusion because they have been used in other modeling systems. Examples are network problems and production planning models. These models permit the user to compare how problems are set up and solved in different modeling systems.

On most mainframe computer systems the models will be stored with the GAMS system files, and can be copied into your working directory as needed by using the GAMSLIB command. Additional information on how to access the library can be obtained by typing

```
GAMSLIB or GAMSLIB ?
```

The computer will respond by displaying instructions on how to access specific models and how to get more information about the models in the library.

On personal computer systems the model library is available on several 360 kilobyte diskettes. Files must be copied to your hard disk using the DOS copy command. If you choose to keep the entire library (1.2 megabytes) on your hard disk, then a supplied GAMSLIB procedure (.BAT file) can be used to copy models between subdirectories, either by specifying a model name or a sequence number.

Some of the models in the library are large and expensive to solve: a few are too large to solve on a DOS-based personal computer, and these are marked with an asterisk in Section 19.2. In general, the more lines there are in the input file, the larger the resulting model will be.

Some of the models containing integer or binary variables are solved as RMIPs, which means that the default linear solver can be used. Others are solved as MIPs, which means that a mixed integer solver must be available: otherwise these models will produce error messages. However, if the MIP specification is changed to RMIP, then the models will compile and the relaxed problem (see Chapter 9 for a complete discussion of the difference) will be solved.

Similarly, if your GAMS system has no nonlinear solver (NLP) you will not be able to solve nonlinear models. The models in the library are characterized by solution method in Section 19.2.

Some of the models in the library contain option statements to control the solve statements. If a model is known to take more than 1000 iterations to solve, then it is likely that an OPTION ITERLIM will have been used to prevent the default limit of 1000 from causing premature termination. If there is more than one solve statement, then LIMCOL and LIMROW will probably have been used to suppress equation and column listings for SOLVES after the first. Some of the MIP models also have non-default settings for OPTCR and OPTCA.

19.2   THE MODELS   ■

This section contains a listing of each model by area of application, its sequence number and the model name (models marked with an asterisk are too large to be solved on a personal computer, e.g., *TURKEY), the number of lines in the model, and columns indicating the number of linear (LP), nonlinear (NLP), and mixed integer (MIP) solve statements in each model. This is followed by a last column citing reference names in the next section (Section 19.3).

Agricultural Economics	Sequence Number	Name	Number of Lines	LP	NLP	MIP	Reference
Chance Constrained Feed Mix Problem	26	CHANCE	48	1	1		BRAC68
Farm Credit and Income Distribution Model	49	SARF	488	1			HUSA77
Pakistan Punjab Livestock Model	55	PAKLIVE	176	1			WB 77A
Organic Fertilizer Use in Intensive Farming	56	CHINA	398	1			WIEN85
Egypt Agricultural Model	75	EGYPT	900	1			KUTC80
Turkey Agricultural Model with Risk	86	*TURKEY	1132	1	2		LESI82
North-East Brazil Regional Agricultural Model	87	*NEBRAZIL	1049	5			KUTC81
Agricultural Farm Level Model of NE Brazil	88	AGRESTE	310	2			KUTC81
Indus Surface Water Network Submodule	89	ISWNM	684				DULO84
Indus Agricultural Model	90	INDUS	1062	1			DULO84
Simple Farm Level Model	91	DEMO1	130	1			KUTC88
Nonlinear Simple Agricultural Sector Model	92	DEMO7	235	1	1		KUTC88

*Model is too large to be solved on a personal computer.

	Sequence Number	Name	Number of Lines	LP	NLP	MIP	Reference
Applied General Equilibrium							
Cameroon General Equilibrium Model	81	CAMCGE	444		1		COND87
Macroeconomic Framework for India	97	GANGES	1349		1		MITR86
General Equilibrium Model for Korea	100	KORCGE	474		1		LEWI86
Chemistry and Chemical Engineering							
Alkylation Process Optimization	20	PROCESS	76		2		BRAC68
Chemical Equilibrium Problem	21	CHEM	46		1		BRAC68
Chemical Equilibrium Problem	76	WALL	24		1		WALL87
Econometrics							
Linear Regression with Various Criteria	23	LINEAR	103	1	12		BRAC68
Nonlinear Regression Problem	24	LEAST	44		2		BRAC68
Maximum Likelihood Estimation	25	LIKE	52		1		BRAC68
Economic Development							
Substitution and Structural Change	33	CHENERY	229		1		CHEN79
Optimal Patterns of Growth and Aid	34	PAK	127	1			CHEN79B
DINAMICO, A Dynamic Multisectoral, Multiskill	35	DINAM	849	1			MANN73
Market Equilibrium and Activity Analysis	41	PROLOG	175		3		NORT81
Savings Model by Ramsey	63	RAMSEY	130		1		RAMS26
Energy Economics							
Optimal Pricing and Extraction for OPEC	28	PINDYCK	54		1		PIND78
Investment Planning in the Oil Shale Industry	46	SHALE	707	1			MELT82
OPEC Trade and Production	47	OTPOP	105		1		BLIT75
Investment Planning in the Korean Oil-Petro Indst	48	*KORPET	495			1	SUH 81
Single-Region Contingency Planning Model	52	SRCPM	199	1	1		MANN82
International Gas Trade Model	53	GTM	156		1		MANN84
Turkey Power Planning Model	54	TURKPOW	215	1			TURV77
Tabora Rural Development—Fuelwood Production	57	TABORA	160	7			WB 77B
ETA-MACRO Energy Model for the USA	80	ETAMAC	267		1		MANN77
Strategic Petroleum Reserve	82	MARKOV	67	1			TEIS81
Industrial Pollution Control	96	POLLUT	99		1		MANG73
Engineering							
Structural Optimization	22	SHIP	87		1		BRAC68
Design of a Water Distribution Network	68	WATER	107		1		BROO85
Finance							
Simple Portfolio Model	50	PORT	38	1	2		CDC 84
Repayment Factors for Loans	72	REPAY	38				BROO88
Forestry							
Antalya Forestry Model—Steady State	61	TFORSS	160	4			BERG80
Antalya Forestry Model—Dynamic	62	TFORDY	235	2			BERG80
International Trade							
World Aluminum Model	31	*ALUM	1760			1	BROW83
Modeling Investment in the World Copper Industry	45	*COPPER	910			1	DAMM85
Macroeconomics							
A Miniature Version of Orani 78	40	ORANI	230	1	2		KEND84
Optimal Growth Model	43	CHAKRA	59		1		KEND71
Linear Quadratic Control Problem	64	ABEL	89		1		KEND82
Household Optimization Problem by Fair	69	HHFAIR	86		1		FAIR84

*Model is too large to be solved on a personal computer.

Management/Operations Research	Sequence Number	Name	Number of Lines	LP	NLP	MIP	Reference
A Transportation Problem	1	TRNSPORT	66	1			DANT63
Blending Problem I	2	BLEND	47	2			DANT63
A Production Mix Problem	3	PRODMIX	38	1			DANT63
Simple Warehouse Problem	4	WHOUSE	39	1			DANT63
On-the-Job Training	5	JOBT	51	1			DANT63
The Shortest Route Problem	6	SROUTE	52	1			DANT63
Aircraft Allocation Under Uncertain Demand	8	AIRCRAFT	107	2			DANT63
APEX—Production Scheduling Model	9	PRODSCH	139			1	CDC 80
ARCNET—Production Distribution and Inventory	10	PDI	116	1			ARC 82
UIMP—Production Scheduling Problem	11	UIMP	123	2			ELLI82
Magic Power Scheduling Problem	12	MAGIC	74			1	WILL72
Weapons Assignment	18	WEAPONS	59		1		BRAC68
Relational Database Example	29	ZLOOF	121				ZLOO77
Elementary Production and Inventory Model	37	ROBERT	57	1			FOUR83
Opencast Mining	39	MINE	58	1			WILL78
Ajax Paper Company Production Schedule	60	AJAX	68	1			CDC 84A
Platoform Example Refinery	65	FAWLEY	281	1			PALM84
AMPL Sample Problem	74	AMPL	54	1			FOUR87
Aluminum Alloy Smelter Sample Problem	79	IBM1	114	5			IBM 79
Minimum Spanning Tree	94	MST	52				HILL67
Thai Navy Problem	98	THAI	80			1	CHOY86
Shortest Route Algorithm	93	SROUTEX	53				DANT63

Mathematics

	Sequence Number	Name	Number of Lines	LP	NLP	MIP	Reference
Area of Hexagon Test Problem	36	HIMMEL16	53		1		HIMM72
Three-Dimensional Noughts and Crosses	42	CUBE	57			1	WILL74
Piecewise Linear Approximation	59	IMSL	102	2			IMSL84
Examples of Extended Arithmetic	67	CRAZY	106				BROO88
Simple Gaussian Elimination	70	PIVOT	31				BROO88
Matrix Inversion with Full Pivoting	71	GAUSS	59				BROO88
Great Circle Distances	73	GREAT	72				BROO88
Rosenbrock Test Function	83	RBROCK	15		1		ROSE60
Nonlinear Test Problem	84	MHW4D	22		1		WRIG76
Himmelblau Testproblem Number 11	95	HIMMEL11	29		1		HIMM72
House Plan Design	99	HOUSE	46		1		BORL87

Microeconomics

	Sequence Number	Name	Number of Lines	LP	NLP	MIP	Reference
Stigler's Nutrition Model	7	DIET	54	1			DANT63
Egypt—Static Fertilizer Model	13	FERTS	427	1			CHOK80
Egypt—Dynamic Fertilizer Model	14	FERTD	690			1	CHOK80
Mexico Steel—Small Static	15	MEXSS	192	1			KEND84
Mexico Steel—Small Dynamic	16	*MEXSD	333			1	KEND84
Mexico Steel—Large Static	17	MEXLS	1241	1			KEND84
Bid Evaluation	19	BID	75			1	BRAC68
Vietoriscz/Manne Fertilizer Model 1961	30	VIETMAN	122			2	VIET63
Mini Oil Refining Model	32	MARCO	191	2			KEND81
Sample Database of the US Economy	38	RDATA	157			1	KEND82
Andean Fertilizer Model	44	ANDEAN	1399	3		1	MENN86
Yemen Cement Model	51	YEMCEM	319			1	WB 82
Economies of Scale and Investment over Time	58	WESTMIP	191	1		1	CHEN79A
Morocco Fertilizer Distribution—Mode Selection	66	*MSM	268	5			MEER85
Sea Distances for World Phosphate Model	78	*PHOSDIS	625	7			MEER85
Models of Spatial Competition	85	HARKER	146		11		HARK86

*Model is too large to be solved on a personal computer.

Statistics	Sequence Number	Name	Number of Lines	LP	NLP	MIP	Reference
Stratified Sample Design	27	SAMPLE	58		2		BRAC68
Social Accounting Matrix Balancing Problem	77	SAMBAL	50		1		ZENI86

19.3 REFERENCES ■

ARC 82 Analysis, Research and Computation Inc. (1982), *Arcnet User Guide*, Austin, Texas.

BERG80 Bergendorff, H., P. Glenshaw, and A. Meeraus (1980), *The Planning of Investment Programs in the Paper Industry*, The World Bank, Washington, D.C.

BLIT75 Blitzer, C., A. Meeraus, and A. Stoutjesdijk (1975), "A Dynamic Model of OPEC Trade and Production," *Journal of Development Economics*, Number 2, pp. 318–35.

BORL87 Borland (1987), *EUREKA: The Solver*, Borland International, Scotts Valley, California.

BRAC68 Bracken, J., and G.P. McCormick (1963), *Selected Applications of Nonlinear Programming*, John Wiley and Sons, New York and London.

BROO85 Brooke, A., A. Drud, and A. Meeraus (1985), "Modeling Systems and Nonlinear Programming in a Research Enviroment," in R. Raghavan and S. M. Rohde (eds.), *Computers in Engineering 1985*, The American Society of Mechanical Engineers, New York.

BROO88 Brooke, A., D. Kendrick, and A. Meeraus (1988), *GAMS: A User's Guide*, The Scientific Press, Redwood City, California.

BROW83 Brown, M., A. Dammert, A. Meeraus, and A. Stoutjesdijk (1983), "Worldwide Investment Analysis—The Case of Aluminum," World Bank Staff Working Paper Number 603, The World Bank, Washington, D.C.

CDC 80 Control Data Corporation (1980), *Apex-III Reference Manual Vers. 1.2*, PN 76070000, Minneapolis.

CDC 84 Control Data Corporation (1984), *IFPS/OPTIMUM User's Guide*, Minneapolis.

CDC 84A Control Data Corporation (1984), "PDS/APEX Sample Model Library," Cybernet, Minneapolis.

CHEN79 Chenery, H. B. (1979), *Structural Change and Development Policy*, Oxford University Press, New York and Oxford.

CHEN79A Chenery, H. B., and L. Westphal (1979), "Economies of Scale and Investment over Time," in H. B. Chenery (ed.), *Structural Change and Development Policy*, Oxford University Press, New York and Oxford.

CHEN79B Chenery, H. B., and A. MacEwan (1979), "Optimal Pattern of Growth and Aid," in H. B. Chenery (ed.), *Structural Change and Development Policy*, Oxford University Press, New York and Oxford.

CHOK80 Choksi, A. M., A. Meeraus, and A. Stoutjesdijk (1980), *The Planning of Investment Programs in the Fertilizer Industry*, The Johns Hopkins University Press, Baltimore and London.

CHOY86 Choypeng, P., P. Puakpong, and R. E. Rosenthal (1986), "Optimal Ship Routing and Personnel Assignment for Naval Recruitment in Thailand," *Interfaces*, Volume 16, Number 4, pp. 356–66.

COND87   Condon, T., H. Dahl, and S. Devarajan, "Implementing a Computable General Equilibrium Model on GAMS: The Cameroon Model," DRD Discussion Paper 290, The World Bank, Washington, D.C.

DAMM85   Dammert, A., and S. Palaniappan (1985), *Modeling Investment in the World Copper Sector*, The University of Texas Press, Austin, Texas.

DANT63   Dantzig, G. B. (1963), *Linear Programming and Extensions*, Princeton University Press, Princeton, New Jersey.

DAY 82   Day, R. E., and H. P. Williams (1982), "Magic—The Design and Use of an Interactive Modeling Language for Mathematical Programming," Department of Business Studies, University of Edinburgh, Edinburgh.

DULO84   Duloy, J. H., and G. T. O'Mara (1984), "Issues of Efficiency and Interdependence in Water Resource Investments: Lessons from the Indus Basin of Pakistan," World Bank Staff Working Paper Number 665, The World Bank, Washington, D.C.

ELLI82   Ellison, E.F.D., and G. Mitra (1982), "UIMP—User Interface for Mathematical Programming," *ACM Transactions on Mathematical Software*, Volume 8, Number 2.

FAIR84   Fair, R. (1984), *Specification, Estimation and Analysis of Macroeconomic Models*, Harvard University Press, Cambridge, Massachusetts.

FOUR83   Fourer, R. (1983), "Modeling Languages Versus Matrix Generators for Linear Programming," *ACM Transaction of Mathematical Software*, Volume 9, Number 2, pp. 143–83.

FOUR87   Fourer, R., D. M. Gay, and B. W. Kernighan (1987), "AMPL: A Mathematical Programming Language," Computing Science Technical Report 133, AT&T Bell Laboratories, Murray Hill, New Jersey.

HARK86   Harker, P.T. (1986), "Alternative Models for Spatial Competition," *Operations Research*, Volume 34, Number 3, pp. 410–25.

HILL67   Hillier, F. S., and G. J. Lieberman (1967), *Introduction to Operations Research*, Holden-Day, San Francisco.

HIMM72   Himmelblau, D. M. (1972), *Applied Nonlinear Programming*, McGraw Hill, New York.

HUSA77   Husain, T., and R. Inman (1977), "A Model For Estimating the Effects of Credit Pricing on Farm Level Employment and Income Distribution," World Bank Staff Working Paper Number 261, The World Bank, Washington, D.C.

IBM 78   IBM (1978), *MPSX/370 Introduction to the Extended Control Language*, Document Number SH19-1147-1, IBM, Endicot, New York.

IBM 79   IBM (1979), *MPSX/370 Primer*, Document Number GH19-1091-1, IBM, Endicot, New York.

IMSL84   IMSL (1984), "LP/PROTRAN—A Problem Solving System for Linear Programming," IMSL Inc., Houston, Texas.

KEND71   Kendrick, D., and L. Taylor (1971), "Numerical Methods and Nonlinear Optimization Models for Economic Planning," in H. Chenery (ed.) *Studies of Development Planning*, Harvard University Press, Cambridge, Massachusetts.

KEND81   Kendrick, D., A. Meeraus, and J. S. Suh (1981), "Oil Refinery Modeling with the GAMS Language," Center for Energy Studies, Research Report Number 14, The University of Texas, Austin, Texas.

KEND82 Kendrick, D. (1982), "A Relational Database of the US Economy," in C. P. Kindleberger and G. DiTella (eds.), *Economics in the Long View*, MacMillan, London.

KEND82A Kendrick, D. (1982), "Caution and Probing in a Macroeconomic Model," *Journal of Economic Dynamics and Control*, Volume 4, Number 2.

KEND84 Kendrick D., A. Meeraus, and J. Alatorre (1984), *The Planning of Investment Programs in the Steel Industry*, The Johns Hopkins University Press, Baltimore and London.

KEND84A Kendrick, D. (1984), "Style in Multisector Modeling," in A. J. Hughes-Hallet (ed.), *Applied Decision Analysis and Economic Behavior*, Kluwer and Nijhoff, Boston and The Hague.

KUTC80 Kutcher, G. (1980), "The Agro-economic Model," Technical Report Number 16, Master Plan for Water and Resources Development, UNDP-EGY/73/024, Cairo.

KUTC81 Kutcher, G., and P. Scandizzo (1981), *The Agricultural Economy of Northeast Brazil*, The Johns Hopkins University Press, Baltimore and London.

KUTC88 Kutcher, G., A. Meeraus, and G. T. O'Mara (1988), "Modeling for Agricultural Policy and Project Analysis," The World Bank, Washington, D.C.

LESI82 Le-Si, V., P. Scandizzo, and H. Kasnagoklu, "Turkey Agricultural Sector Model," AGREP Working Paper Number 67, The World Bank, Washington, D.C.

LEWI86 Lewis, J., and S. Robinson (1986), Chapter 11 in *Industrialization and Growth: A Comparative Study*, edited by H. B. Chenery, S. Robinson, and M. Syrquin, Oxford University Press, London.

MANG73 Mangasarian, O. L. (1973), *Nonlinear Programming*, McGraw Hill, New York.

MANN73 Manne, A. S. (1973), "Dinamico, A Multisector, Multiskill Model," in L. M. Goreux and A. S. Manne (eds.), *Multilevel Planning: Case Studies in Mexico*, North-Holland, Amsterdam.

MANN77 Manne, A. S. (1977), "ETA-MACRO: A Model of Energy-Economy Interactions," in C. J. Hitch (ed.), *Modeling Energy-Economy Interactions*, Resources for the Future, Washington, D.C.

MANN82 Manne, A. S., C. R. Nelson, K. C. So, and J. P. Weyant (1982), "CPM: A Contingency Planning Model of the International Oil Market," International Energy Report, Stanford University, Stanford.

MANN84 Manne, A. S., and M. A. Beltramo (1984), "GTM: An International Gas Trade Model," International Energy Report, Stanford University, Stanford.

MEER85 Meeraus, A., and Y. Smeers (1985), "Transport Cost Estimates via Linear Programming," The World Bank, Washington, D.C.

MELT82 Melton, J. W.(1982), "An Investment Planning Model for an Oil Shale Industry in the Piceance Basin," Center for Economic Research, University of Texas, Austin, Texas.

MENN86 Mennes, L., and A. Stoutjesdijk (1986), *Multicountry Investment Analysis*, The John Hopkins University Press, Baltimore and London.

MITR86 Mitra, P., and S. Tendulkar (1986), "Coping with Internal and External Exogenous Shocks: India, 1973/74 to 1983/84," CPD Discussion Paper Number 1986/21, The World Bank, Washington, D.C.

MURT82   Murtagh, B. A., and M. A. Sauders (1982), "A Projected Lagrangian Algorithm and Its Implementation for Sparse Nonlinear Constraints," *Mathematical Programming Study 16*, pp. 84–117.

NORT81   Norton, R., and P. L. Scandizzo (1981), "Market Equilibrium Computations in Activity Analysis Models," *Operations Research*, Volume 29, Number 2.

PALM84   Palmer, K. H. (1985), *A Model Management Framework for Mathematical Programming*, Exxon Monograph Series, John Wiley and Sons, New York.

PIND78   Pindyck, R. S. (1978), "Gains to Producers from the Cartelization of Exhaustible Resources," *Review of Economics and Statistics*, Volume 60, pp. 238–51.

RAMS26   Ramsey, F. P. (1926), "A Mathematical Theory of Savings," *Economics Journal*.

ROSE60   Rosenbrock, H. H. (1960), "An Automatic Method for Finding the Greatest and Least Value of a Function," *Computer Journal*, Volume 3, pp. 175–84.

SUH 81   Suh, J. S. (1981), "An Investment Planning Model for the Oil-Refining and Petrochemical Industries in Korea," Center for Economic Research, University of Texas, Austin, Texas.

TEIS81   Teisberg, T.J. (1986), "A Dynamic Programming Model of the U.S. Strategic Petroleum Reserve," *Bell Journal of Economics*, Autumn 1981.

TURV77   Turvey, R., and D. Anderson (1977), *Electricity Economics: Essays and Case Studies*, Chapter 8, Johns Hopkins University Press, Baltimore and London.

VIET63   Vietoriscz, T., and A. S. Manne (1963), "Chemical Processes, Plant Location and Economies of Scale," in A. S. Manne and H. M. Markowitz (eds.), *Studies in Process Analysis*, John Wiley and Sons, New York.

WALL87   Wall, T. W., D. Greening, and R.E.D. Woolsey (1987), "Solving Complex Chemical Equilibria Using a Geometric Programming Based Technique," *Operations Research*, Volume 34, Number 3.

WB 77A   World Bank (1977), "Pakistan Punjab Livestock Project: Staff Project Report," Report Number 1193-PAK, Annexes I and II, Washington, D.C.

WB 77B   World Bank (1977), "Tanzania: Appraisal of the Tabora Rural Development Project," Report Number 1360-TA, Annex 7, Washington, D.C.

WB 82   World Bank (1982), "Yemen Arab Republic—Manufacturing Industry: Performance, Policies and Prospects," Report Number 3651-YAR, Appendix II, Washington, D.C.

WIEN85   Wiens, T. B. (1985), "The Economics of High-Yield Agriculture in China: Triple-Cropping at the Baimano People's Commune," The World Bank, Washington, D.C.

WILL74   Williams, H. P. (1974), "Experiments in the Formulation of Integer Programming," *Mathematical Programming Study 2*.

WILL78   Williams, H. P. (1978), *Model Building in Mathematical Programming*, John Wiley and Sons, New York.

WRIG76   Wright, M. H. (1976), "Numerical Methods for Nonlinearly Constraint Optimization," Ph.D. dissertation, Stanford University, Stanford.

ZENI86   Zenios, S. A., A. Drud, and J. M. Mulvey (1986), "Balancing Some Large Social Accounting Matrices with Nonlinear Network Programming," Technical Report, Department of Civil Engineering, Princeton University, Princeton.

ZLOO77   Zloof, M. M. (1977), "Query-By-Example: A Database Language," *IBM Systems Journal*, Volume 16, Number 5, pp. 324–43.

APPENDICES

THE GAMS CALL A

The entire GAMS system appears to the user as a single program that reads the input file and produces an output file. Several options are available at this level to define the overall layout of the output page, and when to save and restore the entire environment. Although details will vary with the type of computer and operating system used, the general operating principles are the same on all machines. For your particular machine we recommend that you follow the instructions in the online documentation, which can be found by issuing the command "GAMS" and following the instructions that are produced. We give details for three popular machines below.

One very important point is system initialization. All GAMS systems require that an access path be established to the program files. How this is done is machine specific. On DOS-based personal computers a "path" must be established, and this is normally done at the time the system is installed; GAMS is then automatically available to all users of the machine. Complete details about the installation process are given in the Installation Section at the end of this manual. On mainframe computers an operating system command file must be executed at "login" time, separately for each user needing GAMS access. Your GAMS coordinator can show you how to do this, and can probably arrange for it to be done automatically. You will not even be able to find the online help file until the access mechanism is set up.

A.1 THE GENERIC "NO FRILLS" GAMS CALL ∎

The simplest way to start GAMS is to enter the command

```
GAMS "file"
```

from the system prompt and GAMS will compile and execute the GAMS statements in the file "file." If a file with this name cannot be found, GAMS on MS-DOS micros or VMS VAX machines will look for a file with the extended name "file.GMS." On IBM/CMS mainframes the input file must be "file GAMS A." The output will be written on the disk file "file.LST" on DOS machines, "file.LIS" on VAXes and "file LISTING A" on IBM/CMS mainframes.

A.2   THE GENERIC "OPTION" CALL   ■

The option call allows more flexibility. It is the same as the "no frills" call except that it is followed by a sequence of keyword-value pairs drawn from the list below. Restart and save were discussed in detail in Chapter 14 on work files. The details given below apply specifically to personal computers running DOS, but the principles apply to all.

```
SAVE = "filename-stem"
S = "filename-stem"
```

This option causes GAMS to save files that will enable the problem to be restarted and extended later. Restart files are not created unless this option is specified and no detectable errors occur. The files saved have a unique naming convention depending on the system, and any existing files with these names are overwritten.

```
RESTART = "filename-stem"
R = "filename-stem"
```

This option is used to restart from previously saved SAVE files. The default is not to restart, but to assume that the input file contains a complete problem definition.

```
PW = "integer"
```

This is used to alter the print width (maximum output line length in characters) on the GAMS output file. The default value depends on the computer system but is usually 79 or 130. Many GAMS models from mainframes have input lines that wrap with small settings, and one may want to increase PW to make the compiler listing more readable. The minimum value for PW is 72, and the maximum is normally 255, although on some machines it is only 137. (Consult your online help to find out.) Beware: many printers cannot print files having lines longer than some limit: 137 characters is a common maximum for traditional mainframe printers.

```
PS = "integer"
```

This is used to set the maximum number of lines printed per page, with a page break issued after this many lines or at the beginning of a new logical page. The default is normally 60, and this is also used if a value less than 30 is entered. Users with laser printers may need to use a smaller value (55 should be safe) to avoid spurious page breaks when output files are printed. The largest legal value for PS is 9999. The user may elect PS = 9999 to prevent page headers from breaking up output viewed on the screen, or to make it easier for the output to be processed by another program.

```
O = "filename"
```

This is used to give the output file a name of your choice. On some operating systems, notably IBM CMS, this option does not exist.

```
A = "string"
```

This is used for those rare cases when you do not want to execute the input file after compiling it. If you specify "A=C" GAMS will stop after compiling the input file.

A.3 EXAMPLES OF CALLING SEQUENCES FOR MS-DOS MICROS ■

GAMS TRNSPORT

This statement compiles and executes the example problem TRNSPORT.GMS from the distribution diskette. The output goes to the disk file TRNSPORT.LST and the output line length is 79 characters.

GAMS TRNSPORT O=CON

This statement also compiles and executes TRNSPORT.GMS, but the output goes directly to the DOS device CON, (console i.e., the screen). If you toggle [Ctrl-P] it will be echoed to your printer simultaneously.

GAMS RAMSEY PW=130

This statement compiles and executes the example problem RAMSEY.GMS from the distribution diskette. The output goes to the disk file RAMSEY.LST and the output line length is 130 characters. The file cannot be 'typed' without suffering from line wrap, but various editors and listing programs can be used to view it without wrap. It can be printed on 8.5 inch paper with the printer in 'compressed' mode (mode lpt1:132) or normally on 14 inch paper.

GAMS TRNSPORT SAVE=XX
GAMS CTRNSPRT RESTART=XX

This two-step sequence shows how to do restarts. The first step is the compilation and execution of TRNSPORT.GMS from the distribution diskettes, with files for restarting the problem being saved as XX.G01 to XX.G08 where XX is a filename of the user's choice. The second step is a restart of this model, with the file CTRNSPRT.GMS (also distributed with GAMS) containing a continuation of the problem definition.

A.4 EXAMPLES OF CALLING SEQUENCES FOR IBM CMS SYSTEMS ■

GAMS GAMS1

This is the standard no frills call for CMS. The input file in this case is "GAMS1 GAMS A" and the output file will be "GAMS1 LISTING A." The output line length is normally 130 characters, but may be changed by individual sites. It is not possible to give the output file a different name.

GAMS GAMS1 PW 80 SAVE GAMS1SAV

Notice that on CMS the separator between the keyword and value (for example between "PW" and "80") is a blank and not an "=" sign as on the PC. The work files in this case will be named "GAMS1SAV WORK1 A" to "GAMS1SAV WORK8 A" (eight files as always). There is a useful shorthand for for IBM CMS only: a single equals sign "=" means "use the name provided for the input file." So the command

GAMS GAMS1 SAVE =

means that the names of the saved work files will be "GAMS1 WORK1 A" to "GAMS1 WORK8 A."

A.5   EXAMPLES OF CALLING SEQUENCES FOR VAX VMS SYSTEMS   ■

```
GAMS GAMS1
```

This is also the standard no frills call for VMS. The input file in this case is "GAMS1" or, if this file does not exist, "GAMS1.GMS." The output file will be "GAMS1.LIS." The output line length is normally 130 characters, but may be changed by individual sites. The output file name can be changed with the "O" keyword as on the personal computer:

```
GAMS GAMS1 O=SYS$OUTPUT PW=79
```

This command puts the output on the screen with 79 character lines (the longest that will not overflow). The separator on VMS is again the "=," and blanks are *not* allowed on either side of it.

```
GAMS GAMS1 PW=80 SAVE=GAMS1SAV
```

This is how work files are saved. In this case the files will be called GAMS1SAV.G01 to GAMS1SAV.G08.

DOLLAR CONTROL OPTIONS B

The Dollar Control Options (DCO) are used to indicate compiler directives and options. DCOs are not part of the GAMS language and must be entered on separate lines recognized by a "$" symbol in the first column. A DCO line may be placed anywhere within a GAMS program. The "$" symbol is followed by one or more options identified by spaces. Since the DCOs are not part of the GAMS language, they do not appear on the compiler listing unless an error had been detected. DCO lines are not case sensitive and a continued compilation uses the previous settings.

The DCOs are grouped into three major functional categories controlling (1) input format, (2) output format, and (3) reference maps.

A summary of all the DCOs is given in Table B.1.

B.1 INPUT FORMAT CONTROLS ■

DCOs in this group determine the interpretation of the input file and can therefore alter the meaning of a GAMS program. They can be used to change the "$" symbol or the "*" symbol into other symbols, to set the left and right margin of interpreted text, and to skip over input text. The eight options in this group are:

DOLLAR <char>   Changes the current "$" symbol to <char>, which can be any character except the current "$" or "*" symbol.

COMMENT <char>   Changes the current "*" symbol to <char>, which can be any character except the current "$" or "*" symbol.

MINCOL <int>   Sets the left margin to column number <int>; text in columns 1 to <int> -1 will be ignored.

MAXCOL <int>   Sets the right margin to column number <int>; text in columns <int> +1 to 120 will be ignored.

ONTEXT   All lines following will be treated as comments until a closing $OFFTEXT is encountered; line numbers in the compiler listing will be supressed to mark the skipped lines.

OFFTEXT   Ends an ONTEXT sequence; no spaces are allowed between the "$" symbol and "OFFTEXT."

ONDIGIT   Turns on the precision check on numbers; if the stated precison of a number exceeds the machine precison an error will be reported; the maximum number of digits for popular machines is as shown below:

IBM PC	10
Burroughs	12
IBM CMS and MVS	15
Apollo	15
VAX Unix	16
VAX VMS	16

OFFDIGIT   Turns off the precision check on numbers; numbers will be rounded to fit into machine precison.

Table B.1: Dollar Control Option Summary

Option		Description
COMMENT	< char >	sets the comment character to < char >
DOLLAR	< char >	sets the dollar character to < char >
DOUBLE		double spaced listing follows
EJECT		advance to next page
HIDDEN	< text >	ignore < text > and do not list
LINES	< int >	next < int > lines have to fit on page
MAXCOL	< int >	ignore text beyond < int > column
MINCOL	< int >	ignore text before < int > column
OFFDIGIT		off number precison check
OFFDOLLAR		off DCO listing
OFFMARGIN		off margin marking
OFFSYMLIST		off symbol list
OFFSYMXREF		off symbol cross reference listing
OFFTEXT		off text mode
OFFUELLIST		off unique element listing
OFFUELXREF		off unique element cross reference
OFFUPPER		off upper case printing
ONDIGIT		on number precision check
ONDOLLAR		on DCO listing
ONMARGIN		on margin marking
ONSYMLIST		on symbol list
ONSYMXREF		on symbol cross reference listing
ONTEXT		on text mode—following lines are comments
ONUELLIST		on unique element listing
ONUELXREF		on unique element cross reference listing
ONUPPER		on upper case printing
SINGLE		single spaced listing follows
STITLE	< text >	set subtitle and reset page
TITLE	< text >	set title, reset subtitle and page

All DCOs are interpreted from column one to MAXCOL and the minimum value for MAXCOL is 15, in order to permit a resetting if needed. The compiler is initialized to use "$" and "*" for the DOLLAR and COMMENT symbol, MINCOL and MAXCOL are set to 1 and 120, OFFTEXT and ONDIGITS are in effect. Any change in the margins via MAXCOL or MINCOL will be reported in the listing file with the message that gives the valid range of input columns. For example, the DCO $MINCOL 20 MAXCOL 110 will trigger the message NEW MARGIN = 20-110.

Non-default settings are reported before the file summary at the end of a GAMS listing as a reminder for future continued compilations. This is only relevant if a restart file has been requested with the GAMS call.

Computers work with different internal precisions. Sometimes a GAMS program has to be moved from a machine with high precision to one with a lower precision. Instead of changing numbers that have too much precision, i.e., too many digits, the $OFFDIGIT control option can be used to tell GAMS to use as much precision as possible and ignore the remaining digits.

B.2 OUTPUT FORMAT CONTROLS ■

The DCOs in this group only change the format of the compiler listing, leaving the meaning of the input file unaltered. Their main use is to control page breaks and page headings. The thirteen options are:

TITLE < text >   Sets the title in the page header to < text > and clears the subtitle to blanks; the next output line will appear on a new page.

STITLE < text >   Sets the subtitle in the page header to < text > ; the next output line will appear on a new page.

EJECT   Advances the output to a new page.

LINES < int >   Guarantees that the next < int > lines will fit on the same or current page; may advance to the next page.

SINGLE   Single-spaced listing follows.

DOUBLE   Double-spaced listing follows.

HIDDEN < text >   < text > will be ignored; used to write comments only relevant to the person manipulating the file.

ONMARGIN   Turns the margin marking on.

OFFMARGIN   Turns the margin marking off.

ONDOLLAR   Turns the listing of DCO lines on.

OFFDOLLAR   Tturns the listing of DCO lines off.

ONUPPER   Following lines will be printed in uppercase.

OFFUPPER   Following lines will be printed as entered.

The system is initialized as follows:

```
$TITLE GENERAL ALGEBRAIC MODELING SYSTEM
$SINGLE OFFMARGIN OFFDOLLAR ONUPPER
```

The definition of the page size (width and length) cannot be changed with a DCO, but rather with the PW and PS parameters in the GAMS call (see Appendix A).

B.3 REFERENCE MAP CONTROLS ■

At the end of the compilation listing various cross reference maps stating the location and context of GAMS symbols or identifiers are listed. These eight options are:

ONSYMXREF OFFSYMXREF	Symbols following this line will (not) be contained in the symbol cross reference list and (not) in a symbol list by type.
ONSYMLIST OFFSYMLIST	The compiler will (not) generate a list of all symbols and their text in alphabetical order, grouped by symbol type.
ONUELLIST OFFUELLIST	The compiler will (not) generate a list of all unique elements in alphabetical and entry order.
ONUELXREF OFFUELXREF	The elements following this line will (not) be contained in the unique element cross reference list.

The system is initialized as follows:

```
$ONSYMXREF OFFUELLIST OFFUELXREF
```

B.4 EXAMPLE ■

The input and output files for a simple example are shown below. The use of the reference map control options is not demonstrated in this example because their use is explained in detail in the section on reference maps (see Chapter 10).

```
$TITLE Dollar Control Option Tests (dcotest)
*  Lines starting with an '*' are treated as comments and are not part
*  of the language. The following lines will demonstrate the resetting
*  of the left and right margin.  The listing appears now exactly
$ OFFUPPER
*  as entered. This was done with the $ OFFUPPER above.  Also note that
*  this DCO was not printed and there is a break in the numbering.
$wrong
*   Only wrong DCOs will be listed (or requested via $ONDOLLAR).
*   Now we can return to resetting of the margins.
$mincol 20 maxcol 50
Anything between    SET i plant / Vienna, London /   This defines i
column 1 and 19     SCALAR x some text / 3.145 /    A scalar example.
is ignored.         PARAMETER a, b, c;              Define some
                                                    parameters.

$onmargin
Now we have turned   a(i) = x; b(i) = sqr(a(i));    Assignments of a
on the margin                                       and b.
marking.
```

```
$offmargin ontext
```
A group of input lines can be ignored by using the $ontext and $offtext
options. Now the numbers to the left have disappeared in order to
indicate that these lines are comments only.

```
          set i demand / abcd /
```

A $offtext returns us into normal mode.
```
$offtext dollar % comment #
```
The comment character has been changed to # and the dollar character
to %. Let's reset everything to standard settings before we go on.
```
% dollar $ comment * mincol 1 maxcol 120
$ hidden These lines  contain text only of interest to the person
$ hidden manipulating the file.
$ontext
```
Computers work with different internal precision. Sometimes a GAMS
problem has to be moved from a machine with high precison to one
with lower precison. Instead of changing numbers with too much
precision the $OFFDIGIT tells GAMS to use as much precision as
possible and ignore the rest of the number.

```
$offtext
PARAMETER y list of values / toolarge 12345678912.1223
$OFFDIGIT
```

                    ignored   12345678912.1223 /

The output produced by this program is as follows:

```
GAMS 2.05 PC AT/XT                      87/09/15 00:24:59  PAGE     1
DOLLAR CONTROL OPTION TESTS (DCOTEST)

   2   *  LINES STARTING WITH AN '*' ARE TREATED AS COMMENTS AND ARE NOT PART
   3   *  OF THE LANGUAGE. THE FOLLOWING LINES WILL DEMONSTRATE THE RESETTING
   4   *  OF THE LEFT AND RIGHT MARGIN.   THE LISTING APPEARS NOW EXACTLY
   6   *  as entered. This was done with the $ OFFUPPER above. Also note that
   7   *  this DCO was not printed and there is a break in the numbering.
   8   $wrong
****   $210
   9   *  Only wrong DCOs will be listed (or requested via $ONDOLLAR).
  10   *  Now we can return to resetting the margins.
                                             NEW MARGINS: 20 - 50
  12   Anything between    SET i plant / Vienna, London / This defines i
  13   column 1 and 19     SCALAR x some text / 3.145 /   A scalar example.
  14   is ignored.         PARAMETER a, b, c;             Define some
  15                                                      parameters.
  17   Now we have turned  . a(i) = x; b(i) = sqr(a(i)); . Assignments of a
  18   on the margin       .                             . and b.
  19   marking.            .                             .
```

A group of input lines can be ignored by using the $ontext and $offtext options. Now the numbers to the left have disappeared in order to indicate that these lines are comments only.
set i demand / abcd /
A $offtext returns us into normal mode.

29   # The comment character has been changed to # and the dollar character

30   # to %. Let's reset everything to standard settings before we go on.
NEW MARGINS: 1 - 120

Computers work with different internal precisions. Sometimes a GAMS problem has to be moved from a machine with high precison to one with a lower precison. Instead of changing numbers with too much precision the $OFFDIGIT tells GAMS to use as much precision as possible and ignore the rest of the number.

43   PARAMETER y list of values / toolarge 12345678912.1223

**** $103

45   ignored   12345678912.1223 /

GAMS 2.05 PC AT/XT   87/09/15 00:24:59   PAGE   2
DOLLAR CONTROL OPTION TESTS (DCOTEST)
ERROR MESSAGES

103   TOO MANY DIGITS IN NUMBER
       ($OFFDIGIT CAN BE USED TO IGNORE TRAILING DIGITS)

210   UNKNOWN DOLLAR CONTROL OPTION. VALID ARE -
       ONMARGIN OFFMARGIN   ONDOLLAR OFFDOLLAR
       ONSYMLIST OFFSYMLIST   ONUELLIST OFFUELLIST
       ONSYMXREF OFFSYMXREF   ONUELXREF OFFUELXREF
       SINGLE DOUBLE EJECT   (LISTING CONTROL)
       ONUPPER OFFUPPER   (SHOW SOURCE TEXT AS ENTERED)
       ONTEXT OFFTEXT   (BRACKET A BLOCK OF COMMENT LINES)
       ONDIGIT OFFDIGIT   (OFF IGNORES PRECISION ON INPUT
       LINES   (FOLLOWED BY LINE COUNT)
       TITLE STITLE   (FOLLOWED BY NEW TITLE/SUBTITLE)
       MINCOL MAXCOL   (FOLLOWED BY COLUMN POSITION)
       DOLLAR COMMENT   (FOLLOWED BY 1 CHARACTER)
       HIDDEN   (FOLLOWED BY UNLISTED COMMENT)

THE OPTION STATEMENT C

The OPTION statement is used to set various global system parameters that control output detail, solution processes and the layout of displays. It starts with the keyword OPTION or OPTIONS followed by one or more name/value pairs separated by commas or end-of-line. There are five possible formats:

1. A DISPLAY specifier.
2. A recognized name, no following = sign or value.
3. A recognized name, an = sign, then an unsigned integer value.
4. A recognized name, an = sign, then an unsigned real number.
5. A recognized name, an = sign, then either of two recognized words.

An example is:

```
OPTIONS EJECT, LIMCOL = 10 , SOLVEOPT = REPLACE , XX:0:3:2 ;
```

A list of option identifier names and their meaning is given in Table C.1. A few of them are used to control solver-specific details, and we have not listed those: you should check in your online help file for details. Option names are distinct from other GAMS names and therefore do not conflict with other uses of their name. The use of specific options is described in more detail in the corresponding sections of Chapters 9, 13, 15 and 16.

Table C.1: Option Value Summary

Name	Default	Description
(a) This is the DISPLAY specifier.		
ident:d ident:d:r:c		Defines print formats for ident; d is the number of decimal places, r is the number of index positions printed as row labels, c is the number of index positions printed as column labels; the remaining index positions (if any) will be used to index the planes (index order: plane, row, column); if r is zero list format will be used.
(b) This one has no associated value.		
EJECT	None	Advances output to the next page.

Table C.1: Option Value Summary   *(continued)*

Name	Default	Description

(c) This group must be followed by an integer number.

DECIMALS	3	Number of decimals printed for symbols not having a specific print format attached.
SEED	3141	Resets the seed for the pseudo random number generator.
LIMCOL	3	The first LIMCOL columns of each variable will be printed by the solve statement.
LIMROW	3	The first LIMROW rows for each equation will be printed by the solve statement.
ITERLIM	1000	Iterative solution procedures will be interrupted after ITERLIM iterations and the current solution values will be returned to GAMS.
DOMLIM	0	Number of domain (evaluation) errors in the function and derivative calculations of a subsystem called by SOLVE before the solution procedure is interrupted.

(d) This group must be followed by a real number.

RESLIM	1000	Solution procedures will be interrupted after having used up RESLIM resource units and the current solution values returned to GAMS.
BRATIO	0.25	Certain solution procedures, such as linear programs, can restart from an advanced basis that is constructed automatically. The use of this basis is rejected if the number of basic variables is smaller than BRATIO times the size of the basis. A BRATIO of zero accepts any basis and a BRATIO of 1 always rejects the basis. This option does not apply to GAMS/ZOOM.
OPTCR	0.1	The relative optimality criterion for mixed integer problems. The solution process stops if it can guarantee that the best solution found is within 100*OPTCR percent of the global optimal.
OPTCA	0	The absolute optimality criterion for mixed integer problems. The solution process stops if it can guarantee that the best solution found is within OPTCA of the global optimal.

(e) This group must be followed by one of two recognized words.

SOLVEOPT	MERGE	Controls the way solution values from a solve are returned to GAMS.
	MERGE	Old and new values are merged together, new values overwrite old ones.
	REPLACE	All old values associated with a variable or equation are reset to default values before the new solution values are returned.
Solver	DEFAULT	Tells GAMS which specific algorithm to use for a generic problem. "Solver" stands for LP, NLP, MIP, etc.
	DEFAULT	GAMS selects the best suited algorithm available at a given installation.
	system	Name of a specific algorithm or subsystem to be used as solver. The names of this subsystem are location specific. The more common names are MINOS5, ZOOM, BDMLP, CONOPT, GRG3, MPSX, APEX4 and SCICONIC.

Table C.1: Option Value Summary   *(continued)*

Name	*Default*	*Description*
SYSOUT	OFF	Controls the printing of subsytem printing.
	ON	Prints the system output file of the solver.
	OFF	No subsystem output appears on output file unless a fatal subsystem error has occured.
SOLPRINT	ON	Controls printing of solution.
	ON	The solution is printed one line per row and column.
	OFF	Solution detail is not printed.

GAMS/MINOS D

by Philip E. Gill, Walter Murray,
Bruce A. Murtagh, Michael A. Saunders,
& Margaret H. Wright

Many of the models created with GAMS are solved with a special adapted version of the MINOS optimizer called GAMS/MINOS. You need to know whether your model is linear or nonlinear when you ask for it to be solved, but ideally you should not have to know *how* your model is solved, as long as a solution is obtained.

In practice, of course, not all models will solve successfully. Some background information is given here to help you interpret the output produced by GAMS/MINOS during the optimization process. GAMS allows you to specify values for many parameters that control GAMS/MINOS, and with careful experimentation you may be able to influence the solution process in a helpful way.

D.1 OVERVIEW OF GAMS/MINOS ■

GAMS/MINOS is a FORTRAN-based system designed to solve large-scale optimization problems expressed in the following form:

$$\underset{x,y}{\text{minimize}} \quad F(x) + c^T x + d^T y \tag{1}$$

$$\text{subject to} \quad f(x) + A_1 y \lessgtr b_1, \tag{2}$$

$$A_2 x + A_3 y \lessgtr b_2, \tag{3}$$

$$l \le \begin{pmatrix} x \\ y \end{pmatrix} \le u, \tag{4}$$

where the vectors c, d, b_1, b_2, l, u and the matrices A_1, A_2, A_3 are constant, $F(x)$ is a smooth scalar function, and $f(x)$ is a vector of smooth functions. The $\lessgtr$ signs mean that individual constraints may be defined using $\le$, $=$ or $\ge$, corresponding to the GAMS constructs =L=, =E= and =G=.

The components of x are called the nonlinear variables, and the components of y are the linear variables. Similarly, the equations in (2) are called the nonlinear constraints, and the equations in (3) are the linear constraints. Equations (2) and (3) together are called the general constraints.

Let m_1 and n_1 denote the number of nonlinear constraints and variables, and let m and n denote the *total* number of (general) constraints and variables. Thus, A_3 has $m - m_1$ rows and $n - n_1$ columns.

The constraints (4) specify upper and lower bounds on all variables. These are fundamental to many problem formulations and are treated specially by the solution algorithms in GAMS/MINOS. Some of the components of l and u may be $-\infty$ or $+\infty$ respectively, in accordance with the GAMS use of -INF and +INF.

The vectors b_1 and b_2 are called the right-hand side, and together are denoted by b.

Linear Programming ∎

If the functions $F(x)$ and $f(x)$ are absent, the problem becomes a *linear program*. Since there is no need to distinguish between linear and nonlinear variables, we use x rather than y. GAMS/MINOS converts all general constraints into equalities, and the only remaining inequalities are simple bounds on the variables. Thus, we write linear programs in the form

$$\underset{x,s}{\text{minimize}} \quad c^T x \quad \text{subject to} \quad Ax + Is = 0, \quad l \le \begin{pmatrix} x \\ s \end{pmatrix} \le u,$$

where the elements of x are your own GAMS variables, and s is a set of *slack variables*: one for each general constraint. For computational reasons, the right-hand side b is incorporated into the bounds on s.

In the expression $Ax + Is = 0$, we write the identity matrix explicitly if we are concerned with columns of the associated matrix $(A \quad I)$. Otherwise we will use the equivalent notation $Ax + s = 0$.

GAMS/MINOS solves linear programs using a reliable implementation of the *primal simplex method* (Dantzig, 1963), in which the constraints $Ax + Is = 0$ are partitioned into the form

$$Bx_B + Nx_N = 0,$$

where the *basis matrix* B is square and nonsingular. The elements of x_B and x_N are called the basic and nonbasic variables respectively. Together, they are a permutation of the vector (x, s).

Normally, each nonbasic variable is equal to one of its bounds, and the basic variables take on whatever values are needed to satisfy the general constraints. (The basic variables may be computed by solving the linear equation $Bx_B = -Nx_N$.) It can be shown that if an optimal solution to a linear program exists, then it has this form.

The simplex method reaches such a solution by performing a sequence of *iterations*, in which one column of B is replaced by one column of N (and vice versa), until no such interchange can be found that will reduce the value of $c^T x$.

As indicated, the nonbasic variables usually satisfy their upper and lower bounds. If any components of x_B lie significantly outside their bounds, we say that the current point is *infeasible*. In this case, the simplex method uses a Phase 1 procedure to reduce the sum of infeasibilities to zero. This is similar to the subsequent Phase 2 procedure that optimizes the true objective function $c^T x$.

If the solution procedures are interrupted, some of the nonbasic variables may lie strictly *between* their bounds: $l_j < x_j < u_j$. In addition, at a "feasible" or "optimal" solution, some of the basic variables may lie slightly outside their bounds: $l_j - \delta < x_j < l_j$

or $u_j < x_j < u_j + \delta$, where δ is a *feasibility tolerance* (typically 10^{-6}). In rare cases, even a few nonbasic variables might lie outside their bounds by as much as δ.

GAMS/MINOS maintains a sparse LU factorization of the basis matrix B, using a Markowitz ordering scheme and Bartels-Golub updates, as implemented in the Fortran package LUSOL (Gill, *et al.* 1987). (See Bartels and Golub, 1969; Bartels, 1971; Reid, 1976 and 1982.) The basis factorization is central to the efficient handling of sparse linear and nonlinear constraints.

Problems with a Nonlinear Objective   ■

When nonlinearities are confined to the term $F(x)$ in the objective function, the problem is a linearly constrained nonlinear program. GAMS/MINOS solves such problems using a *reduced-gradient* algorithm (Wolfe, 1962) combined with a *quasi-Newton* algorithm (Davidon, 1959) that generally leads to superlinear convergence. The implementation follows that described in Murtagh and Saunders (1978).

In the reduced-gradient method, the constraints $Ax + Is = 0$ are partitioned into the form

$$Bx_B + Sx_S + Nx_N = 0,$$

where x_S is a set of *superbasic variables*. At a solution, the basic and superbasic variables will lie somewhere between their bounds (to within the feasibility tolerance δ), while the nonbasic variables will normally be equal to one of their bounds, as before. Let the number of superbasic variables be s, the number of columns in S. (The context will always distinguish s from the vector of slack variables.) At a solution, s will be no more than n_1, the number of nonlinear variables. In many practical cases we have found that s remains reasonably small, say 200 or less, even if n_1 is large.

In the reduced-gradient algorithm, x_S is regarded as a set of "independent variables" or "free variables" that are allowed to move in any desirable direction, namely one that will improve the value of the objective function (or reduce the sum of infeasibilities). The basic variables can then be adjusted in order to continue satisfying the linear constraints.

If it appears that no improvement can be made with the current definition of B, S and N, some of the nonbasic variables are selected to be added to S, and the process is repeated with an increased value of s. At all stages, if a basic or superbasic variable encounters one of its bounds, that variable is made nonbasic and the value of s is reduced by one.

A step of the reduced-gradient method is called a *minor iteration*. For linear problems, we may interpret the simplex method as being the same as the reduced-gradient method, with the number of superbasic variables oscillating between 0 and 1.

A certain matrix Z is needed now for descriptive purposes. It takes the form

$$Z = \begin{pmatrix} -B^{-1}S \\ I \\ 0 \end{pmatrix},$$

though it is never computed explicitly. Given an LU factorization of the basis matrix B, it is possible to compute products of the form Zq and $Z^T g$ by solving linear equations involving B or B^T. This in turn allows optimization to be performed on the superbasic variables, while the basic variables are adjusted to satisfy the general linear constraints.

An important part of GAMS/MINOS is a stable implementation of a quasi-Newton algorithm for optimizing the superbasic variables. This can achieve superlinear convergence during any sequence of iterations for which the B, S, N partition remains constant. A *search direction q* for the superbasic variables is obtained by solving a system of the form

$$R^T R q = -Z^T g,$$

where g is the gradient of $F(x)$, $Z^T g$ is the *reduced gradient*, and R is a dense upper-triangular matrix. GAMS computes the gradient vector g analytically, using symbolic differentiation. The matrix R is updated in various ways in order to approximate the *reduced Hessian* according to $R^T R \approx Z^T H Z$, where H is the matrix of second derivatives of $F(x)$ (the *Hessian*).

Once q is available, the search direction for all variables is defined by $p = Zq$. A *linesearch* is then performed to find an approximate solution to the one-dimensional problem

$$\underset{\alpha}{\text{minimize}} \quad F(x + \alpha p) \quad \text{subject to} \quad 0 \le \alpha \le \beta,$$

where β is determined by the bounds on the variables. Another important part of GAMS/MINOS is the step-length procedure used in the linesearch to determine the step-length α (see Gill *et al.*, 1979). The number of nonlinear function evaluations required may be influenced by setting the Linesearch tolerance, as discussed in Section D.3.

As in linear programming, an equation $B^T \pi = g_B$ is solved to obtain the *dual variables* or *shadow prices* π, where g_B is the gradient of the objective function associated with basic variables. It follows that $g_B - B^T \pi = 0$. The analogous quantity for superbasic variables is the reduced-gradient vector $Z^T g = g_S - S^T \pi$; this should also be zero at an optimal solution. (In practice its components will be of order $r\|\pi\|$, where r is the *optimality tolerance*, typically 10^{-6}, and $\|\pi\|$ is a measure of the size of the elements of π.)

Problems with Nonlinear Constraints   ∎

If any of the constraints are nonlinear, GAMS/MINOS employs a *projected Lagrangian* algorithm, based on a method due to Robinson (1972); see Murtagh and Saunders (1982). This involves a sequence of *major iterations*, each of which requires the solution of a *linearly constrained subproblem*. Each subproblem contains linearized versions of the nonlinear constraints, as well as the original linear constraints and bounds.

At the start of the k-th major iteration, let x_k be an estimate of the nonlinear variables, and let λ_k be an estimate of the Lagrange multipliers (or dual variables) associated with the nonlinear constraints. The constraints are linearized by changing $f(x)$ in equation (2) to its linear approximation:

$$\tilde{f}(x, x_k) = f(x_k) + J(x_k)(x - x_k),$$

or more briefly

$$\tilde{f} = f_k + J_k(x - x_k),$$

where $J(x_k)$ is the *Jacobian matrix* evaluated at x_k. (The i-th row of the Jacobian is the gradient vector for the i-th nonlinear constraint function. As for the objective gradient, GAMS calculates the Jacobian using symbolic differentiation.)

The subproblem to be solved during the k-th major iteration is then

$$\underset{x,y}{\text{minimize}} \quad F(x) + c^T x + d^T y - \lambda_k^T(f - \tilde{f}) + \frac{1}{2}\rho(f - \tilde{f})^T(f - \tilde{f}) \qquad (5)$$

$$\text{subject to} \qquad \tilde{f} + A_{1y} \lessgtr b_1, \qquad\qquad\qquad\qquad\qquad\qquad (6)$$

$$A_2 x + A_3 y \lessgtr b_2, \qquad\qquad\qquad\qquad\qquad\qquad (7)$$

$$l \le \begin{pmatrix} x \\ y \end{pmatrix} \le u. \qquad\qquad\qquad\qquad\qquad\qquad (8)$$

The objective function (5) is called an *augmented Lagrangian*. The scalar ρ is a *penalty parameter*, and the term involving ρ is a modified *quadratic penalty function*.

GAMS/MINOS uses the reduced-gradient algorithm to minimize (5) subject to (6)–(8). As before, slack variables are introduced and b_1 and b_2 are incorporated into the bounds on the slacks. The linearized constraints take the form

$$\begin{pmatrix} J_k & A_1 \\ A_2 & A_3 \end{pmatrix}\begin{pmatrix} x \\ y \end{pmatrix} + \begin{pmatrix} I & 0 \\ 0 & I \end{pmatrix}\begin{pmatrix} s_1 \\ s_2 \end{pmatrix} = \begin{pmatrix} J_k x_k - f_k \\ 0 \end{pmatrix}.$$

This system will be referred to as $Ax + Is = 0$ as in the linear case. The Jacobian J_k is treated as a sparse matrix, the same as the matrices A_1, A_2 and A_3.

Unfortunately, there is no guarantee that the algorithm just described will converge from an arbitrary starting point. The concerned modeller can influence the likelihood of convergence as follows:

1. Specify initial activity levels for the nonlinear variables as carefully as possible (using the GAMS suffix .L).

2. Include sensible upper and lower bounds on all variables.

3. Specify a Major damping parameter that is lower than the default value, if the problem is suspected of being highly nonlinear.

4. Specify a Penalty parameter ρ that is higher than the default value, again if the problem is highly nonlinear.

In rare cases it may be safe to request the values $\lambda_k = 0$ and $\rho = 0$ for all subproblems, by specifying Lagrangian = No. However, convergence is much more likely with the default setting, Lagrangian = Yes. The initial estimate of the Lagrange multipliers is then $\lambda_0 = 0$, but for later subproblems, λ_k is taken to be the Lagrange multipliers associated with the (linearized) nonlinear constraints at the end of the previous major iteration.

For the first subproblem, the default value for the penalty parameter is $\rho = 100.0/m_1$, where m_1 is the number of nonlinear constraints. For later subproblems, ρ is reduced in stages when it appears that the sequence $\{x_k, \lambda_k\}$ is converging. In many cases it is safe to specify $\rho = 0$, particularly if the problem is only mildly nonlinear. This may improve the overall efficiency.

In the output from GAMS/MINOS, the term Feasible subproblem indicates that the *linearized constraints* have been satisfied. In general, the nonlinear constraints are satisfied only in the limit, so that *feasibility* and *optimality* occur at essentially the same time. The nonlinear constraint violation is printed every major iteration. Even if it is zero early on (say at the initial point), it may increase and perhaps fluctuate before tending to zero. On "well behaved" problems, the constraint violation will decrease quadratically (i.e., very quickly) during the final few major iterations.

Restrictions ■

GAMS/MINOS is designed to find solutions that are *locally optimal*. The nonlinear functions in a problem must be *smooth* (i.e., their first derivatives must exist). The functions need not be separable. Integer restrictions cannot be imposed directly.

A certain region is defined by the linear constraints in a problem and by the bounds on the variables. If the nonlinear objective and constraint functions are convex within this region, any optimal solution obtained will be a *global optimum*. Otherwise there may be several local optima, and some of these may not be global. In such cases the chances of finding a global optimum are usually increased by choosing a starting point that is "sufficiently close," but there is no general procedure for determining what "close" means, or for verifying that a given local optimum is indeed global.

Storage ■

GAMS/MINOS uses one large array of main storage for most of its workspace. The implementation places no fixed limit on the size of a problem or on its shape (many constraints and relatively few variables, or *vice versa*). In general, the limiting factor will be the amount of main storage available on a particular machine, and the amount of computation time that one's budget and/or patience can stand. On current personal computers with 640K of main memory, problem size is limited to perhaps 300 constraints and 500 variables for linear models, and somewhat less if there are many nonlinear variables. Machines with virtual memory can process several thousand constraints and variables.

Some detailed knowledge of a particular model will usually indicate whether the solution procedure is likely to be efficient. An important quantity is m, the total number of general constraints in (2) and (3). The amount of workspace required by GAMS/MINOS is roughly $100m$ words, where one "word" is the relevant storage unit for the floating-point arithmetic being used. This usually means about $800m$ bytes for workspace. A further 300K bytes, approximately, are needed for the program itself, along with buffer space for several files. Very roughly, then, a model with m general constraints requires about $(m + 300)$K bytes of memory.

Another important quantity is n, the total number of variables in x and y. The above comments assume that n is not much larger than m, the number of constraints. A typical ratio is $n/m = 2$ or 3.

If there are many nonlinear variables (i.e., if n_1 is large), much depends on whether the objective function or the constraints are highly nonlinear or not. The degree of nonlinearity affects s, the number of superbasic variables. Recall that s is zero for purely linear problems. We know that s need never be larger than $n_1 + 1$. In practice, s is often very much less than this upper limit.

In the quasi-Newton algorithm, the dense triangular matrix R has dimension s and requires about $\frac{1}{2}s^2$ words of storage. If it seems likely that s will be very large, some aggregation or reformulation of the problem should be considered.

D.2   FORMAT OF THE GAMS/MINOS OPTIONS FILE ■

The performance of GAMS/MINOS is controlled by a number of parameters or "options." Each option has a default value that should be appropriate for most problems. (The defaults are given in the next section.) For special situations it is possible to specify non-standard values for some or all of the options, in a file containing statements of the following general form:

```
BEGIN GAMS/MINOS options
    Iterations limit          500
    Major damping parameter   0.5
    Feasibility tolerance     1.0E-7
    Scale all variables
END GAMS/MINOS options
```

We shall call such a file a GAMS/MINOS options file. It starts with the keyword BEGIN and ends with END. The file is in free format. Each line specifies a single option, using one or more items as follows:

1. A *keyword* (required for all options).

2. A *phrase* (one or more words) that qualifies the keyword (only for some options).

3. A *number* that specifies an integer or real value (only for some options). Such numbers may be up to 16 contiguous characters in Fortran 77's I, F, E or D formats, terminated by a space.

The items may be entered in upper or lower case or a mixture of both. Some of the keywords have synonyms, and certain abbreviations are allowed, as long as there is no ambiguity. Blank lines and comments may be used to improve readability. A comment begins with an asterisk (*), which may appear anywhere on a line. All subsequent characters on the line are ignored.

We discussed the file-naming conventions necessary for the options file in Section 15.2 (e). Your online help document will provide the name that is to be used for your system: any options file you provide will be ignored unless it has the correct name. If you need to specify different options for different solves, you will have to use work files to interrupt processing between the solves so you can change option files.

It may be useful to include a comment on the first (BEGIN) line of the file. This line is echoed to the GAMS/MINOS summary file, and appears on the screen in an interactive environment. It also serves as a useful warning if an old or inappropriate file is used. Remember that the content of your options file will always be listed as part of your output.

The following example illustrates the use of certain options that might be helpful for "difficult" models involving nonlinear constraints. Experimentation may be necessary with the values specified, particularly if the sequence of major iterations does not converge using default values.

```
BEGIN GAMS/MINOS options

  * These options might be relevant for very nonlinear models.

    Major damping parameter  0.2 * may prevent divergence.
    Minor damping parameter  0.2 * if there are singularities
                                 * in the nonlinear functions.
    Penalty parameter       10.0 * or 100.0 perhaps—a value
                                 * higher than the default.

      Scale linear variables     * (This is the default.)
END GAMS/MINOS options
```

Conversely, nonlinearly constrained models that are very nearly linear may optimize more efficiently if some of the "cautious" defaults are relaxed:

```
BEGIN GAMS/MINOS options

 * Suggestions for models with MILDLY nonlinear constraints.

   Completion             Full
   Minor iterations limit  200
   Penalty parameter      0.0 * or 0.1 perhaps—a value
                              * smaller than the default.

 * Select one of the following:

   Scale all variables       * if starting point is VERY GOOD.
   Scale linear variables    * if they need it.
   Scale                 No  * otherwise.
END GAMS/MINOS options
```

Most of the options described in the next section should be left at their default values for any given model. If experimentation is necessary, we recommend changing just one option at a time.

D.3   GAMS/MINOS OPTIONS   ■

The following is an alphabetical list of the keywords that may appear in the GAMS/ MINOS options file, and a description of their effect. The letters i and r denote integer and real values. The number ϵ denotes machine precision (typically 10^{-15} or 10^{-16}). Options not specified will take the default values shown.

```
   Check frequency      i     Default = 30
```
Every i-th iteration after the most recent basis factorization, a numerical test is made to see if the current solution x satisfies the general linear constraints (including linearized nonlinear constraints, if any). The constraints are of the form $Ax + s = 0$, where s is the set of slack variables. To perform the numerical test, the residual vector $r = Ax + s$ is computed. If the largest component of r is judged to be too large, the current basis is refactorized and the basic variables are recomputed to satisfy the general constraints more accurately.

```
   Completion    Full    Default
   Completion    Partial
```
When there are nonlinear constraints, this determines whether subproblems should be solved to moderate accuracy (partial completion), or to full accuracy (full completion). GAMS/MINOS implements the option by using two sets of convergence tolerances for the subproblems.

Use of partial completion may reduce the work during early major iterations, unless the Minor iterations limit is active. The optimal set of basic and superbasic variables will probably be determined for any given subproblem, but the reduced gradient may be larger than it would have been with full completion.

An automatic switch to full completion occurs when it appears that the sequence of major iterations is converging. The switch is made when the nonlinear constraint error is reduced below 100*(Row tolerance), the relative change in λ_k is 0.1 or less, and the previous subproblem was solved to optimality.

Full completion tends to give better Lagrange-multiplier estimates. It may lead to fewer major iterations, but may result in more minor iterations.

Crash option	i	Default = 1
Crash tolerance	r	Default = 0.1

If a restart is not being performed, an initial basis will be selected from certain columns of the constraint matrix $(A \ \ I)$. The value of i determines which columns of A are eligible. Columns of I are used to fill "gaps" where necessary.

i

0   The initial basis will contain only slack variables: $B = I$.

1   All columns of A are considered (except those excluded by the Start assigned nonlinears option).

2   Only the columns of A corresponding to the linear variables y will be considered.

3   Variables that appear nonlinearly in the objective will be excluded from the initial basis.

4   Variables that appear nonlinearly in the constraints will be excluded from the initial basis.

If $i > 0$, three passes are made through the relevant columns of A, searching for a basis matrix that is essentially triangular. A column is assigned to "pivot" on a particular row if the column contains a suitably large element in a row that has not yet been assigned. (The pivot elements ultimately form the diagonals of the triangular basis.)

Pass 1 selects pivots from free columns (corresponding to variables with no upper and lower bounds). Pass 2 requires pivots to be in rows associated with equality (=E=) constraints. Pass 3 allows the pivots to be in inequality rows.

For remaining (unassigned) rows, the associated slack variables are inserted to complete the basis.

The Crash tolerance r allows the starting procedure CRASH to ignore certain "small" nonzeros in each column of A. If a_{max} is the largest element in column j, other nonzeros a_{ij} in the column are ignored if $|a_{ij}| \leq a_{max} \times r$. (To be meaningful, r should be in the range $0 \leq r < 1$.)

When $r > 0.0$ the basis obtained by CRASH may not be strictly triangular, but it is likely to be nonsingular and almost triangular. The intention is to obtain a starting basis containing more columns of A and fewer (arbitrary) slacks. A feasible solution may be reached sooner on some problems.

For example, suppose the first m columns of A are the matrix shown under LU factor tolerance; i.e., a tridiagonal matrix with entries -1, 4, -1. To help CRASH choose all m columns for the initial basis, we would specify Crash tolerance r for some value of $r > 1/4$.

Damping parameter	r	Default = 2.0

See Major damping parameter.

Debug level   *i*   Default = 0

This causes various amounts of information to be output. Most debug levels will not be helpful to GAMS users, but they are listed here for completeness.

i

0   No debug output.

2   (or more) Output from M5SETX showing the maximum residual after a row check.

40   Output from LU8RPC (which updates the *LU* factors of the basis matrix), showing the position of the last nonzero in the transformed incoming column.

50   Output from LU1MAR (which computes the *LU* factors each refactorization), showing each pivot row and column and the dimensions of the dense matrix involved in the associated elimination.

100   Output from M2BFAC and M5LOG listing the basic and superbasic variables and their values at every iteration.

Expand frequency   *i*   Default = 10000

This option is part of an anti-cycling procedure designed to guarantee progress even on highly degenerate problems.

For linear models, the strategy is to force a positive step at every iteration, at the expense of violating the bounds on the variables by a small amount. Suppose the specified feasibility tolerance is δ. Over a period of *i* iterations, the tolerance actually used by GAMS/MINOS increases from 0.5δ to δ (in steps of $0.5\delta/i$).

For nonlinear models, the same procedure is used for iterations in which there is only one superbasic variable. (Cycling can occur only when the current solution is at a vertex of the feasible region.) Thus, zero steps are allowed if there is more than one superbasic variable, but otherwise positive steps are enforced.

Increasing *i* helps reduce the number of slightly infeasible nonbasic basic variables (most of which are eliminated during a resetting procedure). However, it also diminishes the freedom to choose a large pivot element (see Pivot tolerance).

Factorization frequency   *i*   Default = 50

At most *i* basis changes will occur between factorizations of the basis matrix.

1. With linear programs, the basis factors are usually updated every iteration. The default *i* is reasonable for typical problems. Higher values up to $i = 100$ (say) may be more efficient on problems that are extremely sparse and well scaled.

2. When the objective function is nonlinear, fewer basis updates will occur as an optimum is approached. The number of iterations between basis factorizations will therefore increase. During these iterations a test is made regularly (according to the Check frequency) to ensure that the general constraints are satisfied. If necessary the basis will be refactorized before the limit of *i* updates is reached.

3. When the constraints are nonlinear, the Minor iterations limit will probably preempt *i*.

Feasibility tolerance r Default = 1.0E-6

When the constraints are linear, a *feasible solution* is one in which all variables, including slacks, satisfy their upper and lower bounds to within the absolute tolerance r. (Since slacks are included, this means that the general linear constraints are also satisfied to within r.)

1. GAMS/MINOS attempts to find a feasible solution before optimizing the objective function. If the sum of infeasibilities cannot be reduced to zero, the problem is declared infeasible. Let *SINF* be the corresponding sum of infeasibilities. If *SINF* is quite small, it may be appropriate to raise r by a factor of 10 or 100. Otherwise, some error in the data should be suspected.

2. If *SINF* is not small, there may be other points that have a significantly smaller sum of infeasibilities. GAMS/MINOS does not attempt to find a solution that minimizes the sum.

3. If Scale option = 1 or 2, feasibility is defined in terms of the scaled problem (since it is then more likely to be meaningful).

4. A nonlinear objective function $F(x)$ will be evaluated only at feasible points. If there are regions where $F(x)$ is undefined, every attempt should be made to eliminate these regions from the problem. For example, for a function $F(x) = \sqrt{x_1} + \log x_2$, it would be essential to place lower bounds on both variables. If Feasibility tolerance = 10^{-6}, the bounds $x_1 \geq 10^{-5}$ and $x_2 \geq 10^{-4}$ might be appropriate. (The log singularity is more serious; in general, keep variables as far away from singularities as possible.)

If the constraints are nonlinear, the above comments apply to each major iteration. A "feasible solution" satisfies the current linearization of the constraints to within the tolerance r. The associated subproblem is said to be feasible.

1. As for the objective function, bounds should be used to keep x more than r away from singularities in the constraint functions $f(x)$.

2. At the start of major iteration k, the constraint functions $f(x_k)$ are evaluated at a certain point x_k. This point always satisfies the relevant bounds $(l \leq x_k \leq u)$, but may not satisfy the general linear constraints.

3. During the associated minor iterations, $F(x)$ and $f(x)$ will be evaluated only at points x that satisfy the bounds *and* the general linear constraints (as well as the linearized nonlinear constraints).

4. If a subproblem is infeasible, the bounds on the linearized constraints are relaxed temporarily, in several stages.

5. Feasibility with respect to the nonlinear constraints themselves is measured against the Row tolerance (not against r). The relevant test is made at the *start* of a major iteration.

Hessian dimension r Default = Superbasics limit

This specifies that an $r \times r$ triangular matrix R is to be available for use by the quasi-Newton algorithm (to approximate the reduced Hessian matrix according to $Z^T H Z \approx R^T R$). Suppose there are s superbasic variables at a particular iteration. *Whenever possible, r should be greater than s.*

1. If $r \geq s$, the first s columns of R will be used to approximate the reduced Hessian in the normal manner. If there are no further changes to the set of superbasic variables, the rate of convergence will ultimately be superlinear.

2. If $r < s$, a matrix of the form

$$R = \begin{pmatrix} R_r & 0 \\ & D \end{pmatrix}$$

will be used to approximate the reduced Hessian, where R_r is an $r \times r$ upper triangular matrix and D is a *diagonal* matrix of order $s - r$. The rate of convergence will no longer be superlinear (and may be arbitrarily slow).

3. The storage required is of order $\frac{1}{2}r^2$, which is substantial if r is as large as 200 (say). In general, r should be a slight over-estimate of the final number of superbasic variables, whenever storage permits. It need not be larger than $n_1 + 1$, where n_1 is the number of nonlinear variables. For many problems it can be much smaller than n_1.

4. If Superbasics limit s is specified, the default value of r is the same number, s (and conversely). This is a safeguard to ensure superlinear convergence wherever possible. If neither r nor s is specified, GAMS chooses values for both, using certain characteristics of the problem.

Iterations limit i Default = 1000

This is the maximum number of minor iterations allowed (i.e., iterations of the simplex method or the reduced-gradient method).

1. Iters or Itns are alternative keywords.

2. If $i = 0$, no minor iterations are performed, but the starting point is tested for both feasibility and optimality.

3. This option, if set, overrides the GAMS ITERLIM specification.

Lagrangian   Yes   Default
Lagrangian   No

This determines the form of the objective function used for the linearized subproblems. The default value Yes is highly recommended. The Penalty parameter value is then also relevant.

If No is specified, the nonlinear constraint functions will be evaluated only twice per major iteration. Hence this option may be useful if the nonlinear constraints are very expensive to evaluate. However, in general there is a great risk that convergence may not occur.

Linesearch tolerance r Default = 0.1

For nonlinear problems, this controls the accuracy with which a step-length α is located in the one-dimensional problem

$$\underset{\alpha}{\text{minimize}} \quad F(x + \alpha p) \quad \text{subject to} \quad 0 < \alpha \leq \beta.$$

A linesearch occurs on most minor iterations for which x is feasible. [If the constraints are nonlinear, the function being minimized is the augmented Lagrangian in equation (5).]

1. r must be a real value in the range $0.0 \leq r < 1.0$.

2. The default value $r = 0.1$ requests a moderately accurate search. It should be satisfactory in most cases.

3. If the nonlinear functions are cheap to evaluate, a more accurate search may be appropriate; try $r = 0.01$ or $r = 0.001$. The number of iterations should decrease, and this will reduce total run time if there are many linear or nonlinear constraints.

4. If the nonlinear functions are expensive to evaluate, a less accurate search may be appropriate; try $r = 0.5$ or perhaps $r = 0.9$. (The number of iterations will probably increase, but the total number of function evaluations may decrease enough to compensate.)

Log frequency $\quad i \quad$ Default $= 100$ or 1

In general, one line of the iteration log is printed every i-th minor iteration. A heading labels the printed items, which include the current iteration number, the number and sum of infeasibilities (if any), the subproblem objective value (if feasible), and the number of evaluations of the nonlinear functions.

1. A value such as $i = 10$, 100 or larger is suggested for those interested only in the final solution.

2. Log frequency 0 may be used as shorthand for Log frequency 99999.

3. If Print level $= 0$, the default value of i is 100.

4. If Print level > 0, the default value of i is 1.

5. If Print level $= 0$ and the constraints are nonlinear, the minor iteration log is not printed (and the Log frequency and Summary frequency are ignored). Instead, one line is printed at the beginning of each major iteration.

LU factor tolerance $\qquad r_1 \qquad$ Default $= 10.0$
LU update tolerance $\qquad r_2 \qquad$ Default $= 10.0$
LU singularity tolerance $\quad r_3 \qquad$ Default $= \epsilon^{2/3} \approx 10^{-11}$

The first two tolerances affect the stability and sparsity of the basis factorization $B = LU$ during refactorization and updates respectively. The values specified must satisfy $r_i \geq 1.0$. The matrix L is a product of matrices of the form

$$\begin{pmatrix} 1 & \\ \mu & 1 \end{pmatrix}$$

where the multipliers μ will satisfy $|\mu| \leq r_i$.

1. The default values $r_i = 10.0$ usually strike a good compromise between stability and sparsity.

2. For large and relatively dense problems, $r_i = 25.0$ (say) may give a useful improvement in sparsity without impairing stability to a serious degree.

3. For certain very regular structures (e.g., band matrices) it may be necessary to set r_1 and/or r_2 to values smaller than the default in order to achieve stability. For example, if the columns of A include a submatrix of the form

$$\begin{pmatrix} 4 & -1 & & & & \\ -1 & 4 & -1 & & & \\ & -1 & 4 & -1 & & \\ & & \cdot & \cdot & \cdot & \\ & & & -1 & 4 & -1 \\ & & & & -1 & 4 \end{pmatrix},$$

it would be judicious to set both r_1 and r_2 to values in the range $1.0 \le r_i < 4.0$.

The singularity tolerance r_3 helps guard against ill-conditioned basis matrices. When the basis is refactorized, the diagonal elements of U are tested as follows: if $|U_{jj}| \le r_3$ or $|U_{jj}| < r_3 \max_i |U_{ij}|$, the j-th column of the basis is replaced by the corresponding slack variable. (This is most likely to occur after a restart, or at the start of a major iteration.)

In some cases, the Jacobian matrix may converge to values that make the basis exactly singular. (For example, a whole row of the Jacobian could be zero at an optimal solution.) Before exact singularity occurs, the basis could become very ill-conditioned and the optimization could progress very slowly (if at all). Setting $r_3 = 1.0\text{E-}5$, say, may help cause a judicious change of basis.

Major damping parameter r Default = 2.0

This parameter may assist convergence on problems that have highly nonlinear constraints. It is intended to prevent large relative changes between subproblem solutions (x_k, λ_k) and (x_{k+1}, λ_{k+1}). For example, the default value 2.0 prevents the relative change in either x_k or λ_k from exceeding 200 per cent. It will not be active on well behaved problems.

The parameter is used to interpolate between the solutions at the beginning and end of each major iteration. Thus, x_{k+1} and λ_{k+1} are changed to

$$x_k + \sigma(x_{k+1} - x_k) \quad \text{and} \quad \lambda_k + \sigma(\lambda_{k+1} - \lambda_k)$$

for some step-length $\sigma < 1$. In the case of nonlinear equations (where the number of constraints is the same as the number of variables) this gives a *damped Newton method*.

1. This is a very crude control. If the sequence of major iterations does not appear to be converging, one should first re-run the problem with a higher Penalty parameter (say 10 or 100 times the default ρ). (Skip this re-run in the case of nonlinear equations: there are no degrees of freedom and the value of ρ is irrelevant.)

2. If the subproblem solutions continue to change violently, try reducing r to 0.2 or 0.1 (say).

3. For implementation reasons, the shortened step σ applies to the nonlinear variables x, but not to the linear variables y or the slack variables s. This may reduce the efficiency of the control.

Major iterations i Default = 50

This is the maximum number of major iterations allowed. It is intended to guard against an excessive number of linearizations of the nonlinear constraints, since in some cases the sequence of major iterations may not converge.

The progress of the major iterations can be best monitored using `Print level` 0 (the default).

`Minor damping parameter` r Default = 2.0

This parameter limits the change in x during a linesearch. It applies to all nonlinear problems, once a "feasible solution" or "feasible subproblem" has been found.

1. A linesearch of the form $\text{minimize}_\alpha \ F(x + \alpha p)$ is performed over the range $0 < \alpha \leq \beta$, where β is the step to the nearest upper or lower bound on x. Normally, the first steplength tried is $\alpha_1 = \min(1, \beta)$.

2. In some cases, such as $F(x) = ae^{bx}$ or $F(x) = ax^b$, even a moderate change in the components of x can lead to floating-point overflow. The parameter r is therefore used to define a limit
$$\bar{\beta} = r(1 + \|x\|)/\|p\|,$$
and the first evaluation of $F(x)$ is at the potentially smaller steplength $\alpha_1 = \min(1, \bar{\beta}, \beta)$.

3. Wherever possible, upper and lower bounds on x should be used to prevent evaluation of nonlinear functions at meaningless points. The `Minor damping parameter` provides an additional safeguard. The default value $r = 2.0$ should not affect progress on well behaved problems, but setting $r = 0.1$ or 0.01 may be helpful when rapidly varying functions are present. A "good" starting point may be required. An important application is to the class of nonlinear least-squares problems.

4. In cases where several local optima exist, specifying a small value for r may help locate an optimum near the starting point.

`Minor iterations` i Default = 40

This is the maximum number of minor iterations allowed between successive linearizations of the nonlinear constraints.

1. A moderate value (e.g., $20 \leq i \leq 50$) prevents excessive effort being expended on early major iterations, but allows later subproblems to be solved to completion.

2. The limit applies to both infeasible and feasible iterations. In some cases, a large number of iterations (say K) might be required to obtain a feasible subproblem. If good starting values are supplied for variables appearing nonlinearly in the constraints, it may be sensible to specify $i > K$, to allow the first major iteration to terminate at a feasible (and perhaps optimal) subproblem solution. (If a "good" initial subproblem is arbitrarily interrupted by a small i, the subsequent linearization may be less favorable than the first.)

3. In general it is unsafe to specify a value as small as $i = 1$ or 2. (Even when an optimal solution has been reached, a few minor iterations may be needed for the corresponding subproblem to be recognized as optimal.)

4. The `Iterations limit` provides an independent limit on the total minor iterations (across all subproblems).

5. If the constraints are linear, only the `Iterations limit` applies; the `Minor iterations` value is ignored.

`Multiple price` i Default = 1

"Pricing" refers to a scan of the current nonbasic variables to determine if any should be changed from their current value (by allowing them to become superbasic or basic).

If multiple pricing is in effect, the i best nonbasic variables are selected for admission to the superbasic set. ("Best" means the variables with largest reduced gradients of appropriate sign.) If partial pricing is also in effect, the i best variables are selected from the current partition of A and I.

1. The default value $i = 1$ is best for linear programs, since an optimal solution will have zero superbasic variables.

2. *Warning*: If $i > 1$, GAMS/MINOS will use the *reduced-gradient method* (rather than the simplex method) even on purely linear problems. The subsequent iterations do *not* correspond to the efficient "minor iterations" carried out by commercial linear programming systems using multiple pricing. (In the latter systems, the classical simplex method is applied to a tableau involving i dense columns of dimension m, and i is therefore limited for storage reasons— typically to the range $2 \leq i \leq 7$.)

3. GAMS/MINOS varies all superbasic variables simultaneously. For linear problems its storage requirements are essentially independent of i. Larger values of i are therefore practical, but in general the iterations and time required when $i > 1$ are greater than when the simplex method is used ($i = 1$).

4. On large nonlinear problems it may be important to set $i > 1$ if the starting point does not contain many superbasic variables. For example, if a problem has 3000 variables and 500 of them are nonlinear, the optimal solution may well have 200 variables superbasic. If the problem is solved in several runs, it may be beneficial to use $i = 10$ (say) for early runs, until it seems that the number of superbasics has levelled off.

5. If `Multiple price` i is specified, it is also necessary to specify `Superbasics limit` s for some $s \geq i$.

`Optimality tolerance` r Default = 1.0E-6

This is used to judge the size of the reduced gradients $d_j = g_j - \pi^T a_j$, where g_j is the gradient of the objective function corresponding to the j-th variable, a_j is the associated column of the constraint matrix (or Jacobian), and π is the set of dual variables.

1. By construction, the reduced gradients for basic variables are always zero. Optimality will be declared if the reduced gradients for nonbasic variables at their lower or upper bounds satisfy

$$d_j / \|\pi\| \geq -r \quad \text{or} \quad d_j / \|\pi\| \leq r$$

respectively, and if $|d_j| / \|\pi\| \leq r$ for superbasic variables.

2. In the above tests, $\|\pi\|$ is a measure of the size of the dual variables. It is included to make the tests independent of a scale factor on the objective function.

3. The quantity actually used is defined by

$$\sigma = \sum_{i=1}^{m} |\pi_i|, \qquad \|\pi\| = \max\{\sigma/\sqrt{m}, 1\},$$

so that only *large* scale factors are allowed for.

4. If the objective is scaled down to be very *small*, the optimality test effectively reduces to comparing d_j against r.

Partial price   *i*   Default = 10 (LP) or 1 (NLP)

This parameter is recommended for large problems that have significantly more variables than constraints. It reduces the work required for each "pricing" operation (when a nonbasic variable is selected to become basic or superbasic).

1. When $i = 1$, all columns of the constraint matrix $(A \quad I)$ are searched.

2. Otherwise, A and I are partitioned to give i roughly equal segments A_j, I_j ($j = 1$ to i). If the previous pricing search was successful on A_{j-1}, I_{j-1}, the next search begins on the segments A_j, I_j. (All subscripts here are modulo i.)

3. If a reduced gradient is found that is larger than some dynamic tolerance, the variable with the largest such reduced gradient (of appropriate sign) is selected to become superbasic. (Several may be selected if multiple pricing has been specified.) If nothing is found, the search continues on the next segments A_{j+1}, I_{j+1}, and so on.

4. Partial price t (or $t/2$ or $t/3$) may be appropriate for time-stage models having t time periods.

Penalty parameter   *r*   Default = $100.0/m_1$

This specifies the value of ρ in the modified augmented Lagrangian. It is used only when Lagrangian = Yes (the default setting).

    For early runs on a problem with unknown characteristics, the default value should be acceptable. If the problem is known to be highly nonlinear, specify a larger value, such as 10 times the default. In general, a positive value of ρ may be necessary to ensure convergence, *even for convex programs*.

    On the other hand, if ρ is too large, the rate of convergence may be unnecessarily slow. If the functions are not highly nonlinear or a good starting point is known, it will often be safe to specify Penalty parameter 0.0.

    If several related problems are to be solved, the following strategy for setting the Penalty parameter may be useful:

1. Initially, use a moderate value for r (such as the default) and a reasonably low Iterations and/or Major iterations limit.

2. If successive major iterations appear to be terminating with radically different solutions, the penalty parameter should be increased. (See also the Major damping parameter.)

3. If there appears to be little progress between major iterations, it may help to reduce the penalty parameter.

Pivot tolerance   *r*   Default = $\epsilon^{2/3} \approx 10^{-11}$

Broadly speaking, the pivot tolerance is used to prevent columns entering the basis if they would cause the basis to become almost singular. The default value of r should be satisfactory in most circumstances.

1. When x changes to $x + \alpha p$ for some search direction p, a "ratio test" is used to determine which component of x reaches an upper or lower bound first. The corresponding element of p is called the pivot element.

2. For linear problems, elements of p are ignored (and therefore cannot be pivot elements) if they are smaller than the pivot tolerance r.

3. For nonlinear problems, elements smaller than $r\|p\|$ are ignored.

4. It is common (on "degenerate" problems) for two or more variables to reach a bound at essentially the same time. In such cases, the Feasibility tolerance (say t) provides some freedom to maximize the pivot element and thereby improve numerical stability. Excessively small values of t should therefore not be specified.

5. To a lesser extent, the Expand frequency (say f) also provides some freedom to maximize the pivot element. Excessively *large* values of f should therefore not be specified.

Print level i Default = 0

This varies the amount of information that will be output during optimization.

1. Print level 0 sets the default Log and Summary frequencies to 100. It is then easy to monitor the progress of a run.

2. Print level 1 (or more) sets the default Log and Summary frequencies to 1, giving a line of output for every minor iteration.

3. Print level 1 also produces basis statistics, i.e., information relating to *LU* factors of the basis matrix whenever the basis is refactorized.

For problems with nonlinear constraints, certain quantities are printed at the start of each major iteration. The value of i is best thought of as a binary number of the form

Print level   JFLXB

where each letter stands for a digit that is either 0 or 1. The quantities referred to are:

B   Basis statistics, as mentioned above.

X x_k, the nonlinear variables involved in the objective function or the constraints.

L λ_k, the Lagrange-multiplier estimates for the nonlinear constraints. (Suppressed if Lagrangian = No, since then $\lambda_k = 0$.)

F $f(x_k)$, the values of the nonlinear constraint functions.

J $J(x_k)$, the Jacobian matrix.

To obtain output of any item, set the corresponding digit to 1, otherwise to 0. For example, Print level 10 sets X = 1 and the other digits equal to zero; the nonlinear variables will be printed each major iteration.

If J = 1, the Jacobian matrix will be output column-wise at the start of each major iteration. Column j will be preceded by the value of the corresponding variable x_j and a key to indicate whether the variable is basic, superbasic or nonbasic. (Hence if J = 1, there is no reason to specify X = 1 unless the objective contains more nonlinear variables than the Jacobian.) A typical line of output is

     3   1.250000D+01 BS   1   1.00000D+00   4   2.00000D+00

which would mean that x_3 is basic at value 12.5, and the third column of the Jacobian has elements of 1.0 and 2.0 in rows 1 and 4. (Note: the GAMS/MINOS row numbers are usually different from the GAMS row numbers; see the Solution option.)

Radius of convergence r Default = 0.01

This determines when the penalty parameter ρ will be reduced (if initialized to a positive value). Both the nonlinear constraint violation (see *ROWERR* below) and the relative change in consecutive Lagrange multipler estimates must be less than r at the start of a major iteration before ρ is reduced or set to zero.

A few major iterations later, full completion will be requested if not already set, and the remaining sequence of major iterations should converge quadratically to an optimum.

Row tolerance r Default = 1.0E-6

This specifies how accurately the nonlinear constraints should be satisfied at a solution. The default value is usually small enough, since model data is often specified to about that accuracy.

Let *ROWERR* be the maximum component of the residual vector $f(x) + A_1 y - b_1$, normalized by the size of the solution. Thus,

$$ROWERR = \|f(x) + A_1 y - b_1\|_\infty / (1 + XNORM),$$

where *XNORM* is a measure of the size of the current solution (x, y). The solution is regarded as acceptably feasible if $ROWERR \leq r$.

If the problem functions involve data that is known to be of low accuracy, a larger Row tolerance may be appropriate.

Scale option i Default = 2 (LP) or 1 (NLP)
Scale   Yes
Scale   No

Scale linear variables   * Same as Scale option 1
Scale nonlinear variables * Same as Scale option 2
Scale all variables   * Same as Scale option 2

Scale tolerance r Default = 0.9
Scale, Print
Scale, Print, Tolerance = r

Three scale options are available as follows:

i

0   No scaling. If storage is at a premium, this option should be used.

1   Linear constraints and variables are scaled by an iterative procedure that attempts to make the matrix coefficients as close as possible to 1.0 (see Fourer, 1982). This will sometimes improve the performance of the solution procedures.

2   All constraints and variables are scaled by the iterative procedure. Also, a certain additional scaling is performed that may be helpful if the right-hand side b or the solution x is large. This takes into account columns of $(A \quad I)$ that are fixed or have positive lower bounds or negative upper bounds.

Scale option 2 is the default for linear programs.

Scale option 1 is the default for nonlinear problems. (Only linear variables are scaled.)

Scale Yes sets the default. (*Caution*: If all variables are nonlinear, Scale Yes unexpectedly does *nothing*, because there are no linear variables to scale.)

Scale No suppresses scaling (equivalent to Scale option 0).

If nonlinear constraints are present, Scale option 1 or 0 should generally be tried at first. Scale option 2 gives scales that depend on the initial Jacobian, and should therefore be used only if (a) a good starting point is provided, and (b) the problem is not highly nonlinear.

Scale, Print causes the row-scales $r(i)$ and column-scales $c(j)$ to be printed. The scaled matrix coefficients are $\bar{a}_{ij} = a_{ij}c(j)/r(i)$, and the scaled bounds on the variables and slacks are $\bar{l}_j = l_j/c(j)$, $\bar{u}_j = u_j/c(j)$, where $c(j) \equiv r(j - n)$ if $j > n$.

All forms except Scale option may specify a tolerance r where $0 < r < 1$ (for example: Scale, Print, Tolerance = 0.99). This affects how many passes might be needed through the constraint matrix. On each pass, the scaling procedure computes the ratio of the largest and smallest nonzero coefficients in each column:

$$\rho_j = \max_i |a_{ij}|/\min_i |a_{ij}| \qquad (a_{ij} \neq 0).$$

If $max_j\rho_j$ is less than r times its previous value, another scaling pass is performed to adjust the row and column scales. Raising r from 0.9 to 0.99 (say) usually increases the number of scaling passes through A. At most 10 passes are made.

If a Scale option has not already been specified, Scale, Print or Scale tolerance both set the default scaling.

Solution	No	Default
Solution	Yes	

This controls whether or not GAMS/MINOS prints the final solution obtained. There is one line of output for each constraint and variable. The lines are in the same order as in the GAMS solution, but the constraints and variables are labeled with internal GAMS/MINOS numbers rather than GAMS names. (The numbers at the left of each line are GAMS/MINOS "column numbers," and those at the right of each line in the rows section are GAMS/MINOS "slacks.")

The GAMS/MINOS solution may be useful occasionally to interpret certain messages that occur during the optimization, and to determine the final status of certain variables (basic, superbasic or nonbasic).

Start assigned nonlinears	Superbasic	Default
Start assigned nonlinears	Basic	
Start assigned nonlinears	Nonbasic	
Start assigned nonlinears	Eligible for Crash	

This option affects the starting strategy when there is no basis (i.e., for the first solve or when OPTION BRATIO = 1 is used to reject an existing basis).

The option applies to all nonlinear variables that have been assigned non-default initial values and are strictly between their bounds. Free variables at their default value of zero are excluded. Let K denote the number of such "assigned nonlinear variables."

1. Specify superbasic for highly nonlinear models, as long as K is not too large (say $K < 100$) and the initial values are "good."

2. Specify basic for models that are essentially "square" (i.e., if there are about as many general constraints as variables).

3. Specify nonbasic if K is large.

4. Specify eligible for Crash for linear or nearly linear models. The nonlinear variables will be treated in the manner described under Crash option.

5. Note that the *first* and *fourth* keywords are significant.

Subspace tolerance r Default = 0.5

This controls the extent to which optimization is confined to the current set of basic and superbasic variables (Phase 4 iterations), before one or more nonbasic variables are added to the superbasic set (Phase 3).

1. r must be a real number in the range $0 < r \le 1$.

2. When a nonbasic variable x_j is made superbasic, the resulting norm of the reduced-gradient vector (for all superbasics) is recorded. Let this be $\|Z^T g_0\|$. (In fact, the norm will be $|d_j|$, the size of the reduced gradient for the new superbasic variable x_j.)

3. Subsequent Phase 4 iterations will continue at least until the norm of the reduced-gradient vector satisfies $\|Z^T g\| \le r \times \|Z^T g_0\|$. ($\|Z^T g\|$ is the size of the largest reduced-gradient component among the superbasic variables.)

4. A smaller value of r is likely to increase the total number of iterations, but may reduce the number of basis changes. A larger value such as $r = 0.9$ may sometimes lead to improved overall efficiency, if the number of superbasic variables has to increase substantially between the starting point and an optimal solution.

5. Other convergence tests on the change in the function being minimized and the change in the variables may prolong Phase 4 iterations. This helps to make the overall performance insensitive to larger values of r.

Summary frequency i Default = 100 or 1

A brief form of the iteration log is output to the summary file. In general, one line is output every i-th minor iteration. In an interactive environment, the output normally appears at the terminal and allows a run to be monitored. If something looks wrong, the run can be manually terminated.

The Summary frequency controls summary output in the same way as the Log frequency controls output to the print file.

1. A value such as $i = 10$ or 100 is often adequate to determine if the SOLVE is making progress.

2. If Print level $= 0$, the default value of i is 100.

3. If Print level > 0, the default value of i is 1.

4. If Print level $= 0$ and the constraints are nonlinear, the Log frequency and Summary frequency are ignored. Instead, one line is printed at the beginning of each major iteration.

Superbasics limit i Default = Hessian dimension

This places a limit on the storage allocated for superbasic variables. Ideally, i should be set slightly larger than the "number of degrees of freedom" expected at an optimal solution.

For linear problems, an optimum is normally a basic solution with no degrees of freedom. (The number of variables lying strictly between their bounds is no more than m, the number of general constraints.) The default value of i is therefore 1.

For nonlinear problems, the number of degrees of freedom is often called the "number of independent variables."

1. Normally, i need not be greater than $n_1 + 1$, where n_1 is the number of nonlinear variables.

2. For many problems, i may be considerably smaller than n_1. This will save storage if n_1 is very large.

3. This parameter also sets the Hessian dimension, unless the latter is specified explicitly (and conversely). If neither parameter is specified, GAMS chooses values for both, using certain characteristics of the problem.

Unbounded objective value r_1 Default = 1.0E+20
Unbounded step size r_2 Default = 1.0E+10

These parameters are intended to detect unboundedness in nonlinear problems. During a linesearch of the form

$$\min_\alpha F(x + \alpha p),$$

if $|F|$ exceeds r_1 or if α exceeds r_2, iterations are terminated with the exit message PROBLEM IS UNBOUNDED (OR BADLY SCALED).

1. If singularities are present, unboundedness in $F(x)$ may be manifested by a floating-point overflow (during the evaluation of $F(x + \alpha p)$, before the test against r_1 can be made.

2. Unboundedness in x is best avoided by placing finite upper and lower bounds on the variables. See also the Minor damping parameter.

Verify level i Default = 0

Verify objective gradients   * Same as Verify option 1
Verify constraint gradients   * Same as Verify option 2
Verify   * Same as Verify option 3
Verify gradients   * Same as Verify option 3

Verify   Yes   * Same as Verify option 3
Verify   No   * Same as Verify option 0

This option refers to a finite-difference check on the gradients (first derivatives) computed by GAMS for each nonlinear function. GAMS computes gradients analytically, and the values obtained should normally be taken as "correct."

Gradient verification occurs before a problem is scaled, and before the first basis is factorized. (Hence, it occurs before the basic variables are set to satisfy the general constraints $Ax + s = 0$.)

i

0   Only a "cheap" test is performed, requiring three evaluations of the non-linear objective (if any) and two evaluations of the nonlinear constraints.

1   A more reliable check is made on each component of the objective gradient.

2   A check is made on each column of the Jacobian matrix associated with the nonlinear constraints.

3   A detailed check is made on both the objective and the Jacobian.

−1   No checking is performed.

`Weight on linear objective` r Default $= 0.0$

This keyword invokes the so-called *composite objective* technique, if the first solution obtained is infeasible, and if the objective function contains linear terms. While trying to reduce the sum of infeasibilities, the method also attempts to optimize the linear objective.

1. At each infeasible iteration, the objective function is defined to be

$$\underset{x}{\text{minimize}} \quad \sigma w(c^T x) + \text{(sum of infeasibilities)},$$

where $\sigma = 1$ for minimization, $\sigma = -1$ for maximization, and c is the linear objective.

2. If an "optimal" solution is reached while still infeasible, w is reduced by a factor of 10. This helps to allow for the possibility that the initial w is too large. It also provides dynamic allowance for the fact that the sum of infeasibilities is tending towards zero.

3. The effect of w is disabled after five such reductions, or if a feasible solution is obtained.

4. This option is intended mainly for linear programs. It is unlikely to be helpful if the objective function is nonlinear.

D.4   REFERENCES   ■

R. H. Bartels (1971). A stabilization of the simplex method, *Numerische Mathematik* 16, 414–434.

R. H. Bartels and G. H. Golub (1969). The simplex method of linear programming using the *LU* decomposition, *Communications of the ACM* 12, 266–268.

G. B. Dantzig (1963). *Linear Programming and Extensions*, Princeton University Press, Princeton, New Jersey.

W. C. Davidon (1959). Variable metric methods for minimization, A.E.C. Res. and Develop. Report ANL-5990, Argonne National Laboratory, Argonne, Illinois.

R. Fourer (1982). Solving staircase linear programs by the simplex method, *Mathematical Programming* 23, 274–313.

P. E. Gill, W. Murray, M. A. Saunders and M. H. Wright (1979). Two step-length algorithms for numerical optimization, Report SOL 79-25, Department of Operations Research, Stanford University, Stanford, California.

P. E. Gill, W. Murray, M. A. Saunders and M. H. Wright (1987). Maintaining *LU* factors of a general sparse matrix, *Linear Algebra and its Applications* 88/89, 239–270.

B. A. Murtagh and M. A. Saunders (1978). Large-scale linearly constrained optimization, *Mathematical Programming* 14, 41–72.

B. A. Murtagh and M. A. Saunders (1982). A projected Lagrangian algorithm and its implementation for sparse nonlinear constraints, *Mathematical Programming Study* 16, *Algorithms for Constrained Minimization of Smooth Nonlinear Functions*, 84–117.

B. A. Murtagh and M. A. Saunders (1983). MINOS 5.0 User's Guide, Report SOL 83-20, Department of Operations Research, Stanford University, Stanford, California. (Revised as MINOS 5.1 User's Guide, Report SOL 83-20R, 1987.)

J. K. Reid (1976). Fortran subroutines for handling sparse linear programming bases, Report R8269, Atomic Energy Research Establishment, Harwell, England.

J. K. Reid (1982). A sparsity-exploiting variant of the Bartels-Golub decomposition for linear programming bases, *Mathematical Programming* 24, 55–69.

S. M. Robinson (1972). A quadratically convergent algorithm for general nonlinear programming problems, *Mathematical Programming* 3, 145–156.

P. Wolfe (1962). The reduced-gradient method, unpublished manuscript, RAND Corporation.

GAMS/ZOOM E

by Roy E. Marsten
& Jaya Singhal

Linear and mixed-integer models created with GAMS (model types LP, MIP or RMIP) may be solved with a specially modified version of the ZOOM optimizer which we call here GAMS/ZOOM. ZOOM stands for Zero/One Optimization Methods.

Some background information on ZOOM is given in the first section to help you interpret the output produced by ZOOM during the optimization process and to prepare for the discussion of the GAMS/ZOOM options file. The GAMS/ZOOM options file is *not* required but may be useful for influencing the solution process in a helpful way if your model is difficult or expensive to solve.

E.1 OVERVIEW OF ZOOM ∎

ZOOM is a Fortran-based system for solving zero/one mixed-integer programming problems. It is intended for medium-sized problems with no special structure and up to about 200 zero/one variables. GAMS/ZOOM is able to handle integer variables as well, by expressing them as combinations of zero/one variables.

The mathematical form of the MIP problem is:

$$\text{maximize} \quad c_1 x_1 + \cdots + c_N x_N$$
$$\text{subject to} \quad a_{1,1} x_1 + \cdots + a_{1,N} x_N \lessgtr b_1$$

$$a_{M,1} x_1 + \cdots + a_{M,N} x_N \lessgtr b_M$$
$$L_j \le x_j \le U_j \quad \text{for } j = 1, \ldots, N$$
$$L_b = 0, U_b = 1, \text{ and } x_b = 0 \text{ or } x_b = 1 \text{ for the set of binary variables.}$$

(The $\lessgtr$ signs mean that the constraints are general inequalities or equalities, corresponding to the GAMS symbols =G=, =L=, and =E=.)

GAMS automatically converts integer variables into sums of zero/one variables, so GAMS/ZOOM is able to solve the general mixed-integer problem. For example if x_j

can take on values $0, 1, \ldots , U_j$, then we define K new zero/one variables, where K is chosen so that:

$$2^{K-1} \leq U_j < 2^K$$

Then the integer variable x_j is represented as:

$$x_j = y_{j,1} + 2y_{j,2} + 4y_{j,3} + 8y_{j,4} + \cdots + 2^{K-1}y_{j,K}$$

where each $y_{j,K}$ variable is a zero/one variable.

A problem with no zero/one variables is a pure linear program; a problem with all zero/one variables is a pure integer program; these are both special cases of the mixed-integer program. This appendix is written with the mixed-integer problem in mind, but it is both easy and efficient to use GAMS/ZOOM to solve pure linear programs as well. There is no extra work done or storage allocated when the problem is a pure LP. GAMS/ZOOM can solve pure linear programs with many thousands of variables and equations.

This appendix assumes some familiarity with linear and integer programming, in particular the simplex method and the branch-and-bound method. We shall always assume maximization, in order to simplify the discussion.

The data for a given problem consists of the $a_{i,j}$, b_i, c_j, L_j, and U_j. These will all have been specified as parts of the GAMS model. ZOOM is based on the XMP linear programming library (Marsten, 1981) which in turn uses the LA05 basis factorization routines of Reid (Reid, 1982).

GAMS/ZOOM begins by solving the problem as a linear program, and then uses the Pivot and Complement (P&C) heuristic [see Balas and Martin, (1980)] to find an initial integer feasible solution. It then uses a branch-and-bound search to find improved solutions and to verify optimality. The Branch-and-Bound (B&B) procedure uses linear programming to compute bounds. It also has several novel features not found in other programs. These are: fixed order branching, multilevel expansion, the resource space tour, and "cheating." These are explained briefly below. For a more complete exposition, see Singhal, Marsten and Morin (1987).

Initial Linear Program   ∎

The first step in solving a zero/one mixed-integer program is solving the linear programming relaxation. This is obtained by relaxing the $x_j = 0$ or 1 conditions to $0 \leq x_j \leq 1$. GAMS/ZOOM solves this LP relaxation by calling XMP. If the LP relaxation is infeasible, then so is the original mixed-integer program, and we are finished. If the LP relaxation has a natural integer optimal solution, then this solution is also optimal for the original mixed-integer program, and we are finished. Notice that this is the case if all of the zero/one variables are non-basic (or basic and degenerate) in the LP solution.

If neither of the above events occurs, we still get a bound on the optimal value of the mixed-integer program. Let v_{LP} denote the optimal value of the LP relaxation, and let v_{MIP} denote the optimal value of the mixed-integer program. Then $v_{LP} \geq v_{MIP}$, assuming maximization.

Pivot and Complement Heuristic   ∎

We will not discuss the Pivot and Complement (P&C) heuristic in detail here, since the reader can consult Balas and Martin (1980). In general terms, the method searches in the vicinity of the optimal solution of the LP relaxation for an integer feasible solution. It conducts this search by trying to force any basic integer variable (which is necessarily fractional unless it is degenerate) out of the basis. This is done by performing pivots. Non-basic integer variables can also be complemented, i.e. flipped from zero to one or one to zero. Both one-at-a-time and two-at-a-time complements are attempted. If a feasible solution is found, then additional complements are performed in an attempt to improve it.

This Pivot and Complement heuristic has worked very well in our experience to date, and it is quite fast (the pairwise complements are not done on more than 500 zero/one variables). Good solutions can be found for many large mixed-integer problems by doing just the initial linear program and the P&C heuristic. Doing branch-and-bound generally takes far longer than the initial LP + P&C heuristic combination.

If the P&C heuristic finds a feasible integer solution with value INCUMBENT, and if the relative gap between INCUMBENT and v_{LP} is less than or equal to a user specified TOLERANCE:

$$(v_{LP} - \text{INCUMBENT})/(1 + |v_{LP}|) \leq \text{TOLERANCE}$$

then we are finished. TOLERANCE corresponds to the GAMS OPTCR option: its default value is 0.1. GAMS/ZOOM also uses an absolute tolerance to independently control termination: see OPTCA in Section E.2.

Branch-and-Bound ■

If the LP relaxation is feasible but does not have a natural integer solution, and if the heuristic does not find an integer feasible solution that satisfies the TOLERANCE, then we have to resort to Branch-and-Bound (B&B).

B&B can be described in general terms in the following way. Assume that we are maximizing, and that INCUMBENT is the objective function value of the best integer feasible solution that has been found so far. We begin by creating a search tree consisting of a single node that represents the original problem (MIP). This node is the permanent root of the tree and is temporarily a leaf as well. The value of the LP relaxation, v_{LP}, is attached to this node as a label. One "iteration" of the branch-and-bound method is to:

BB$_1$ Select some leaf node in the current search tree. This node represents a problem which we denote CP for "candidate problem." Initially, CP = MIP. (If the search tree is empty, we are done.)

BB$_2$ Choose a zero/one variable, say x_k, and split CP into two new problems NP$_1$ and NP$_2$ by appending the mutually exclusive constraints: $x_k = 0$ and $x_k = 1$. Add two new leaf nodes to the tree for NP$_1$ and NP$_2$ (see Figure E.1). The node for CP is no longer a leaf.

BB$_3$ Solve the LP relaxation LP$_1$ of NP$_1$. Eliminate the node for NP$_1$ if LP$_1$ is infeasible, or if $v_{LP_1} \leq$ INCUMBENT, or if LP$_1$ has a natural integer solution. In the latter case, update the value of the INCUMBENT. If the NP$_1$ node survives, then attach v_{LP_1} to it as a label. Do the same for NP$_2$. If NP$_1$ and NP$_2$ are both eliminated, then CP may be eliminated as well.

This cycle (select, split, solve) is then repeated. The B&B search is finished when the search tree is empty, or the INCUMBENT value satisfies the TOLERANCE, whichever comes first. The largest LP-value label over all leaves in the current tree is the best available upper bound on v_{MIP}, and we call this bound GLOBAL.

$$\text{INCUMBENT} \leq v_{MIP} \leq \text{GLOBAL}$$

Figure E.1:   Schematic of Branch-and-Bound Tree

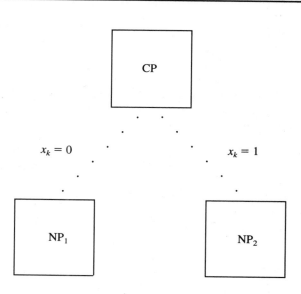

Initially, GLOBAL $= v_{LP}$. The search is halted if either of the termination criteria is satisfied.

If the search tree is empty, then the INCUMBENT value is guaranteed to be optimal. (Assuming that we really have a solution with value INCUMBENT and are not bluffing. Bluffing is explained under GAP in Section E.4.) Thus B&B is a race between creating nodes at step BB_2 and eliminating them at step BB_3.

Fixed Order Branching ■

In the general B&B procedure described above, we can use any zero/one variable to split node CP into two new nodes. (More precisely, any zero/one variable that has not already been fixed on the path from the root of the tree to the node for CP.) In GAMS/ZOOM we restrict this freedom of choice. Any node in the search tree has a "level," which is the number of arcs on the path from that node up to the root of the tree. (Or the number of zero/one variables already fixed in the problem associated with that node.) We shall designate a specific zero/one variable for each level in the tree. For level d, we shall denote the index of this variable as SORT_d. Then whenever any node at level d is split into two new nodes, this will be done with the constraints:

$$x_{\text{SORT}_{(d+1)}} = 0 \quad \text{and} \quad x_{\text{SORT}_{(d+1)}} = 1$$

We shall also use "depth" to mean "level."

The reason for imposing a fixed branching order will be explained below in the section on the resource space tour. The fixed order is determined in the following way. Consider the LP relaxation of the original problem (MIP). The optimal LP solution partitions the zero/one variables into three groups: basic (BS), non-basic at upper bound

(UB), and non-basic at lower bound (LB). The BS variables are sorted according to their values, the UB variables are sorted according to their relative profits, and the LB variables are sorted according to the negatives of their relative profits. The relative profit (or reduced cost) for variable x_j is:

$$d_j = c_j - u_1 a_{1,j} - \cdots - u_M\, a_{M,j}$$

where the $u_1, \ldots, u_M$ are the shadow prices. Then if ORDER = 1 in the options file, the branching order is taken as first the BS variables as sorted, then the UB variables as sorted, and finally the LB variables as sorted. If ORDER = 2, then the UB variables are placed before the BS variables.

Multi-level Expansion ∎

In the B&B procedure described above, we always select one node and split it into two nodes at the next level. In GAMS/ZOOM we employ a more general strategy. We may select several nodes which are at the same level in the current tree and split them several times to create new nodes which are several levels below the selected nodes. The user may specify two parameters, SELECT and EXPAND in the options file. GAMS/ZOOM will then take SELECT nodes which are at the same level, say level d, and split them EXPAND times to create SELECT*(2**EXPAND) nodes at level d+EXPAND. For example, the default values are SELECT = 2 and EXPAND = 3. This causes 2 nodes at some level d to be expanded into 16 nodes at level $d + 3$. The standard strategy is obtained by setting SELECT = 1 and EXPAND = 1.

We have found empirically that it is advantageous to use values greater than 1 for SELECT and EXPAND in an algorithm based on fixed order branching and resource space tours.

The question of what level the SELECT nodes should be taken from is addressed in the next section. As to which nodes are actually selected, we always take the ones with the SELECT best LP-value labels. (If there are fewer than SELECT nodes, then we take all of them.)

Diving vs. Best Bound ∎

The first step in each B&B iteration is deciding on the level in the tree from which the nodes to be expanded are to be selected. GAMS/ZOOM permits two alternative strategies: diving and best bound. In the diving strategy we always choose the deepest level in the current tree. This tends to produce natural integer solutions as soon as possible, which is useful if the INCUMBENT value is far from the optimum.

In the best bound strategy, we always choose the level that has the leaf node with the largest LP-value label in the current tree. That is, the leaf node with LP-value = GLOBAL. This tends to reduce GLOBAL as fast as possible. This is useful when we have an optimal or near-optimal solution and are trying to satisfy the TOLERANCE. The choice between diving and best bound is made in the options file.

The Resource Space Tour ∎

We will now explain the motivation for the fixed order branching. This section requires a knowledge of LP duality theory and parametric linear programming.

Suppose that SELECT = 2 and EXPAND = 3. Then we will select the two best nodes from some level d and expand them into 16 nodes at level $d + 3$. These 16 nodes have

16 associated linear programs: LP_1, . . . , LP_{16}. We are going apply bounding tests to these 16 nodes and eliminate as many as we can. The bounding tests will be based on LP generated information, but we will not be solving the 16 LP's completely separately from one another. We will be making a "resource space tour."

Because of the fixed order branching, the 16 linear programs are identical except for their right-hand-sides. They all have the same set of fixed zero/one variables: $SORT_1$, . . . , $SORT_{(d + 2)}$. The fixed variables are moved from the left-hand-side of the constraints to the right-hand-side, giving 16 different reduced right-hand-side vectors. We imagine the 16 nodes as represented by 16 points in the M-dimensional space of right-hand-side vectors. Starting at the point for LP_1, we shall make a tour that visits some or all of these 16 points. We begin by solving LP_1. Then we use parametric programming to obtain the solution of LP_2.

The 16 linear programs have the same dual feasible region, hence any dual feasible solution can be used to compute an upper bound on v_{LP_q} for every q, and hence to perform a bounding test on all 16 nodes. Since we are doing parametric programming on the right-hand-side, every pivot produces a new dual feasible solution that can be used to perform a bounding test on all of the still surviving nodes.

If we are traveling, by parametric programming, from the point for LP_q to the point for LP_r and we succeed in eliminating some other point, say LP_s ($q < r < s$), we call it an "indirect hit." If we eliminate the current destination, LP_r, we call it a "direct hit." If LP_r is eliminated, we immediately change direction and head toward the next still surviving point.

If LP_r survives, then we check to see if its LP solution is naturally integer and then strike off for the next still surviving node (which will be $LP_r + 1$ if it still exists). At the end of the tour we have eliminated some of the nodes (points) and obtained the LP solutions of the others (some of which may be naturally integer and hence new incumbents).

We have discovered empirically that with fixed order branching and the resource space tour, the standard SELECT = 1, EXPAND = 1 strategy gives poor results. It is much more effective to spread the LP computational overhead among more nodes and take advantage of indirect hits. In one series of experiments, the best strategy was SELECT = 5, EXPAND = 4, giving 80 nodes for each tour.

If EXPAND = 3, then we will only be performing tours at levels 3, 6, 9, . . . , in the search tree. GAMS/ZOOM will save one "hot" LP basis for each of these levels. A tour at level 9 will start with the hot basis for level 9 if one is available, otherwise with the hot basis for level 6, or level 3, or level 0 (root) in that order of preference. The "MAX SAVE" option in the options file allows the user to decide how many hot bases should be saved. If "MAX SAVE 5" is specified, then the root basis and four other hot bases will be held at any one time. Saving more hot bases should speed up the tours, but each one saved takes up COLUMNS/2 + ROWS words of work space.

Locking Zero/One Variables   ∎

GAMS/ZOOM will lock zero/one variables automatically, based on the solution to the initial LP relaxation. After solving the initial LP we compute the relative profits d_j for each variable x_j, j in binary. Assuming a maximization problem, if x_j is at its upper bound (UB) and

$$d_j \geq v_{LP} - \text{INCUMBENT}$$

then x_j can be locked permanently at one. On the other hand, if x_j is at its lower bound (LB) and

$$-d_j \geq v_{\text{LP}} - \text{INCUMBENT}$$

then x_j can be locked permanently at zero. The d_j and v_{LP} values are saved and whenever a new INCUMBENT value is found during the heuristic or the branch-and-bound search we attempt to lock additional variables.

The Algorithm ∎

We summarize the above discussion in a concise statement of the main steps in the algorithm. Capitalized names refer to options and parameters from the options file or to program variables. We assume maximization, and an initial INCUMBENT value (see the INCUMBENT and GAP keywords in the options file).

Step 1. Solve the initial linear program. If it is infeasible, stop. If it has a natural integer solution, stop. Otherwise initialize the search tree by creating a node with LP-value label $= v_{\text{LP}}$. (If the problem is a pure LP, stop.)

Step 2. Compute the relative profits, d_j, of all the zero/one variables and lock as many of them as possible using v_{LP} and INCUMBENT.

Step 3. If HEURISTIC = 'YES', then use the Pivot and Complement heuristic to attempt to find an integer feasible solution. If P&C finds an improved INCUMBENT, try to lock additional variables.

Step 4. If INCUMBENT satisfies either of the termination tolerances (OPTCA or OPTCR), stop.

Step 5. If BRANCH = 'NO', stop. Otherwise use ORDER to determine the branching order. Set IMPROV = .FALSE..

Step 6. If the search tree is empty, stop. The INCUMBENT value is optimal (unless it is a bluff).

Step 7. Set GLOBAL = the largest LP-value label over all leaves in the current tree. Stop if $(\text{GLOBAL} - \text{INCUMBENT})/(1 + |\text{GLOBAL}|) \leq \text{TOLERANCE}$.

Step 8. Stop if IMPROV = .TRUE. and QUIT = 'YES'.

Step 9. Stop if the LIMIT on LP iterations has been exceeded.

Step 10. If DIVE = 'YES', choose d = the deepest level in the current tree. Otherwise, choose d = the level that has the leaf with LP-value label = GLOBAL.

Step 11. Take the SELECT nodes at level d that have the best LP-value labels, and expand them into SELECT*(2**EXPAND) nodes at level d+EXPAND. If there are fewer than SELECT nodes at level d, then just take all of them.

Step 12. Do a resource space tour at level d+EXPAND. If a natural integer solution is found that gives an improved INCUMBENT value, then set IMPROV = .TRUE.. Keep track of all LP iterations for comparison with LIMIT. Label each surviving node with its LP-value.

Step 13. If IMPROV = .TRUE., purge the tree. That is, eliminate any leaf that has LP-value label $\leq$ INCUMBENT.

Step 14. If IMPROV = .TRUE., use the saved d_j and v_{LP} values to attempt to lock additional variables.

Step 15. Go to Step 6.

Cheating   ■

In this section we examine the bounding test that is used in the branch-and-bound procedure. Consider any node in the search tree. Suppose it represents sub-problem CP_q with LP relaxation LP_q. We may eliminate (discard) this node if

$$UB_q \leq \text{INCUMBENT}$$

where UB_q is an upper bound on v_{CP_q}, the optimal value of CP_q. UB_q may be v_{LP_q}, or it may be an upper bound on v_{LP_q} computed using a dual feasible solution of LP_q during a resource space tour. It may happen that

$$v_{CP_q} \leq \text{INCUMBENT} \leq UB_q$$

i.e., CP_q does not contain any solution better than the current incumbent, but we cannot discard it since UB_q is too loose an estimate of v_{CP_q}. (Remember that v_{CP_q} is unknown.) It may also happen that

$$\text{INCUMBENT} < UB_q < v_{MIP}$$

i.e., CP_q does not contain an optimal solution of MIP, but we cannot discard it because it may contain a solution that is better than the current (poor) incumbent.

Because of the error involved in making the LP relaxation, UB_q is too big. And INCUMBENT, because it is not, in general, optimal, is too small. We would like to decrease UB_q and increase INCUMBENT to correct for these errors. Of course the amount of correction needed is unknown, but the form of the correction would be:

$$UB_q(1 - A) \leq \text{INCUMBENT}(1 + B)$$

where $0 \leq A < 1$ and $B > 0$. This is equivalent to:

$$UB_q \leq \text{INCUMBENT}(1 + \epsilon)$$

If $\epsilon > 0.0$, then we may discard nodes that would not normally ($\epsilon = 0.0$) be discarded. Clearly if ϵ is large, we will eliminate too many nodes and almost surely miss the optimal solution. We can, however, determine the maximum possible error in our final answer.

During the B&B search we simply keep track of the largest UB_q value over all discarded nodes. That is, the best bound that gets thrown away. We call this value DISCARD. During the search, we modify the definition of GLOBAL to be either DISCARD or the largest LP-value label over all the leaves in the tree, whichever is larger. At the end of the search,

$$\text{GLOBAL} = \max(\text{DISCARD}, \text{INCUMBENT})$$

Thus the incumbent is optimal if DISCARD $\leq$ INCUMBENT, and otherwise the relative error is no greater than

$$(\text{GLOBAL} - \text{INCUMBENT})/\text{GLOBAL}$$

So we can determine the consequences of cheating (i.e., using $\epsilon > 0.0$) simply by keeping track of the single number DISCARD.

In deciding on the numerical value to use for ϵ, our first observation is that ϵ should be smaller when we are deep in the tree than when we are near the top of the tree. We would also like ϵ to depend on the apparent relative gap between the MIP and LP optimal values for the problem at hand. GAMS/ZOOM uses the following method for computing ϵ values when CHEAT = 'YES' is specified in the options file.

Let NBR be the number of zero/one variables that have to be branched on, i.e. the original number minus any that are locked. Let SHRINK and EXPAND be as given in the options file, or by default. Suppose we are performing a resource space tour at level d + EXPAND. Then we use the bounding test:

$$\text{UB}_q \leq \text{INCUMBENT}(1 + \epsilon)$$

where $\epsilon = \text{GAP}_d[1 - (\text{SHRINK} + \text{EXPAND} - 1)/(\text{NBR} - d)]$

                             if   SHRINK + EXPAND $- 1 < $ NBR $- d$;

or $= 0.0$ otherwise

and $\text{GAP}_d = (\text{BESTUB}_d - \text{INCUMBENT})/\text{INCUMBENT}$

and BESTUB_d = the largest LP-value label obtained so far at depth d.

Thus we cheat more if the estimate GAP_d of the relaxation error at depth d is large. The SHRINK parameter is required to be at least 1.0, and the larger it is, the less we are cheating.

If CHEAT = 'YES', then the ϵ value will be printed out at the beginning of each resource space tour (and again during the tour if a new INCUMBENT value causes ϵ to be revised). The value of DISCARD will also be printed.

E.2 GAMS/ZOOM OPTIONS SPECIFIED IN YOUR PROGRAM ■

The most important of the options used to control the behavior of GAMS/ZOOM must be included in your program as GAMS OPTION statements, rather than in the options file. These have been discussed in Chapters 10 and 16, enumerated in Appendix C, and are listed again below in the sequence *option, value,* and *default*.

OPTCR   A real number in the range 0 to 1   Default $= 0.1$

Controls the termination of GAMS/ZOOM. If (assuming maximization) an integer feasible solution is found in which

$$v_{\text{MIP}} \geq \text{BESTUB}(1 - \text{OPTCR})$$

then GAMS/ZOOM is stopped and this solution reported. BESTUB is the best objective value possible. It decreases during B&B. *Warning:* setting OPTCR $= 0.0$ can result in extremely long-run times for even small problems that have a great many optimal and near optimal solutions (unless OPTCA, below, has been set different from zero). It is much safer to use a very small value like 0.0001 than an exact 0.0.

OPTCA   A positive real number   Default $= 0.0$

Controls the termination of GAMS/ZOOM. If (assuming maximization) an integer feasible solution is found in which

$$v_{\text{MIP}} \geq \text{BESTUB} - \text{OPTCA}$$

then GAMS/ZOOM is stopped and this solution reported. This control operates *independently* of that provided by OPTCR.

ITERLIM   A positive integer   Default = 1000

Limits the number of iterations that will be performed by GAMS/ZOOM. If the problem is an MIP this limit will be approximate and not exact.

RESLIM   A positive real number   Default = Varies, often 1000

Controls the amount of computer time used by GAMS/ZOOM. The units are machine specific.

SYSOUT   ON or OFF   Default = OFF

If set to ON, you will receive a listing of all GAMS/ZOOM output on your output file. This information is essential for investigating or changing the behavior of GAMS/ZOOM. Use the options file PRINT keyword to control the amount and type of output.

WORK   A positive integer   Default = Estimated by GAMS/ZOOM

Use to control the size of the table of waiting B&B nodes. If you have trouble with the node table size, messages will tell you how big it was.

BRATIO

This option has no effect on GAMS/ZOOM, since we are unable (for technical reasons) to provide an advanced start for it.

E.3. FORMAT OF THE GAMS/ZOOM OPTIONS FILE   ■

The options file contains general information about the problem to be solved, and the user's choices for the many algorithmic parameters and options.

The options file is a file with a fixed name, and it must be in the current directory if you have a directory-based file system. The name is constructed from two parts. The first is most likely ZOOM: the name you would use in your program to specify that GAMS/ZOOM be used (e.g., OPTION MIP = ZOOM;). The second is a machine-specific suffix or type that would apply to all solvers on a particular machine: on personal computers "OPT," giving a complete filename "ZOOM.OPT." The same principles lead to the name "ZOOM OPTIONS A" on IBM/CMS systems. Consult your online GAMS documentation for exact details on your machine.

If you do not provide an options file, GAMS/ZOOM will use reasonable defaults that are satisfactory for most problems.

> *If an options file is used (whether you provided it intentionally or not), then its contents will be listed as part of your output.*
>
> *It is your responsibility to ensure that, if a file with the matching name exists, then its contents are applicable to the model at hand.*

The first line of the options file must contain the keyword 'BEGIN', and the last line must contain the keyword 'END'. Every line between the 'BEGIN' and 'END' must either be a comment line (first non-blank character '*' or '!') or contain one of the keywords listed in Section E.4 as its first non-blank characters. For each of the valid keywords there may be a modifier and/or a value. The lines are free form in that there may be any number of blanks or '=' signs separating items. Every line must look like:

```
   keyword
or keyword   modifier
or keyword   value
or keyword   modifier   value
```

Any line may end with a comment whose first character is '*' or '!'. The ordering of the lines (i.e., of the keywords) is not important. Only the first three characters of each keyword are significant. Only the first four characters of each modifier are significant. All of the keywords have default values that are intended to reduce the number of values that the user has to specify.

Numeric values for the keywords may consist of up to eight characters, the first of which must be numeric. The number may be either an integer or a real constant. A number will be treated as real if any character other than the first is '.', 'E', or 'D'. Real numbers may be expressed in F, E, or D FORTRAN formats. Any other numbers will be treated as integers. (Note that .001 is invalid, but 0.001 is valid.)

All text must be in uppercase. If a real number is required, it must contain a decimal point.

E.4 GAMS/ZOOM OPTIONS

The following is the list in sequence of valid keywords with their associated modifiers, values, and default values. Please note the following:

1. The GAMS options RESLIM and ITERLIM (Chapter 9) may be used to control resource usage, and OPTCA and OPTCR (Chapter 16) control termination. The node table size can be set with the GAMS WORK option. The ZOOM options TOLERANCE and MAX NODES are not recognized by GAMS/ZOOM.
2. GAMS/ZOOM is not able to use basis or tree information from a previous solve to provide an advanced start to your problem.
3. GAMS/ZOOM accepts only a subset of keywords available to programmers using ZOOM. None of the problem size parameters are applicable, and several of the methods and settings are not available. They are:
   (a) The Dual method.
   (b) The ZOOM SAVE/RESTORE capability.
   (c) The ability to provide a user-specified branching order.
4. GAMS/ZOOM provides an additional pre-specified branching order (ORDER = 3) that has been found to work well with general integer variables. The meaning of ORDER = 3 is thus different from the meaning in the Fortran program ZOOM.

GAMS/ZOOM Option List ■

BRANCH   'YES', 'NO'   Default = 'YES'

Specifies whether or not a branch-and-bound search is to be performed.

CHEAT   'YES', 'NO'   Default = 'NO'

Specifies whether or not the cheating strategy is to be used during the branch-and-bound search.

DIVE   'YES', 'NO'   Default = 'YES'

Specifies whether or not to use the diving strategy in the branch-and-bound search. Diving is recommended as a first attack on the problem, especially if the heuristic fails or finds a relatively poor solution. 'NO' means use the best-bound strategy. In the diving strategy, we always select nodes from the deepest level in the current search tree. In the best-bound strategy, we choose the level in the tree that has the best associated LP bound. If GAMS/ZOOM is diving and it finds an improved integer feasible solution (i.e., new incumbent), it will automatically switch over to the best-bound strategy.

EXPAND   1, . . . , 6   Default = 3

During the branch-and-bound search, each node that is selected is expanded EXPAND levels down in the search tree, resulting in 2**EXPAND new nodes.

FACTOR or INVERT   1, . . . , 100   Default = 50

The number of iterations to be allowed between refactorizations of the basis matrix. A value of 50 is suitable for most problems. It should be reduced in the presence of serious numerical instability. The accuracy of the current solution is checked every FACTOR/2 iterations and an early refactorization done if necessary.

GAP   Non-negative real   Default = $+\infty$

An estimate of the relative gap between the value of the integer program, v_{MIP}, and the value of the linear program, v_{LP}. That is, GAP is an *a priori* estimate of $(v_{\mathrm{LP}} - v_{\mathrm{MIP}})/(1 + |v_{\mathrm{LP}}|)$. After computing v_{LP}, the code will compute an estimate of v_{MIP} using GAP. It will use this as the incumbent value (see Keyword: INCUMBENT) at the beginning of the branch-and-bound search (unless a better incumbent value has been found by the heuristic). If the true gap is larger than GAP, and the corresponding estimate of v_{MIP} is not improved by the heuristic, then the branch-and-bound search will not find any solutions. Guessing a GAP can save a lot of work in the early part of the search, until a true incumbent solution is found. It is a bluff, however, and fails if it is too optimistic (too small). A value specified with the INCUMBENT keyword will always override the value of GAP. The default of $+\infty$ has the effect of not using the GAP feature at all. Suggested value: 0.25.

HEURISTIC   'YES', 'NO'   Default = 'YES'

Specifies whether or not the search for an integer feasible solution starts with the Pivot and Complement heuristic.

INCUMBENT   Real   Default $= -\infty$ for maximization; $+\infty$ for minimization

The objective function value of the best integer feasible solution that is known so far. This is used to eliminate nodes in the search tree whose LP values are not better than INCUMBENT. You can also bluff and hope that the search turns up a solution with a better value than INCUMBENT. If you bluff, however, and the value you give for INCUMBENT is better than the true optimal value, then the branch-and-bound search will not find any solutions. A value specified with the INCUMBENT keyword will always override the GAP value. (*See* Keyword: GAP.)

INVERT   *See:* FACTOR

MAX   Modifier: SAVE   Positive integer   Default $= 5$

An upper limit on the number of hot LP bases saved during the branch-and-bound search. Saving more bases should speed up the search, but each one saved takes up (COLUMNS/2 + ROW) words of work space.

MULTIPLE   Positive integer   Default $= 5$

Multiple pricing parameter for the simplex method. This is the number of attractive non-basic variables saved during a major iteration for basis entry during the subsequent series of minor iterations.

ORDER   1, 2, 3   Default $= 1$, or 3 if integer variables

Specifies the branching order for branch-and-bound. If BS, UB, and LB denote the sets of zero/one variables that are basic, at upper bound, and at lower bound respectively in the optimal solution of the initial linear program, and if the variables in these sets are ordered as described in Section 2, then:

> 1 means BS, UB, LB
> 2 means UB, BS, LB
> 3 means an order that may provide improved performance with integer variables.

PARTIAL   Positive integer   Default $= 500$

Partial pricing parameter for the simplex method. The number of columns priced out during a major iteration. A major iteration consists of pricing out PARTIAL columns and saving the MULTIPLE best ones.

PRINT   Modifier: LP1   0, 1, 2, 3   Default $= 2$

Output level for XMP while solving the initial linear program. Higher values give more output.

PRINT   Modifier: LP2   0, 1, 2, 3   Default $= 0$

Output level for XMP during the Pivot and Complement heuristic. Higher values give more output.

PRINT   Modifier: LP3   0, 1, 2, 3   Default $= 0$

Output level for XMP during the branch-and-bound search. Higher values give more output.

PRINT   Modifier: HEURISTIC   0, 1, 2, 3   Default = 0

Output level for the Pivot and Complement heuristic. Higher values give more output.

PRINT   Modifier: BRANCH   0, 1, 2, 3   Default = 1

Output level for the branch-and-bound search. Higher values give more output.

PRINT   Modifier: TOUR   0, 1, . . . , 6   Default = 0

Output level for the Resource Space Tour during the branch-and-bound search. Higher values give more output. Values 2, . . . ,6 are intended for serious debugging.

QUIT   'YES', 'NO'   Default = 'NO'

Specifies whether or not the branch-and-bound search should be halted when an improved incumbent solution is found.

SELECT   Positive integer   Default = 2

The number of nodes to be selected for each expansion during the branch-and-bound search. One expansion consists of choosing a level in the search tree (*see* Keyword: DIVE), selecting the SELECT best nodes at that level, and expanding them down EXPAND levels, resulting in SELECT*(2**EXPAND) nodes (*see* Keyword: EXPAND.)

SHRINK   Positive real ≥ 1.0   Default = 5.0

The control parameter for the cheating strategy (*see* Keyword: CHEAT). The smaller the value of SHRINK, the more you are cheating. The more you cheat, the faster the branch-and-bound search goes, but the less likely you are to find the optimal solution.

E.5   ADVICE FOR CONTROLLING BRANCH-AND-BOUND   ■

The time and computational effort required to solve a mixed-integer program by Branch-and-Bound is notoriously unpredictable. GAMS/ZOOM has many options and parameters that you can set in your search for an optimal, or near-optimal, integer solution. Here, in the currently fashionable form of *if-then* rules, are some suggestions about using these parameters.

1. If the model you want to solve is new, unfamiliar, or large, then plan on making more than one run.
2. If you are going to make more than one run *and* this is your first run, then use HEURISTIC = 'YES' and BRANCH = 'NO'.
3. If (the heuristic has found a feasible integer solution *or* an earlier B&B search has found a feasible integer solution *or* you know a feasible integer solution), then set INCUMBENT to the value of that solution and compute:
$$\text{CRITERION} = (v_{\text{LP}} - \text{INCUMBENT})/(1 + |v_{\text{LP}}|).$$
4. If you have not found any feasible integer solutions, then set CRITERION = 100.

5. If CRITERION < 0.10, then make a B&B search with BRANCH = 'YES', DIVE = 'NO' and QUIT = 'NO'.

6. If 0.10 < CRITERION < 0.25, then make a B&B run with BRANCH = 'YES', DIVE = 'NO' and QUIT = 'YES'.

7. If CRITERION > 0.25 *and* you have not tried B&B yet, then make a B&B run with BRANCH = 'YES', DIVE = 'YES', QUIT = 'YES', SELECT = 1, and EXPAND = 4.

8. If CRITERION > 0.25 *and* you have already tried B&B, then bluff, i.e., use the INCUMBENT or GAP parameter to pretend that you have a feasible integer solution that is within 25 percent of v_{LP}.

9. If CRITERION > 0.25 *and* you have already tried bluffing, then cheat, i.e., use the CHEAT and SHRINK parameters to try to find a better feasible integer solution.

10. If you found an improved feasible integer solution during a B&B run with cheating, then make another B&B run with cheating, but cheat less, i.e., increase SHRINK.

11. If you have made several B&B runs *and* you have a feasible integer solution *and* CRITERION > 0.50 *and* the current upper bound on v_{MIP} is almost the same as v_{LP}, then you should give up on trying to satisfy your stopping TOLERANCE. In this event, B&B is just not going to bring the upper bound down in any reasonable amount of time. Any further B&B runs should be pure diving raids (DIVE = 'YES', QUIT = 'YES'), perhaps with bluffing or cheating, looking for improved integer solutions (i.e., increase INCUMBENT).

E.6 REFERENCES ■

Marsten, R. E., "The design of the XMP linear programming library," *ACM Transactions on Mathematical Software*, Vol. 7, No. 4, December, 1981, 481–497.

Reid, J. K., "A sparsity-exploiting variant of the Bartels-Golub decomposition for linear programming bases," *Mathematical Programming*, Vol. 24, No. 1, September, 1982, 55–69.

Balas, E. and C. H. Martin, "Pivot and Complement—a heuristic for 0–1 programming," *Management Science*, Vol. 26, No. 1, January, 1980, 86–96.

Singhal, J. A., R. E. Marsten, and T. L. Morin, "Fixed Order Branch-and-Bound Methods for Mixed-Integer Programming: The ZOOM System," Dept. of Management Information Systems, University of Arizona, Tucson, AZ, 85721, December, 1987.

GRAMMAR F

In this section the syntax of GAMS is presented using the Backus-Naur Form (BNF) notation. BNF defines the syntax by using a set of rules expressed in terms of the meta-symbols defined below:

    ::=   is defined as

    | or

    { }   enclosed construct may be repeated zero or more times

    [ ]   enclosed construct is optional

    Symbols appearing only on the right side of a rule (production) are terminal symbols. Although GAMS makes no distinction between lower and upper case letters, the terminal symbols below are typed in upper case and non-terminal symbols use lower case to improve readability.

    The numbered notes below each group of rules describe additional conventions that are best written using English instead of BNF.

GAMS Problem

```
gams-problem    ::=   unit { ; unit } [ ; ]
unit            ::=   definition I statement I solve
definition      ::=   scalar-def I set-def I param-def I table-def I
                      variable-def I equation-def I model-def I alias-def I
                      acronym-def I equ-spec
statement       ::=   assignment I display I abort I option I loop
```

1. The semicolon (;) can be omitted if the following unit starts with a reserved word. The only two units not starting with a reserved word are the equ-spec and the assignment statement.

2. Spaces can be used freely unless indicated.

3. Line boundaries are not recognized except in table-def and before text.

4. When used as a list separator the comma (,) can be omitted at the end or beginning of a line. The commas used to separate index positions and function arguments and the sum-operator comma (see primary) cannot be omitted and should not be the first symbol on a line.

Lexical Items

A number of lexical items need to be defined first. These items define basic building blocks of the language like words in English.

ident	::=	symbol composed of letters and digits starting with a letter and no longer than 10 characters
label	::=	one to ten long sequence of letters, digits, + and - | "labtext"
labtext	::=	one to ten long sequence of any character except EOL
text	::=	one to eighty long sequence of characters not starting with .. and = and separated by at least one space from the preceeding symbol, which must be on the same line; the sequence is terminated by , / ; EOL | "one to eighty long sequence of any character"
number	::=	[.]integer[exponent] | integer.[integer][exponent]
exponent	::=	E[sign]integer
integer	::=	digit{digit}

Rules for Definitions and Statements

In order to define compactly the rules for all definitions and statements, we need to define the common concepts of declaration, element, expression, primary and signed number. The definitions of these major rules are given in alphabetical order below.

ABORT Statement

abort	::=	ABORT [$ primary] display-entry { , display-entry }
display-entry	::=	extended-id | "any text"
extended-id	::=	ident[extension]
extension	::=	.LO | .UP | .L | .M

1. If the primary exists or evaluates to non-zero, all the display entries are printed as in a DISPLAY statement and the program is aborted (terminated)

ACRONYM Definition

acronym-def	::=	ACRONYM[S] ident [text] { , ident [text] }

1. An ident defined as an ACRONYM can be used like a number; it has no numerical value, however, and only the operations 'eq' and 'ne' are allowed.

ALIAS Definition

alias-def	::=	ALIAS alias-list { , alias-list }
alias-list	::=	(ident , ident { , ident })

1. Exactly one ident must be a known set name and all other idents must be unknown.

2. The dimension of the known set name must be one: if the dimension is not known it will be set to one.

3. All unknown names will become sets of dimension one and can only be used as driving index sets or in domain list definitions.

Assignment Statement

assignment	::=	ident-ref [$ primary] = expression
ident-ref	::=	ident[extension] [(index { , index })]
extension	::=	.LO I .UP I .L I .M I .FX
index	::=	"labtext" I ident [lag-operator primary]
lag-operator	::=	- I + I -- I ++

1. .FX is a short way of setting .LO, .L and .UP to the same value.
2. References in primary and expression must have values.
3. Variables and equations can only be used with extensions.
4. Set idents with lag-operations force the set to be static and ordered.

Declaration

declaration	::=	ident [(domain-id { , domain-id })] [text]
domain-id	::=	ident I *

1. At least one space is required before the text.
2. No EOL is allowed before the text.
3. The domain-id ident must be a one-dimensional defined set that cannot be redefined.

DISPLAY Statement

display	::=	DISPLAY [$ primary] display-entry { , display-entry }
display-entry	::=	extended-id I "any text"
extended-id	::=	ident[extension]
extension	::=	.LO I .UP I .L I .M

1. The display entries are not printed if the primary evaluates to zero.

Element

element	::=	s-element { . s-element }
s-element	::=	label { * label } I (element { , element })

1. No EOL is allowed before a . or *.
2. Spaces around . and * can be used freely except in two situations when the dimensionality of the element is not known. Spaces in front of a "." are not allowed in:
   (a) the first row if the overall dimensionality of the table is not known and
   (b) the first element in a PARAMETER list if the dimensionality is not known.
3. No restrictions apply inside ( ).
4. The s-element label1 * label2 is expanded into a list of labels by interpreting the variant part of strings label1 and label2 as ranges for a numeric sequence.

EQUATION Definition

equation-def	::=	EQUATION[S] declaration { , declaration }

Equation Specification

equ-spec	::=	eq-reference [$ primary] .. expression type expression
eq-reference	::=	ident I ident (index { , index })
index	::=	"labtext" I ident [lag-operator primary]
lag-operator	::=	- I + I -- I ++
type	::=	=E= I =L= I =G= I =N=

1. An equation name can only appear once on the left side of an equation detail.

2. Only controlling sets must have values assigned: referenced sets, parameters and equations or variables in extended form (.L, .M, .LO, .UP) do not need values assigned.

3. Expression can include variables.

4. A lag-operation is only possible if the associated set is static and ordered.

Expression

expression	::=	primary I [unary] expression [binary expression]
unary	::=	- I + I NOT
binary	::=	$ I ** I * I / I + I - I LT I LE I EQ I NE I GE I GT I AND I
		OR I XOR

1. The unary and binary operators have an eight-level precedence order as defined below from highest to lowest:

$
**
*
/
- + (unary and binary)
LT LE EQ NE GE GT
NOT
AND
OR XOR

2. Operations must have compatible data types that are set-valued or numeric.

3. Only the $ operator allows mixed mode.

4. Note that the $ symbol can be used for two different purposes, as a binary operator and as a domain restriction, as in other constructs.

LOOP Statement

loop	::=	LOOP (control [$ primary] , statement { ; statement })
statement	::=	assignment I display I abort I option I loop

MODEL Definition

model-def	::=	MODEL[S] model-detail { , model-detail }
model-detail	::=	ident [text] [/ model-list /]
model-list	::=	ALL I ident { , ident }

1. ALL is a short form for including all previously declared equations.

2. Idents in a model-list must be known (declared) names but need not have numeric or symbolic values.

3. If idents have different types, they must appear in the partial order set, parameters, equations and variables.

OPTION Statement

option	::=	OPTION[S] option-value { , option-value }
option-value	::=	ident I ident = ident I ident = number I ident:integer{:integer:integer}

PARAMETER Definition

param-def	::=	PARAMETER[S] param-detail { , param-detail }
param-detail	::=	declaration [/ value-pair { , value-pair } /]
value-pair	::=	element [=] signed-num

Primary

primary	::=	number I NA I EPS I INF I YES I NO I ORD (ident) I CARD (ident) I extended-id I extended-id (index { , index }) I function (expression { , expression }) I sum-operator (control [$ primary] , expression) I (expression)
extended-id	::=	ident[extension]
extension	::=	.LO I .UP I .L I .M
index	::=	"labtext" I ident [lag-operator primary]
control	::=	ident I (ident { , ident })
function	::=	ABS I ARCTAN I CEIL I COS I ERRORF I EXP I FLOOR I LOG I LOG10 I MAPVAL I MAX I MIN I MOD I NORMAL I POWER I ROUND I SIN I SIGN I SQR I SQRT I TRUNC I UNIFORM
sum-operator	::=	PROD I SMAX I SMIN I SUM
lag-operator	::=	- I + I -- I ++

1. The use of the ORD(ident) function forces the associated set, which must have a dimension of one, to be static and ordered.

2. Note that the $ symbol is used here as a domain restriction rather than as a binary operator.

SCALAR Definition

scalar-def	::=	SCALAR[S] scalar-detail { , scalar-detail }
scalar-detail	::=	ident [text] [/ signed-num /]

1. No EOL between ident and text.

SET Definition

set-def	::=	SET[S] set-detail { , set-detail }
set-detail	::=	declaration [/ element [text] { , element [text] } /]

1. No EOL allowed between element and text.

Signed Number

signed-num	::=	[sign] number	NA	EPS	ident	[sign] INF
sign	::=	-	+

1. Spaces are allowed between sign and number or INF. No EOL is allowed between them, however.

2. The ident must be of type ACRONYM.

SOLVE Statement

solve	::=	SOLVE ident USING process [direction ident]	
		SOLVE ident direction ident USING process
process	::=	LP	NLP	DNLP	RMIP	MIP	RMIDNLP	MIDNLP
direction	::=	MAXIMIZING	MINIMIZING

TABLE Definition

table-def	::=	TABLE declaration EOL table-body
table-body	::=	columns rows { EOL + columns rows }
columns	::=	element { element }
rows	::=	EOL element { signed-num } { EOL element { signed-num } }

1. The relative positions of all entries in a table are significant. This is the only statement where end of line (EOL) has semantic meaning.

2. The column section has to fit on one input line.

3. The sequence of signed numbers forming a row must be on the same line.

4. The element definition of a row can span more than one line.

5. A specific column can appear only once in the entire table.

6. Can only be used with parameter-type data.

VARIABLE Definition

variable-def	::=	[var-type] VARIABLE[S] declaration { , declaration }
var-type	::=	FREE	POSITIVE	NEGATIVE	BINARY	INTEGER

1. If no var-type is specified, FREE is assumed unless redefined with another variable definition.

2. Once a var-type has been defined, or the ident without explicit var-type is referenced or assigned, the type is frozen.

GLOSSARY

REFERENCES

INDEX

GLOSSARY

ACRONYM

A GAMS data type used to give logical classifications to data points.

ALIAS

An alternative name for a set.

ALGORITHM

This term may be used in two ways. It is either a prescription for how to solve a problem, or a particular solver system.

ASSIGNMENT

The statement used to change values associated with an identifier.

BASIC

A classification of a row or column that is in the basis maintained by solution methods that use linear programming iterations.

BINDING

An inequality constraint is binding when the value of the associated slack is zero.

BOUNDS

Upper and lower limits on the possible values that a column may assume in a feasible solution. May be "infinite," meaning that no limit is imposed.

COLUMN

An individual decision variable in the model seen by a solver program. Many may be associated with one GAMS variable.

COMPILATION

The initial phase of GAMS processing, when the program is being checked for syntax and consistency.

CONSTANT SET

A set is constant if it remains unchanged. It has to be initialized with a set definition statement and cannot be changed using assignment statements. Sets used in domain definitions must be constant. Sets used in lag operations must be ordered as well. Sometimes the word static is used instead of constant.

CONSTRAINT

A relationship between columns that must hold in a feasible solution. There may be many constraints associated with one GAMS equation.

CONTINUOUS

There are two contexts. First, a classification of a function. A plot of the function values will be a line without breaks in it. Second, a classification of variables. A continuous variable may assume any value within its bounds.

CONTROLLING SETS

See driving sets.

COORDINATOR

See GAMS COORDINATOR.

DATA TYPES

Each symbol or identifier has to be declared to be one of the six data types, which are SET, PARAMETER, VARIABLE, EQUATION, MODEL and ACRONYM. The keywords SCALAR and TABLE do not introduce separate data types but rather comprise a shorthand way to declare a symbol to be a PARAMETER that will use a particular format for specifying initial values.

DECLARATION

The entry of a symbol and the specification of its data type. A declaration may include the specification of initial values, and then it is more properly called a definition.

DEFAULT

The value used, or the action taken, if the user provides no information.

DEFINITION

The definition of the algebraic relationships in an equation or the assignment of initial values to parameters or of elements to sets as part of the initial declaration of the identifier.

DEFINITION STATEMENTS

Units that describe symbols, assign initial values to them, and describe symbolic relationships. Some examples are the SET, PARAMETER, TABLE, VARIABLE, and MODEL statements, and the equation definition statement.

DIRECTION

Either maximization or minimization, depending on whether the user is interested in the largest or the smallest possible value for the objective function.

DISCONTINUOUS

A classification of a function. A plot of the function values will be a line with breaks in it.

DISCRETE

A discrete variable (type *binary* or *integer*) may not assume *any* value between the bounds, but must assume integer values.

DOLLAR CONTROL OPTION (or DIRECTIVE)

Directives or options used to control input or output detail associated with the GAMS compiler.

DOLLAR OPERATOR

An operator used for exception handling in assignment statements and in equation definitions.

DOMAIN CHECKING

The check that ensures that only legal label combinations are used on every assignment to, or reference of, an identifier.

DOMAIN OF DEFINITION

The label combinations whose data will be updated in an assignment statement, or that will generate an individual constraint in an equation definition.

DOMAIN RESTRICTION CONDITION

The alteration to the domain of definition caused when a dollar operator is used on the left (of the "=" in an assignment or of the ".." in an equation definition).

DRIVING SETS

The sets that determine the domain of definition, or that control an index operation such as SUM.

DYNAMIC SET

A set is dynamic if it has been changed with an assignment statement. Dynamic sets cannot be used with lag operations or in domain definitions.

ENDOGENOUS

Data values that change when a solve statement is processed. In GAMS most often associated with VARIABLES.

EQUATION

The GAMS data type used to specify required relationships between activity levels of variables.

EXECUTION

The second phase of GAMS processing, when GAMS is actually carrying out data transformations or generating a model.

EXECUTION STATEMENTS

Instructions to carry out actions such as data transformations, model solutions, and report generation. Some examples are the assignment and the OPTION, DISPLAY, LOOP and SOLVE statements.

EXOGENOUS

Data values known before a SOLVE statement is processed, and not changed by the solve. In GAMS most often parameters.

EXPLANATORY TEXT

See TEXT.

EXPONENT

A scale factor used to conveniently represent very large or small numbers.

EXTENDED ARITHMETIC

The usual computer arithmetic is extended to include plus and minus infinity (+INF and -INF) and a special value for an arbitrarily small number (i.e., one which is close to zero) known as epsilon (EPS). Also, not available (NA) can be used to indicate missing data, and undefined (UNDF) is the result of any illegal operation. GAMS allows extended arithmetic for all operations and functions. The library problem [CRAZY] demonstrates extended arithmetic by showing the results for all operations and functions.

E-FORMAT

The representation of numbers when an exponent is used explicitly. For example, 1.1E+07.

FEASIBLE

Often used to describe a model that has at least one feasible solution (see below).

FEASIBLE SOLUTION

A solution to a model in which all column activity levels are within the bounds and all the constraints are satisfied.

GAMS COORDINATOR

The person who looks after the administration of a GAMS system, and who will know what solvers are available and can tell you who to approach for help with GAMS problems. This person's name should be given in the online 'help' file. Unlikely to apply to personal computer versions.

HERCULES

A system for formulating and solving macroeconomic models that are based on social accounting matrices. See Drud and Kendrick (1986).

IDENTIFIERS

Names given to data entities. Also called symbols.

INDEX POSITION(S)

Another way of describing the set(s) that must be used when referencing a symbol of dimensionality one or more (i.e., a vector or a matrix).

INEQUALITY CONSTRAINT

A constraint in which the imposed relationship between the columns is not fixed, but must be either greater than or equal to, or less than or equal to, a constant. The GAMS symbols =G= and =L= are used in equation definitions to specify these relationships.

INFEASIBLE

Used to describe either a model that has no feasible solution, or an intermediate solution that is not feasible (although feasible solutions may exist). See FEASIBLE, above.

INITIALIZATION

Associating initial values with sets or parameters using lists as part of the declaration or definition, or (for parameters only) using TABLE statements.

LABELS

Set elements. Sometimes called unique elements.

LIST

One of the ways of specifying initial values. Used with sets or parameters, most often for one dimensional but also for two and higher dimensional data structures.

LIST FORMAT

One of the ways in which sets and parameters, can be initialized and all symbol classes having data can be displayed. Each unique label combination is specified in full, with the associated non-default value alongside.

MARGINALS

Often called reduced costs or dual values. The values, which are meaningful only for nonbasic rows or columns in optimal solutions, contain information about the rate at which the objective value will change of if the associated bound or right hand side is changed.

MATRIX ELEMENT

See NONZERO ELEMENT.

MODEL GENERATION

The initial phase of processing a SOLVE statement: preparing a problem description for the solver.

MODEL LIST

A list of equations used in a model, as specified in a MODEL statement.

NONBASIC

A column that is not basic and (in nonlinear problems) not superbasic. Its value will be the same as one of the finite bounds (or zero if there are no finite bounds) if the solution is feasible.

NONLINEAR NONZERO

In a linear programming problem, the nonzero elements are constant. In a nonlinear problem, one or more of them vary because their values depend on that of one or more columns. The ratio of nonlinear (varying) to linear (constant) nonzero elements is a good indicator of the pervasiveness of nonlinearities in the problem.

NONOPTIMAL

There are two contexts. First, describing a *variable*: a nonbasic variable that would improve the objective value if made basic. The sign of the marginal value is normally used to test for nonoptimality. Second, for a *solution*: other solutions exist with better objective values.

NONSMOOTH

A classification of a function that does not have continuous first derivatives, but has continuous function values. A plot of the function values will be a line with "kinks" in it.

NONZERO ELEMENT

The coefficient of a particular column in a particular row if it is not zero. Most mathematical programming problems are sparse, meaning that only a small proportion of the entries in the full tableau of dimensions "number of rows" by "number of columns" is different from zero.

OBJECTIVE ROW (or FUNCTION)

Solver systems require the specification of a row or (for nonlinear systems) a function whose value will be maximized or minimized. GAMS users, in contrast, must specify a scalar variable.

OBJECTIVE VALUE

The current value of the objective row or of the objective variable.

OBJECTIVE VARIABLE

The variable specified in the SOLVE statement.

OPTIMAL
> A feasible solution in which the objective value is the best possible.

OPTION
> The statement that allows users to change the default actions or values in many different parts of the system.

ORDERED SETS
> A set is ordered if its content has been initialized with a SET definition statement and the entry order of the individual elements of the set has the same partial order as the chronological order of the labels. A set name alone on the left hand side of an assignment statement destroys the ordered property. LAG and ORD operations rely on the relative position of the individual elements and therefore require ordered sets. Ordered sets are by definition constant.

OUTPUT
> A general name for the information produced by a computer program.

OUTPUT FILE
> A disk file containing output. A GAMS task produces one such file that can be inspected.

PARAMETER
> A constant or group of constants that may be a scalar, a vector, or a matrix of two or more dimensions. One of the six data types in GAMS.

PROBLEM TYPE
> A model class that is dependent on functional form and specification. Examples are linear, nonlinear, and mixed integer programs.

PROGRAM
> A GAMS input file that provides a representation of the model or models.

RELATIONAL OPERATOR
> This term may be used in two ways. First, in an equation definition it describes the type of relationship the equation specifies, for example equality, as specified with the =E= symbol. Second, in a logical expression, the symbols EQ, NE, LT and so on (see Section 6.4 (a)) are also called relational operators, and are used to specify a required relationship between two values.

RIGHT HAND SIDE
> The value of the constant term in a constraint.

SCALAR
> One of the forms of PARAMETER inputs. Used for single elements.

SET
> A collection of elements (labels). The SET statement is used to declare and define a set.

SIMPLEX METHOD
> The standard algorithm used to solve linear programming problems.

SLACK
> The amount by which an inequality constraint is not binding.

SLACK VARIABLE

> An artificial column introduced by a solver into a linear programming problem. Makes the implementation of the simplex method much easier.

SMOOTH

> A classification of a function that has continuous first derivatives.

SOLVER

> A computer code used to solve a given problem type. An example is GAMS/MINOS, which is used to solve either linear or nonlinear programming problems.

STATEMENTS

> Sometimes called units. The fundamental building block of GAMS programs. Statements or sentences that define data structures, initial values, data modifications, and symbolic relationships. Examples are TABLE, PARAMETER, VARIABLE, MODEL, assignment, and DISPLAY statements.

STATIC SET

> See CONSTANT SET.

SUPERBASIC

> In nonlinear programming, a variable that it is not in the basis but whose value is between the bounds. Nonlinear algorithms often search in the space defined by the superbasic variables.

SYMBOL

> An identifier.

TABLE

> One of the ways of initializing parameters. Used for two and higher dimensional data structures.

TEXT

> A description associated with an identifier or label.

TYPE

> See DATA TYPE, PROBLEM TYPE or VARIABLE TYPE.

UNIQUE ELEMENT

> A label used to define SET membership.

UNIT

> See STATEMENT. A LOOP is often called a unit since it can contain several statements.

VARIABLE TYPE

> The classification of variables. The default bounds are implicit in the type, and also whether continuous or discrete. The types are FREE, POSITIVE, BINARY, INTEGER and NEGATIVE.

VECTOR

> A one-dimensional array, corresponding to a symbol having one index position.

ZERO DEFAULT

> Parameter values are initially zero. Other values can be initialized using PARAMETER or TABLE statements. Assignment statements have to be used thereafter to change parameter values.

REFERENCES

(Note: references to all models in the Model Library are in Section 19.3.)

Control Data Corporation (1982). *APEX-IV Reference Manual*, CDC Manual 84002550, Minneapolis, Minnesota.

Dantzig, George B. (1963). *Linear Programming and Extensions*, Princeton University Press, Princeton N.J.

Drud, Arne (1985). "CONOPT—A GRG Code for Large Sparse Dynamic Nonlinear Optimization Problems," *Mathematical Programming*, vol. 31, 1985, page 153.

Drud, Arne, and Kendrick, David (1986). "HERCULES: A System for Large Economywide Models," draft report, Development Research Department, The World Bank, October 1986.

Fourer, R. (1983). "Modeling Languages versus Matrix Generators for Linear Programming," *ACM Transactions on Mathematical Software*, vol. 9, pages 143–183.

Fourer, R., Gay, D., and Kernighan, B. (1987). "AMPL: A Mathematical Programming Language," Computing Science Technical Report No. 133, AT&T Bell Laboratories, Murray Hill, New Jersey.

Geoffrion, A. M. (1987). "An Introduction to Structured Modeling," *Management Science*, vol. 33, pages 547–88.

Gill, E. P., Murray, W., Saunders, M. A., and Wright, M. H. (1986). "Users' Guide for NPSOL (Version 4.0): A FORTRAN Package for Nonlinear Programing," Report SOL 86-2, Department of Operations Research, Stanford University.

Henaff, Patrick (1980). "An Input-Output Model of the French Economy," Master's thesis, Department of Economics, University of Maryland.

International Business Machines Corp. (1978). *Mathematical Programming System Extended (MPSX) and Generalized Upper Bounding (GUB)*, IBM Manual SH20-0968-1, White Plains, New York.

Lasdon, Leon S., Waren, Alan D., Jain, A., and Ratner M. (1978). "Design and Testing of a Generalized Reduced Gradient Code for Nonlinear Programming," *ACM Transactions on Mathematical Software*, vol. 4, page 34.

Marsten, Roy E. (1981). "The Design of the XMP Linear Programming Library," *ACM Transactions on Mathematical Software*, vol. 7, No. 4, pages 481–97.

Murtagh, Bruce A., and Saunders, Michael A. (1987). "MINOS 5.1 User's Guide," Report SOL 83-20R, December 1983, revised January 1987, Stanford University.

Mulvey, John M., and Zenios, Stavros A., (1987). "GENOS 1.0: A Generalized Network Optimization System," Report 87-12-03, Decision Science Department, The Wharton School, University of Pennsylvania, Philadelphia.

Paules, Granville E. IV, and Floudas, Christodoulos A. (1988). "Algorithmic Development Methodology for Discrete-Continuous Optimization Problems: A Modeling Language Approach," Operations Research, to appear.

Schrage, L. (1987). "The LINGO Modeling Language," presented at ORSA/TIMS Joint National Meeting, St. Louis, Missouri.

Scicon Ltd (1986). *Scicon V/M User Guide ver 1.40*, Milton Keynes, England.

Singal, Jaya, Marsten, Roy E., and Morin, Thomas (1987). "Fixed Order Branch-and-Bound Methods for Mixed-Integer Programming: The ZOOM System," working paper, Management Information Science Department, The University of Arizona, Tucson, Arizona, December 1987.

Welch, J. S. Jr. (1987). "PAM—A Practitioner's Guide to Modeling," *Management Science*, vol 33, pages 610–25.

INDEX

INSTALLATION INSTRUCTIONS

The installation instructions for GAMS 2.25 can be found on the first distribution disk in a file labeled "README.DAT". Bring the contents of this file to your screen with the DOS command:

```
TYPE A:README.DAT | MORE
```

and follow the instructions. This file also contains some notes about the current release of GAMS. Please—always read the README file in the software you receive. The Addendum printed in this book is for the August, 1992, Release 2.25. Changes and additions to the software at later dates will be described in the README file.

ADDENDUM

Short Notes About Some New Features
in GAMS Release 2.25

The next few pages describe some of the new features in GAMS. Examples are included to clarify the concepts. Most models will run on GAMS 2.20 and 2.23 systems, but for some you will need to have access to GAMS 2.25.

INCLUDE Files ■

Many programming languages (or at least their implementations) contain the concept of an INCLUDE file. At the point where an include statement is found, the compiler reads further input from that file. When it reaches the end of the included file the compiler then switches back to the original file, continuing where it left off.

INCLUDE files not only offer a way of structuring the input of a compiler, they also give more flexibility if the input is coming from different sources (people and/or programs).

The syntax is as follows:

```
$INCLIDE fln
```

or

```
$INCLUDE "fln"
```

where fln is the file name of the file to be included.

A parametrized version of the INCLUDE statement allows for a primitive macro capability. The syntax for the "call" is:

```
$BATINCLUDE "fln" parameter1 parameter2 ...
```

(In the INCLUDE file, use %1 for parameter1, %2 for parameter2, etc.)

Some examples are shown on the following pages.

File: INCLUDE.GMS

```
* include.gms
* this is the main source text
*
* next line instructs compiler to allow for Pascal style {..} comments
$inlinecom{ }
$include "sets.inc"     { set definitions }
$include "declar.inc"   { declarations of vars/constraints }
$include "tables.inc"   { some tables }
$include "model.inc"    { the actual model }

model m /all/;
solve m using lp minimizing z;

<EOF>
```

File: SETS.INC

```
*
*   sets.inc : sets and parameters
*
    SETS
    I    canning plants    / SEATTLE, SAN-DIEGO /
    J    markets           / NEW-+YORK, CHICAGO, TOPEKA / ;
    PARAMETERS      { could be placed in a separate file }
        A(I)  capacity of plant i in cases
           /    SEATTLE      350
                SAN+DIEGO    600  /

        B(J)  demand at market j in cases
           /    NEW+YORK     325
                CHICAGO      300
                TOPEKA       275  / ;

    <EOF>
```

File: DECLAR.INC

```
*
* declar.inc : declarations of variables and equations
*
    VARIABLES
        X(I,J)  shipment quantities in cases
        Z        total transportation costs in thousands of dollars ;
    POSITIVE VARIABLE X ;
        EQUATIONS
            COST        define objective function
            SUPPLY(I)   observe supply limit at plant i
        DEMAND(J)   satisfy demand at market j ;
    <EOF>
```

File: TABLES.INC

```
*
* tables.inc : tables
*

    TABLE D(I,J)  distance in thousands of miles
                   NEW-YORK       CHICAGO     TOPEKA
         SEATTLE     2.5            1.7         1.8
         SAN-DIEGO   2.5            1.8         1.4  ;
    <EOF>
```

File: MODEL.INC

```
*
* model.inc : actual model
*

    SCALAR F  freight in dollars per case per thousand miles /90/ ;
    PARAMETER C(I,J)  transport cost in thousands of dollars per case ;
              C(I,J) = F * D(I,J) / 1000 ;
    COST ..        Z =E=  SUM((I,J), C(I,J)*X(I,J)) ;
    SUPPLY(I) ..   SUM(J, X(I,J))  =L=  A(I) ;
    DEMAND(J) ..   SUM(I, X(I,J))  =G=  B(J) ;
    <EOF>
```

PUT Statement

The standard way to print within GAMS is to use the DISPLAY statement (described in Chapter 13 of the GAMS manual). This statement, however, only writes to the standard GAMS listing file (.LST file), and print control is somewhat limited.

The GAMS PUT statement allows GAMS to output results to a file with the same flexibility as the major programming languages. The PUT statement features include: a wide range of numeric output formats, page formatting, text justification, numeric justification, and multiple files in use at one time.

Before using a PUT statement, specify the file where the GAMS output will be directed using the FILE statement. For example

```
FILE RES /RESULTS.DAT/;
```

Now the logical file RES corresponds to the disk file RESULTS.DAT. Next we specify that the next PUT statements concern this file:

```
PUT RES;
```

This looks somewhat clumsy the first time, but think of the case when you want to write to several files. Then we would have:

```
FILE F1 /file1.dat/;
FILE F2 /file2.dat/;
PUT F1;
    :
    : puts in this part go to f1
    :
PUT F2;
    :
    : puts in this part go to f2
```

The following is an example of the PUT statement:

```
PUT X.L(i):17:6 : output value of X.L(i) with 6 decimals and a width of 17
PUT PAR(k):17:6 : output parameter PAR(k)
PUT i.TL        : output text label of set element
```

One major difference between the PUT statement and the DISPLAY statement is that PUT only works on scalars not on blocks. That is:

```
DISPLAY X.L;
```

will display all the level values of the X(i)'s. To do the same thing with a PUT statement you will need the LOOP statement:

```
LOOP(I,
      PUT X.L(I) /;
    );
```

Note: The "/" character creates a linefeed.

The following shows a complete example with PUTs, based on the TRNSPORT model in the GAMS library.

```
$inlinecom { }
{ The above option allows you to use inline comments.
  In this case we can use curly braces like in Pascal.
  To mimic C use $inlinecom /* */. }

option lp=cplex;    { use cplex as LP solver }
  SETS
      I  sources /KansasCity, StLouis, Chicago/
      J  destinations /NYC, WashDC, LA, Phil, Houston/ ;
  PARAMETERS
      A(I)     capacity of source i
      B(J)     demand at destination j
      C(I,J)   transport cost;

  { fill a, b and c with random numbers, but so that sum(a) = sum(b) }
  a(i)   = uniform(1,100);
  b(j)   = uniform(1,100);
  a('KansasCity') = a('KansasCity') - sum(i,a(i)) + sum(j,b(j));
  c(i,j) = uniform(1,10);
```

```
VARIABLES
   X(I,J)   shipment quantities
   Z        total transportation costs;

POSITIVE VARIABLE X ;

EQUATIONS
   COST         define objective function
   SUPPLY(I)    observe supply limits
   DEMAND(J)    satisfy demand;

COST ..        Z  =E=  SUM((I,J), C(I,J)*X(I,J)) ;
SUPPLY(I) ..   SUM(J, X(I,J))  =L=  A(I) ;
DEMAND(J) ..   SUM(I, X(I,J))  =G=  B(J) ;

MODEL TRANSPORT /ALL/ ;

SOLVE TRANSPORT USING LP MINIMIZING Z ;

{ now write results to RESULTS.DAT }

file res /RESULTS.DAT/;   { res is a file handle to file results.dat }
put res;                  { next puts are to file res }

{ now loop over (i,j) and write i,j and x(i,j) }
{ when writing numbers you may suffix them by  :a:b where }
{ a is the width and b is the number of decimals. }
{ labels may be suffixed by :a, indicating the width. }
{ a slash (/) is the symbol to generate a newline. }

loop ((i,j),
          put i.TL:11,  j.TL:11,  x.L(i,j):15:7 /;
     );
     { we can also output the status of the model: }
put // "Model status: "
put$(transport.modelstat eq 1) "Optimal";
put$(transport.modelstat eq 2) "Locally optimal";
put$(transport.modelstat eq 3) "Unbounded";
put$(transport.modelstat eq 4) "Infeasible";
put$(transport.modelstat eq 5) "Locally infeasible";
put$(transport.modelstat eq 6) "Intermediate infeasible";
put$(transport.modelstat eq 7) "Intermediate nonoptimal";
put$(transport.modelstat eq 8) "Integer solution";
put$(transport.modelstat eq 9) "Intermediate non-integer";
put$(transport.modelstat eq 10) "Integer infeasible";
put$(transport.modelstat eq 12) "Error unknown";
put$(transport.modelstat eq 13) "Error no solution";

put // "Solution time : " transport.resusd
```

The RESULTS.DAT file now reads:

```
KANSASCITY  NYC          30.8126525
KANSASCITY  WASHDC       29.9289996
KANSASCITY  LA            0.0000000
KANSASCITY  PHIL          4.6146537
KANSASCITY  HOUSTON       0.0000000
STLOUIS     NYC           0.0000000
STLOUIS     WASHDC        0.0000000
STLOUIS     LA            0.0000000
STLOUIS     PHIL         31.0185661
STLOUIS     HOUSTON      53.4648379
CHICAGO     NYC           0.0000000
CHICAGO     WASHDC        0.0000000
CHICAGO     LA           23.1812338
CHICAGO     PHIL          0.0000000
CHICAGO     HOUSTON      32.3059264
Model status: Optimal
Solution time:        0.71
```

A summary of the GAMS PUT facility and related statements is shown in the table at the end of this Addendum.

SOLVES Within a Loop   ■

The loop statement is a very powerful device. The manual describes this statement extensively in connection with lagged variables etc. It is also possible to have solves within a loop. This gives the user the possibility to do a solve, change some parameters or levels and repeat this process.

One application for using a solve within a loop is to output point on the efficient curve when doing portfolio models: each QP gives you a point on this curve, and using a loop you can calculate a series of these points. Using the PUT statement, and a graphics package it is possible to draw this frontier.

An example using the solve within a loop follows. This example demonstrates how loops can be nested. The application area is nonlinear MIPS for which soon a solver under GAMS will be available. For tiny problems, the shown complete enumeration method can be used to see how the NLMIPS algorithm performs.

```
$offsymxref  offsymlist
$inlinecom { }
set bin /zero
         one/
    true(bin) /one/;
alias (bin,bin1);
alias (bin,bin2);
alias (bin, opt);
    parameter boole(bin) /zero 0,
                         one  1/;
```

```
variables y1,y2,y3;
Positive variables a,a2,a3,b,b1,b2,b3,c ;
variable z ;

equations e1,e2,e3,e4,e5,i1,i2,i3,obj ;

e1..   b2 - log(1+a2) =e= 0 ;
e2..   b3 - 1.2*log(1+a3) =e= 0 ;
e3..    c - 0.9*b =e= 0 ;
e4..   -b + b1 + b2 + b3  =e= 0 ;
e5..   a - a2 - a3 =e= 0 ;
i1..   b - 5*y1 =l= 0 ;
i2..   a2 - 5*y2 =l= 0 ;
i3..   a3 - 5 * y3 =l= 0 ;
obj..    z =e=  3.5* y1 + y2 + 1.5*y3 + 7*b1 + b2 + 1.2*b3 + 1.8*a - 11*c ;

c.up = 1 ; b2.up = 5 ;
z.lo = -20 ;

option optcr = 0.0 ;
option iterlim = 1000;
option reslim = 1000;

model gk2 /all/ ;

file res /results.dat/;
put res;
put "Results from complete enumeration" /
put "————————————————————————————" //
put "   y1   y2   y3        obj" /
scalar min, optimal;
min = 1.0e10;
   loop(bin,
   loop(bin1,
   loop(bin2,
      y1.fx = boole(bin);
      y2.fx = boole(bin1);
      y3.fx = boole(bin2);    { fix the "binary" variables }
      put boole(bin):5:0 boole(bin1):5:0 boole(bin2):5:0;
      solve gk2 minimizing z using nlp;
      optimal = 1$((gk2.modelstat eq 1) or (gk2.modelstat eq 2));
      loop(true$(boole(true) eq optimal),
         { if optimal then ... }
            put z.l:15:5;
            put$(z.l lt min) " *";
               { if better, mark this line with a * }
            min$(z.l lt min) = z.l;
               { min = min(min,z) }
         );
      put$(not optimal) "  No optimal solution";
      put /;
   )));
```

The file RESULTS.DAT:

RESULTS FROM COMPLETE ENUMERATION

Y1	Y2	Y3	OBJ	
0	0	0	0.00000	*
0	0	1	1.50000	
0	1	0	1.00000	
0	1	1	2.50000	
1	0	0	0.27778	
1	0	1	−1.92310	*
1	1	0	−1.72097	
1	1	1	−1.41100	

Communication with Spreadsheets   ■

Moving data from a spreadsheet to a GAMS model and moving results from a GAMS run into a spreadsheet can be done through the PUT and INCLUDE statements respectively.

A spreadsheet block represents a table. To include such a table, create a print file in your spreadsheet and then use the INCLUDE statement to bring this file into your GAMS model.

To have GAMS print a file that Lotus can read, write data in a "quoted-string," "comma-delimited" format. This format requires a .PC print control suffix of 5. The next example shows how to import a table, and to produce a solution file that can be imported into Lotus 1-2-3.

```
$EOLCOM —
  SETS
      I   canning plants   / SEATTLE, SAN-DIEGO /
      J   markets          / NEW-YORK, CHICAGO, TOPEKA / ;
  PARAMETERS
      A(I)  capacity of plant i in cases
        /   SEATTLE    350
            SAN-DIEGO  600  /
      B(J)  demand at market j in cases
        /   NEW-YORK   325
            CHICAGO    300
            TOPEKA     275  / ;
  TABLE D(I,J)  distance in thousands of miles
  $include '123.prn'
  ;
  — the 123.prn file is a 123 print file of the following table;
  —              NEW-YORK  CHICAGO   TOPEKA
  —    SEATTLE      2.5      1.7      1.8
  —    SAN-DIEGO    2.5      1.8      1.4
  —
```

```
SCALAR F  freight in dollars per case per thousand miles /90/ ;
PARAMETER C(I,J)  transport cost in thousands of dollars per case ;
          C(I,J) = F * D(I,J) / 1000 ;

VARIABLES
   X(I,J)  shipment quantities in cases
   Z          total transportation costs in thousands of dollars ;
POSITIVE VARIABLE X ;
   EQUATIONS
      COST          define objective function
      SUPPLY(I)     observe supply limit at plant i
      DEMAND(J)     satisfy demand at market j ;

COST ..        Z =E= SUM((I,J), C(I,J)*X(I,J)) ;

SUPPLY(I) ..   SUM(J, X(I,J)) =L= A(I) ;

DEMAND(J) ..   SUM(I, X(I,J)) =G= B(J) ;

MODEL TRANSPORT /ALL/ ;

SOLVE TRANSPORT USING LP MINIMIZING Z ;

FILE SOL /'123.sol'/;  — file sol is connected to '123.sol'
PUT SOL;               — start writing to this file
SOL.PC = 5;            — write in comma delimited format
PUT ' ';               — write header
LOOP(J,PUT J.TL);
PUT /;
LOOP(I,
    PUT I.TL;
    LOOP(J,
        PUT X.L(I,J);
        );
    PUT/;
);
```

The output file looks like:

```
" ","NEW-YORK","CHICAGO","TOPEKA"
"SEATTLE",50.00,300.00,0.00
"SAN-DIEGO",275.00,0.00,275.00
```

Priorities for Discrete Variables

Priorities are a simple and effective device to influence the branch-and-bound algorithm. Especially if you are using ZOOM, with its fixed branching order, a user specified branching order may be an enormous improvement. In addition, other codes, even if they use a clever dynamic ordering scheme (most of the time based on so called 'pseudo-costs') can benefit from a user specified ordering. This is the case when variables in the model have a natural hierarchy. To set the priorities, discrete variables have a suffix, .PRIOR, to which you can assign a real number. For instance: BINVAR.PRIOR(I,J) = ORD(I);. Lower values mean higher priorities. The default priority is 1.0. The solver needs an option file entry of MOD.PRIOROPT=1 (where MOD is name of the model). The following model is from the model library, THAI.GMS. At the bottom you will see how we implemented the use of priorities. The results using ZOOM are: 7292 iterations were needed without priorities and 1503 iterations if we turned the priorities on. The option file contained the lines 'nodetable 5000' and 'heuristic no'.

```
$TITLE THAI NAVY PROBLEM (THAI,SEQ=98)
*  THIS MODEL IS USED TO ALLOCATE SHIPS TO TRANSPORT PERSONNEL FROM
*  DIFFERENT PORT TO A TRAINING CENTER.
*
*  REFERENCE: CHOYPENG P, PUAKPONG P AND ROSENTHAL R E, OPTIMAL SHIP
*             ROUTING AND PERSONNEL ASSIGNMENT FOR NAVAL RECRUITMENT
*             IN THAILAND, INTERFACES, VOL 16, NO 4, PP.356-366, 1986.
SETS  I  PORTS          / CHUMPHON, SURAT, NAKON, SONGKHLA /
      J  VOYAGES        / V-01* V-15 /
      K  SHIP CLASSES   / SMALL, MEDIUM, LARGE /
      SC(I,K) SHIP CAPABILITY / CHUMPHON.(SMALL,MEDIUM,LARGE)
                                (SURAT,NAKON).(MEDIUM,LARGE)
                                SONGKHLA.LARGE /
      VC(J,K) VOYAGE CAPABILITY ;
PARAMETER  D(I)  NUMBER OF MEN AT PORT I NEEDING TRANSPORT
                 / CHUMPHON = 475, SURAT    = 659
                   NAKON   = 672, SONGKHLA = 1123 /
           SHIPCAP(K)  SHIP CAPACITY IN MEN / SMALL   100
                                             MEDIUM  200
                                             LARGE   600 /
           N(K)    NUMBER OF SHIPS OF CLASS K AVAILABLE
                   / SMALL  2, MEDIUM  3, LARGE  4 / ;
TABLE   A(J,*)   ASSIGNMENT OF PORTS TO VOYAGES
        DIST  CHUMPHON SURAT NAKON SONGKHLA
V-01    370    1
V-02    460           1
V-03    600                 1
V-04    750                       1
V-05    515    1      1
V-06    640    1            1
V-07    810    1                  1
V-08    665           1     1
V-09    665           1           1
V-10    800                 1     1
V-11    720    1      1     1
V-12    860    1      1           1
V-13    840    1            1     1
V-14    865           1     1     1
V-15    920    1      1     1     1
SCALAR W1 SHIP ASSIGNMENT WEIGHT          / 1.00 /
       W2 SHIP DISTANCE TRAVELED WEIGHT   / .01  /
       W3 PERSONNEL DISTANCE TRAVEL WEIGHT / .0001 / ;
```

```
VC(J,K) = PROD(I$A(J,I), SC(I,K)); DISPLAY VC ;
VARIABLES
    Z(J,K)     NUMBER OF TIMES VOYAGE JK IS USED
    Y(J,K,I)   NUUMBER OF MEN TRANSPORTED FROM PORT I VIA VOYAGE JK
    OBJ ;
INTEGER VARIABLES Z; POSITIVE VARIABLES Y ;
EQUATIONS
    OBJDEF
    DEMAND(I)        PICK UP ALL THE MEN AT PORT I
    VOYCAP(J,K)      OBSERVE VARIABLE CAPACITY OF VOYAGE JK
    SHIPLIM(K)       OBSERVE LIMIT OF CLASS K ;
DEMAND(I)..  SUM((J,K)$(A(J,I)$VC(J,K)), Y(J,K,I))  =G= D(I) ;
VOYCAP(J,K)$VC(J,K)..  SUM(I$A(J,I), Y(J,K,I))  =L= SHIPCAP(K)*Z(J,K) ;
SHIPLIM(K)..  SUM(J$VC(J,K), Z(J,K))   =L=  N(K) ;
OBJDEF..      OBJ =E= W1*SUM((J,K)$VC(J,K), Z(J,K))
                    + W2*SUM((J,K)$VC(J,K), A(J,"DIST")*Z(J,K))
                    + W3*SUM((J,K,I)$(A(J,I)$VC(J,K)), A(J,"DIST")*Y(J,K,I)) ;
    MODEL THAINAVY /ALL/;
Z.UP(J,K)$VC(J,K) = N(K) ;
* Branch first on the large ships
Z.PRIOR(J,"SMALL")  = 3;
Z.PRIOR(J,"MEDIUM") = 2;
Z.PRIOR(J,"LARGE")  = 1;

THAINAVY.OPTCR   =0;
THAINAVY.OPTCA   =0;
THAINAVY.ITERLIM =10000;
THAINAVY.OPTFILE =1;
* we need an option file with NODETABLE 5000 to be able
* to solve THAI to optimality without priorities.

* first solve model without use of priorities
THAINAVY.PRIOROPT=0;
SOLVE THAINAVY MINIMIZING OBJ USING MIP ;
* now solve it with priorities
THAINAVY.PRIOROPT=1;
SOLVE THAINAVY MINIMIZING OBJ USING MIP ;
```

The IF-ELSE Statement   ■

The IF–ELSE statement is useful to branch conditionally around a group of statements. In some cases this can also be written as a set of $ conditioned statements, but the IF statement may be used to make the GAMS code more readable. For instance:

```
P(I)$(f GT 0) = f*P(I);
Q(J)$(f GT 0) = f*Q(J);
```

can also be written as:

```
IF(f GT 0,
    P(I) = f*P(I);
    Q(J) = f*Q(J);
    );
```

An optional ELSE part allows you yo formulate traditional IF–THEN–ELSE constructs. The syntax is:

```
IF(condition,
    statements;
        :
        :
    ELSE
    statements;
        :
        :

    );
```

Example:

```
IF(ml.modelstat EQ 4,
    * model ml was infeasible
    * relax bounds on X

    x.up(j) - 2*x.ip(j);

    * and solve again
    solve ml using lp minimizing lp;
ELSE
    if(ml.modelstat NE 1,
        abort "Error solving models ml";
    );
);
```

Note: It is not allowed to define equations inside an IF statement. For example:

```
IF(s GT 0,
    eq.. sum(j,x(j)) = g = s;
);
```

is *not* legal.

New Solvers ■

Complete information about new GAMS solvers can be found on the first distribution disk in a file labeled "SOLVERS.DAT." You can bring the contents of this file to your screen with the DOS command:

```
TYPE A: SOLVERS.DAT ¦ MORE
```

Summary of the GAMS PUT Facility and Related Statements

Put Statements

Statements	Description	Syntax
FILE	define files	FILE fname text / external file name / where <u>fname</u> is the GAMS internal file name
PUTTL	write to title block	PUTTL fname item(s) fname item(s) ... ; where <u>item(s)</u> are the GAMS values to be printed.
PUTHD	write to header block	PUTHD fname item(s) fname item(s) ... ; where <u>item(s)</u> are the GAMS values to be printed.
PUT	assign current file and write to window	PUT fname item(s) fname item(s) ... ; where <u>item(s)</u> are the GAMS values to be printed.
PUTPAGE	assign current file and write to window with formfeed	PUTPAGE fname item(s) fname item(s) ... ; where <u>item(s)</u> are the GAMS values to be printed.
PUTCLOSE	close file	PUTCLOSE fname item(s) fname item(s) ... ; where <u>item(s)</u> are the GAMS values to be printed.

Control Characters

	item delimiter (blank)
,	item delimiter (comma)
/	carriage return (delimiter)
;	end statement delimiter
:	item display format delimiter
<	left justification
>	right justification
<>	center justification
@	position cursor at specified column
#	position cursor at specified row
' '	quoted text delimiter (paired)
" "	quoted text delimiter (paired)

System Suffixes

.DATE	program execution date
.IFILE	input file name
.OFILE	output file name
.PAGE	current page
.RDATE	restart file date
.RFILE	restart file name
.RTIME	restart file time
.SFILE	save file name
.TIME	program execution time
.TITLE	model title

Variable and Equation Suffixes

.FX	lower, upper, and level
.L	level or primal value
.LO	lower bound
.M	marginal or dual value
.PRIOR	priority value
.SCALE	scale value
.UP	upper bound

Identifier Suffixes

.TE(index)	set element text
.TL	set element labels
.TS	identifier symbol text

(continued)

Summary of the GAMS PUT Facility and Related Statements (*continued*)

File Suffixes

Suffix	Description	Default	Options
.AP	append option	0	0 overwrite 1 append
.BM	bottom margin	0	
.CASE	alphabetic case	0	0 mixed case 1 upper case
.CC	current column	0	
.CR	current row	1	
.ERRORS	number of PUT errors	0	
.HDCC	header current column	0	
.HDCR	header current row	1	
.HDLL	header last line	0	
.LJ	label justification	2	1 right 2 left 3 center
.LL	last line	0	
.LP	last page	0	
.LW	label field width	12	0 variable length
.ND	number of decimals	2	
.NJ	numeric justification	1	1 right 2 left 3 center
.NR	numeric round format	1	0 scientific notation 1 round to fit fields
.NW	numeric field width	12	0 variable length
.NZ	numeric zero tolerance	1E-5	0 round to field size
.PC	print control	2	0 standard paging 1 FORTRAN page format 2 continuous page 3 ASCII page format 4 text quoted, blank delimited 5 text quoted, comma delimited
.PS	page size	60	max 130
.PW	page width	132	max 255
.SJ	set value justification	1	1 right 2 left 3 center
.SW	set value field width	12	0 variable length
.TF	text fill missing .TE	2	0 no fill 1 fill existing only 2 fill always
.TJ	text justification	2	1 right 2 left 3 center
.TLCC	title current column	0	
.TLCR	title current row	1	
.TLLL	title last line	0	
.TM	top margin	0	
.TW	text field width	0	0 variable length
.WS	window size	60	

Summary of the GAMS PUT Facility and Related Statements (*continued*)

Model Suffixes

Suffix	Description	Solve Reset	Global Option
.BRATIO	basis acceptance test	no	BRATIO
.DOMLIM	maximum number of domain violations	no	DOMLIM
.DOMUSD	number of domain violations	yes	
.ITERLIM	iteration limit	no	ITERLIM
.ITERUSD	number of iterations used	yes	
.LIMCOL	number of columns displayed for each block of variables	no	LIMCOL
.LIMROW	number of rows displayed for each block of variables	no	LIMROW
.MODELSTAT	model status	yes	
	1 optimal		
	2 locally optimal		
	3 unbounded		
	4 infeasible		
	5 locally infeasible		
	6 intermediate infeasible		
	7 intermediate nonoptimal		
	8 integer solution		
	9 intermediate non-integer		
	10 integer infeasible		
	11 (unused)		
	12 error unknown		
	13 error no solution		
.NUMEQU	number of single equations generated	yes	
.NUMINFES	number of infeasibilities	yes	
.NUMNOPT	number of non-optimalities	yes	
.NUMNZ	number of non-zero entries in the technological coefficient matrix	yes	
.NUMUNBND	number of unbounded variables	yes	
.NUMVAR	number of single variables generated	yes	
.OPTCA	absolute termination criterion for MIPs	no	OPTCA
.OPTCR	relative termination criterion for MIPs	no	OPTCR
.OPTFILE	option file usage	no	
.RESLIM	maximum number of resource units (usually CP seconds)	no	RESLIM
.RESUSD	resource units used to solve model	yes	
.SOLPRINT	solution print option	no	SOLPRINT
.SOLVEOPT	merge or replace option for solution data	no	SOLVEOPT
.SOLVESTAT	solver status	yes	
	1 optimal		
	2 iteration interrupt		
	3 resource interrupt		
	4 terminated by solver		
	5 evaluation error limit		
	6 unknown		
	7 (unused)		
	8 error preprocessor error(s)		
	9 error setup failure		
	10 error solver failure		
	11 error internal solver		
	12 error post-processor		
	13 error system failure		
.SYSOUT	subsystem print option	no	SYSOUT
.WORKSPACE	size of work array	no	WORK

pairs. Control will be returned to this file only if you use the COMMAND/C invocation of GAMS discussed in (c) below.

(b) Directory search order.

For the greatest efficiency in finding GAMS files, make the GAMS directory the first one mentioned in the 'path'. It is best to keep the number of files in 'path' directories as small as conveniently possible.

(c) Sequences of GAMS tasks.

To run a sequence of GAMS tasks unattended, make a .BAT file that contains a series of lines as below:

COMMAND/C GAMS file options

Each of the GAMS calls will be executed in turn.

This usage requires that you either have a DOS 'path' to your root directory, or that you have a copy of the file COMMAND.COM in a directory that does have a path to it. Also, it uses an extra 3k bytes to load an additional copy of the command processor.

(Note for DOS 2.x users. Because of a bug in DOS, you will get a message 'Invalid directory' while GAMS is erasing scratch files. If your scratch files are in a remote directory, they will not be erased. Just remember to erase them next morning.)

There is no simple way to terminate the sequence of tasks if one should fail because of a compiler or other error. If subsequent tasks depend on 'save' files that should have been created by the failed task, DOS will still attempt to process them and they will all fail. (You might like to use the DOS batch command 'IF NOT EXIST file GOTO end' to check on existence of 'save' files before each task. It is best to check on the existence of <file> .G05, which is the last one to be closed. With DOS 2.x this scheme will only work if the files are in the current directory.) It is probably best to echo the console output to your printer to have a record of what happened, although if there is trouble with any of the errors with 'hexadecimal' codes from Section 11, that evidence will NOT be echoed to the printer.

(d) Output files.

GAMS runs faster if the output goes to a disk file. Some users find development convenient if the output goes to the screen, but they stop it for inspection with a resident stop-scroll utility such as BACKSCROLL.

(e) Memory statistics

You can use the DOS command 'CHKDSK' to find out how much free memory is available. On a 640K machine running DOS 3.1, CHKDSK will report about 612000 bytes available if no non-essential programs or device drivers are loaded. (The memory used by the "files" and "buffers" specified in your file CONFIG.SYS is included in the memory used.)

(f) BUFFERS in the file CONFIG.SYS.

There is nothing magic about the number 10: it just seems to give the best performance. You may want to experiment with other values, since each BUFFER uses 528 bytes. IBM recommends a minimum of 3 for fixed disk machines.

(g) How to get a clean machine.

If you occasionally run large models, but prefer to have resident programs available at other times, you may want to put the following sequence into your file AUTOEXEC.BAT just before it loads the memory resident programs.

```
ECHO Hit ctl-c for a big machine or else . .
PAUSE
```

Then every time the machine is booted, you will have the choice of entering control-C (followed by Y when DOS prompts you) to get all available memory for GAMS, but using any other key will allow Sidekick, your print spooler, etc. to be loaded.

(h) Adding new solvers after the initial installation.

If you ever get additional solver systems, repeat the solver installation procedure outlined in Section 7 (b) AFTER the new files have been copied into the GAMS system directory.

19. Notes on Installation on Networks

GAMS can be installed on a file server and run via a network. The experience is still limited, but some general comments are in order:

(a) GAMS creates many small scratch files that communicate between GAMS itself and the solvers. If the network has a read-only disk then these files must be put on the user's machine. Add SCRDIR A:\ or SCRDIR B:\ in the GAMS.BAT as explained in Section 18, and document it in GAMS.DOC.

(b) If network access is slow with many users you should consider keeping scratch files on a local diskette: see (a) above.

(c) All GAMS files can be made read-only to facilitate simultaneous access by many users.